BUILDING TYPE BASICS FOR

healthcare facilities

BUILDING TYPE BASICS FOR

healthcare facilities

Stephen A. Kliment, Series Founder and Editor

RICHARD L. KOBUS *Tsoi/Kobus & Associates*

RONALD L. SKAGGS *HKS Inc.*

MICHAEL BOBROW and JULIA THOMAS *Bobrow/Thomas and Associates*

THOMAS M. PAYETTE *Payette Associates Inc.*

JOHN WILEY & SONS, INC.

New York, Chichester, Weinheim, Brisbane, Singapore, Toronto

Interior design and layout: Thumb Print and Jeff Baker.

Library of Congress Cataloging-in-Publication Data:

Building type basics for healthcare facilities /Bobrow/Thomas and Associates
   [et. al.]
      p. : cm. —(Building type basics series)
  Includes index.
  ISBN: 0-471-35672-7 (cloth : alk. paper)
  1. Health facilities—Design and construction. I. Bobrow/Thomas and Associates. II. Series.
   [DNLM: 1. Facility Design and Construction. 2. Health Facilities. 3. Health Facility Environment. WX 140 H4233 2000]
RA967 .H434 2000
725'.51—dc21

99-462025

CONTENTS

CONTENTS

PREFACE

STEPHEN A. KLIMENT, *Series Founder and Editor*

This book on healthcare facilities is one of the first in Wiley's "Building Type Basics" series on the principal building types. It is not a coffee-table book lavish with color photography but meager in usable content. Rather, it contains the kind of instant information architects, consultants, and their clients need in their various kinds of work, where, inevitably, time is scarce. As architectural practice becomes more generalized and firms pursue and accept commissions for a widening range of building types, the books in this series will comprise a convenient, hands-on resource providing basic information on the initial design phases of a project and answers to the questions design professionals routinely encounter in those crucial early phases. And each volume will be useful to other interested parties as well. Members of healthcare providers' boards and their architect and engineer selection committees, for example, will find essential information about healthcare programming and the design and construction process.

The healthcare industry today is in a highly unsettled state—coming to grips with some of its most pressing problems. Driving the turbulence are costs: simply put, healthcare providers expect to be paid more for services than most consumers are able or willing to pay. For years, as Richard Kobus, one of the authors of this volume, points out, the healthcare system, made up of hospitals, physicians, insurers, and consumers (i.e., patients), had a very good arrangement under which hospitals and physicians charged actual costs plus (in the case of hospitals) a margin for reinvestment and recapitalization. Insurers passed on cost increases to employers and individuals who paid premiums. The patient, in Kobus' words, was "happy with unlimited choice and few restrictions on access to care."

Left to support the system financially was the great band of those who paid the premiums, and the late 1970s saw a revolt from this sector. The result was a revolution in the way healthcare was dispensed and paid for, a revolution still under way. As the authors of this volume point out, pieces of this story go back one hundred years and more, to the firebrand reforms of Florence Nightingale in late-nineteenth-century England and, notes Thomas Payette, the equally radical reforms of Charles and William Mayo. The Mayos introduced two previously unheard of concepts: an interdisciplinary approach to healthcare, and the idea that in a very large percentage of cases, care can be dispensed to patients without a hospital stay.

The most significant change of the past twenty years has been the gallop toward managed care. The underlying concepts were that prevention costs less than cure and that constraints on physicians' treatment options and on charges by hospitals would help place a lid on costs. Health maintenance organizations (HMOs) would limit providers' choice of and reimbursement for procedures. They would pressure subscribers to use only approved doctors, by charging more for visits to physicians not on their list. This has not worked as well as expected: competition among HMOs drove down revenues; patients and their families began to demand better physical amenities; and government subsidies began to shrink (for the first time since the program began, Medicare payments actually dropped in 1999, by a modest but very significant 1 percent).

But these are not the only makers of change in a changing industry. Other elements whose impact will be ever more felt include the following:

- The nation's demographics. The percentage of Americans over age 75 keeps climbing. In a sense, as people live longer, the healthcare system becomes a victim of its own success. The elderly are far more prone to getting sick, which places growing pressure on facilities but has also spawned an array of alternate facilities designed for varying levels of independent living by the elderly. (Assisted living facilities will be the topic of another volume in this series.)

- The construction boom. While it may end at any time, the present surge's eight-year run, one of the longest on record, has encouraged overworked contractors to raise their bids on healthcare construction and renovation, which has resulted in higher initial and operating costs for facilities.

- The theory, increasingly backed by research, that a pleasant, stress-free environment, both architectural and landscape, helps heal the patient. Color, carpeting, indirect lighting, fine furniture, ample daylight and views—all are part of the healing environment, but they have their price.

- The gargantuan problem embodied by the 44.3 million Americans without health insurance (*New York Times,* 8 November 1999), and the tragedy that severe illness can visit upon the great majority of those millions who cannot afford to pay for care. One result is the enormous pressures felt by hospital emergency departments, the first recourse for the poor uninsured.

- New medical equipment, using new technologies, that promotes healing but must be paid for, hooked up, stored, and maintained. The unknown space and connectivity demands of future new equipment makes a flexible facility essential. The need for such flexibility will lead to what author Michael Bobrow calls universal rooms.

- The embattled position of the teaching hospital, with its three traditional functions of training physicians, providing care to rich and poor, and fostering medical research. The teaching hospital is under siege above all in large inner cities, because those three functions are very costly, and HMOs are reluctant to send patients because of high charges.

- Reduced hospital stays. Stays have declined from 1000 days per 1000 population to 250 days per 1000, and this has left older hospitals with unused, nonproductive beds.

- Rising labor costs. Healthcare labor demands for higher pay dictates buildings that can run with fewer staff. Bobrow cites the intriguing statistic that one nurse or an equivalent pay-level person can save $1 million in construction cost.

- Alternate medical therapies. Alternative therapies are gaining ground and may have some impact on demand for conventional facilities.

Big managed-care organizations have, indeed, tried to control healthcare costs. The Department of Veterans Affairs (VA), which runs 1,032 facilities in 4,332 buildings, both medical centers and outpatient clinics, is switching from a hospital-care model to a patient-centered, community-based privatized healthcare system. Its enhanced-use leasing program is a cooperative arrangement between the VA and the private sector. The VA offers land or long-term lease agreements. The private sector provides capital, design, construction, financing, and business operations. The property is leased to the private concern at nominal rent, and that concern is responsible for day-to-day hospital operations, undertaken for profit.

And one of the largest healthcare providers, Columbia/HCA Healthcare Corporation, hopes to contain costs of facilities by working with a handful of "preferred" architectural firms and contractors. Architects and contractors work at fees at the lower end of the scale in exchange for a steady volume of work (*Engineering News–Record*, November 1999).

In the end, the underlying economics of healthcare delivery is both the system's saving grace and its Achilles' heel. Market forces enforce cost consciousness, but there are drawbacks. Few have said it better than New York state assemblyman Richard Gottfried: "You always have to be careful about applying market forces in healthcare because the values of the marketplace say if something isn't a profit center we cut it out. And in health care there are things we need that are not profitable" (*New York Times*, 27 November 1999).

Kobus makes a similar point, but with a focus on the design process: "In an effort to be responsive to the demands of their clients some [architects] may choose the route that leads to greater efficiency while forgetting their responsibility to the care of their prime consumer—the patient."

Each volume in this series is tightly organized for ease of use. The heart and soul of the volume is a set of twenty questions most frequently asked about a building type in the early phases of design. Answers to those twenty questions are provided throughout the text, supplemented by essential diagrams, drawings, and illustrations. The questions are indexed for the reader's convenience at the front of this book.

This volume is divided into four chapters:

- "Perspective," contributed by Richard Kobus and members of his firm, Tsoi/Kobus & Associates of Cambridge.
- "Ancillary Departments," contributed by Ronald Skaggs and members of their firm, HKS Inc. of Dallas.
- "Inpatient Facilities," contributed by Michael Bobrow and Julia Thomas and members of their firm, Bobrow/Thomas and Associates of Los Angeles.
- "Ambulatory Care Facilities," contributed by Thomas Payette and members of his firm, Payette Associates Inc. of Boston.

"Perspective" is a wide-ranging assessment, from the points of view of architect and provider, of the healthcare field today, and a shrewd look at where it is heading.

"Ancillary Departments" is divided into three parts: public and administrative departments; diagnostic, interventional, and therapy departments; and logistical support departments. Each department is covered from the standpoint of space and interface demands, and as either inpatient or ambulatory or both.

"Inpatient Facilities" takes up in logical order the planning and design of the nursing unit, including plan types and the patient room; interior architectural considerations; overall functional and space programming issues; technical issues, including structural, mechanical, electrical, and lighting; and how to deal with reuse and retrofit challenges.

"Ambulatory Care Facilities" sets out the unique programming, planning, design, and technical issues of such structures and shows how they apply through a series of case studies that focus on the most common ambulatory-care departments.

All the chapters also cover circulation; the unique features of each healthcare category, including design trends; site planning; codes; energy/environmental challenges; structural, mechanical, and electrical systems; information technology; materials; acoustics and lighting; interiors; wayfinding; renovation and retrofit; and operations and maintenance, costs, and financing.

I hope this book serves you well—as guide, reference, and inspiration.

ACKNOWLEDGMENTS

CHAPTER 1

I'd like to thank L. James Wiczai and Kate Reed, good friends and good teachers, for all that they have shared with me about the world of healthcare. I also wish to thank Katy Wolff and Tina Vaz of Tsoi/Kobus & Associates, Inc., for their great assistance in editing and coordinating this manuscript.

Richard L. Kobus, AIA, *Tsoi/Kobus & Associates, Inc.*

CHAPTER 2

A special thanks to the authors of our chapter, including Ralph Hawkins, FAIA, FACHA, Ron Gover, AIA, Craig Beale, FAIA, MPH, Ron Dennis, AIA, Tom Harvey, AIA, Jeff Stouffer, AIA, Eli Osatinski, and Greg Olivet. Their hard work and dedication to healthcare design is exemplified in their writing. A note of appreciation goes to Wei-erh Ko, our graphic designer. His capabilities allow our story to be told in both literarily and graphically. Additionally, we would like to recognize Trish Jerome for her efforts in organizing, coordinating and editing this extensive manuscript.

Ronald L. Skaggs, FAIA, FACHA, *HKS Inc.*

CHAPTER 3

We would like to acknowledge the following individuals for their contribution to this chapter: John Sealander, for technical issues; Lori Selcer, for interior design issues; and Meradith Cherbo, for functional and space programming issues.

Michael Bobrow, FAIA and Julia Thomas, FAIA, *Bobrow/Thomas and Associates*

CHAPTER 4

I would like to extend my gratitude to all of the architects and designers whose insightful descriptions, based on their first-hand experiences with the design of ambulatory care facilities, have greatly enriched this volume. The astute editing of Susan Daylor has brought individual projects into a coherent vision of the contemporary ambulatory care design field and its impact on the healthcare industry.

Thomas M. Payette, FAIA, *Payette Associates Inc.*

BUILDING TYPE BASICS FOR

healthcare
facilities

CHAPTER 1

PERSPECTIVE

RICHARD L. KOBUS *Tsoi/Kobus and Associates*

As the United States moves into the twenty-first century, our system of healthcare delivery is under enormous pressure to change—to reduce its costs to society and to provide greater convenience in a manner more responsive to its consumers. Seldom has an industry that serves all Americans been under such compulsion to reinvent itself and, in doing so, redefine the roles of its component parts—institutions, caregivers, and the physical environment. What is most remarkable about the challenges facing healthcare is that consumers are demanding change in a period of rising consumption and limited supply. Demographics for the United States show significantly increasing populations over the age of 75.

Traditionally, aging populations are the largest users of healthcare services. Perhaps because of this growth in the population, healthcare payors—large employers and the U.S. government—are generating the greatest pressure to contain the cost of healthcare. At the same time, consumers are expressing increasing dissatisfaction with the system, the options available to them, and their experiences in receiving healthcare. To understand this rapidly evolving phenomenon, it is useful to look back at the last 25 years in U.S. healthcare.

As recently as the 1970s, the U.S. healthcare system was, by and large, a cost-plus system of reimbursement. Physicians and hospitals were paid on the basis of actual costs plus a margin for reinvestment and recapitalization. The big winners were *physicians*, who were the

drivers of this lucrative reimbursement system; *hospitals*, for whom a cost-plus environment meant freedom to charge at will; *insurers*, who simply passed on the cost increases to payors through higher premiums; and *healthcare consumers*, who were happy with unlimited choice and few restrictions on access to care.

The big losers were the payors, who woke up in the late 1970s as inflation and the percentage increase of healthcare benefit costs soared into double digits. The first attempts at containing costs included the dawn of managed care and the introduction of diagnosis rate groups (DRGs) by the federal government. Expanding cost-containment measures in the early 1980s sent the first tremors through the healthcare industry, warning of an accelerating cycle of cost-control initiatives. Hospitals and physicians responded to these early attempts by increasing the number of services they provided, which further fed the double-digit inflation and, in turn, caused payors to demand relief through even more aggressive means.

Insurers, responding to their customers—large employers—squeezed providers to achieve lower utilization of healthcare services. Reductions in lengths of stay in hospitals became the norm. Increasingly, patient care was moved to the ambulatory setting.

Inpatient bed utilization in the United States dropped from nearly 1,000 days/per 1,000 population in the early 1970s to as little as 250 days/per 1,000 population in some areas. Reimbursement arrangements became more aggressive,

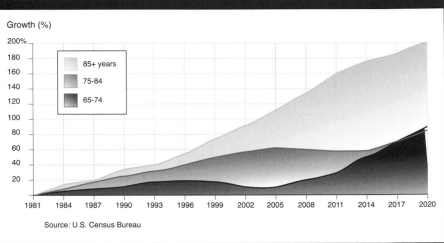

HISTORICAL AND PROJECTED GROWTH IN THE AGING U.S. POPULATION

Growth (%)

Legend:
- 85+ years
- 75-84
- 65-74

Source: U.S. Census Bureau

Hospitals branched out from inpatient care to offer a wide spectrum of healthcare services. More sophisticated players formed integrated delivery systems intended to provide vertical services.

placing the risk for healthcare costs on the provider rather than the insurer. Attempts to establish capitated markets—in which provider organizations bore the risk of healthcare status within a given population—began to appear in the early 1990s, and such arrangements were predicted to become the norm by the turn of the century. Healthcare organizations—hospitals, in particular—lost market clout as the ability to price for services freely gave way to the need to accept market risks that had traditionally resided with healthcare insurers.

Recognizing that the earth had moved beneath them, hospitals began to develop new strategies to regain market standing. They began to consolidate with one another to form healthcare systems.

Hospitals branched out from inpatient care to offer a wide spectrum of healthcare services, including ambulatory care, home care, and extended care for aging and chronically ill patients. More sophisticated players formed integrated delivery systems that were intended to

provide vertical services—ranging from healthcare for individuals and groups to proprietary managed-care networks, from home care services to traditional inpatient care services and extended care services—to lower the cost of providing for aging populations.

Integrated delivery systems (IDSs) represented the full potential of managed care by appearing to address the needs of all parties. They created local brand identification, whereby healthcare became a recognizable consumer product identified as being associated with one institution or another. IDSs also stabilized costs and potentially increased profits by coordinating care within set budgets, at the same time improving the health status of the populations served.

It seemed that managed care had delivered on its promise to contain healthcare costs while creating a highly profitable industry. In the early 1990s cost trends were at a 30-year low. Physician salaries had stabilized, premiums for healthcare insurance products had been reduced, the increase in the aging population spelled phenomenal growth and profit opportunities, and physicians managed their practices more efficiently through the formation of physician practice management organizations. Hospital and hospital system profits climbed throughout the 1990s.

But all was not as rosy as predicted in the industry. Despite prosperity, job growth, and disappearing budget deficits in the general economy, 1998 was disastrous for managed care. And 1999 was predicted to be worse. Well-publicized crashes of managed healthcare provider organizations shook confidence in the industry and raised new questions about the future of managed care. Overall, the health maintenance organization industry lost more than $41 billion in 1998. Large, integrated delivery systems such as Kaiser-Permanente saw unprecedented losses, totaling more than $420 million. For-profit healthcare providers such as Columbia-HCA faced financial and legal troubles, and major East Coast integrated delivery systems sought the protection of Chapter 11 bankruptcy.

Integrated delivery systems, the acclaimed heir apparent of the managed-care dynasty, fared particularly poorly as numerous economic problems beset the integrated system:

- No market share gains
- Declining physician productivity
- Payment rates to the integrated delivery systems flattening or declining
- Negative underwriting cash flows resulting from stabilized payments
- Unrealistic rate guarantees that did not match cost experience

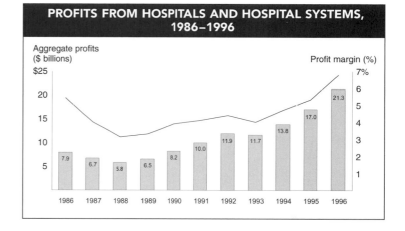

PROFITS FROM HOSPITALS AND HOSPITAL SYSTEMS, 1986–1996

- Sparring over acquisition prices to increase the size and scope of the integrated delivery system

Furthermore, organizational difficulties within integrated delivery systems became insurmountable: Few economies of scale were realized, and transaction costs were higher than expected. Staff morale deteriorated and productivity declined. Economies of scale proved minimal. Coordination of services was difficult, and the relationship between management and care providers was troubled.

As a result, 1999 saw an unprecedented rise in labor union activity among healthcare providers. Nurses, technicians, and even doctors sought protection for themselves, and for the relationship between care providers and patients, through organized labor movements. Even the American Medical Association endorsed union activity for physicians in June 1999, with the avowed intent of increasing physician control over decision making for patients and improving the physician-patient relationship. Clearly, dissatisfaction within the industry reached an all-time high.

Hospital system profits climbed throughout the decade. Despite general prosperity, however, the late 1990s were disastrous for managed care. Integrated delivery systems fared particularly poorly.

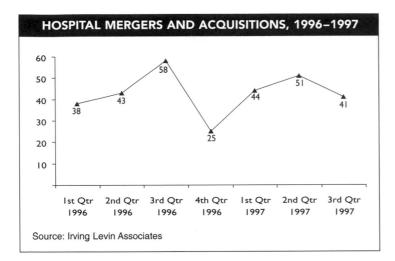

HOSPITAL MERGERS AND ACQUISITIONS, 1996–1997

	1st Qtr 1996	2nd Qtr 1996	3rd Qtr 1996	4th Qtr 1996	1st Qtr 1997	2nd Qtr 1997	3rd Qtr 1997
	38	43	58	25	44	51	41

Source: Irving Levin Associates

Once indomitable stand-alone institutions, hospitals consolidated in the 1990s, forming large, regional, multihospital systems.

Compounding the organizational and economic problems in the industry was an unprecedented, yet enormously powerful, consumer revolt. Managed care, while appeasing payors and providers, had neglected its most important constituency—the consumer. The consumer movement against managed care has been fueled by a backlash against limited choice and access, increased costs, dissatisfaction with service and quality, increased knowledge about health issues, and a more assertive, demanding, educated, and sophisticated consumer. By exerting pressure on a number of fronts, dissatisfied consumers quickly achieved significant clout to increase legal and legislative action and media attention in order to expand care options. Unhappy consumers defected from unsatisfactory relationships with managed-care organizations in droves, opting for other choices that appeared to offer a higher degree of access and satisfaction.

We have entered the age of consumerism in healthcare. Healthcare organizations must understand the link

Healthcare organizations must understand the link between satisfied patients and the generation of revenue.

between satisfied patients and the generation of revenue. Patients are walking, talking advertisements for good or ill. Employers and managed-care organizations will leave providers that do not meet consumer service standards. To retain their consumer base, healthcare organizations must become consumer-driven.

Consumers are increasingly demanding

- participation in healthcare information and decisions,
- a greater choice of providers,
- better relationships with their providers,
- respect, dignity, compassion, and empathy,
- open and ongoing communication so that their views and wishes are considered, and expectations met,
- continuity of care, and
- timely, convenient, and reliable services provided in a high-quality and caring environment.

Healthcare organizations must focus on improving the encounters between patients and care providers in order to make patients feel valued. Healthcare consumers best remember the quality of their contact with staff. Moreover, the quality and character of the environment goes a long way toward supporting positive interactions between caregivers and patients.

A healthcare organization can no longer rely on its reputation, name, or standing in the community to convey a sense of quality to its consumers. There is a phenomenon known as the "take-it-for-granted" attitude, whereby healthcare consumers assume that they will receive the very best healthcare, much as airline passengers assume that their flight will arrive safely, grocery shoppers assume that fresh meat and produce will meet health standards, and new car purchasers assume that their vehicles will deliver trouble-free driving for five years or more. Healthcare consumers take it for granted that the quality of care provided to them will be equal among reputable healthcare providers.

At the same time, healthcare organizations have worked diligently to reduce their costs. Reductions have been so great that few healthcare provider organizations see any way to lower the costs of care through further reductions in staff, increases in economy of scale, or limitations on utilization of healthcare resources.

If healthcare organizations cannot compete on quality or lower costs, they can compete only on perceived quality of contacts, convenience, and continuity of care. The rise of two-income families has further complicated the healthcare consumer picture, as demands on family time become increasingly complex. There simply is less time available to an average family for healthcare activities. The need for convenient and predictable healthcare experiences has led consumers to choose organizations that can structure themselves to provide an "Ideal Patient Encounter"[1] wherein caregivers, technology, information, and the patient can be brought together in the most effective manner to limit the amount of time and the number of steps required for any healthcare experience. Examination, diagnosis, consultation, and follow-up should all be provided within an encapsulated time frame and environment.

Women are particularly demanding of healthcare organizations. Their role as family healthcare decision makers is well known. It is estimated that more than 75 percent of all healthcare decisions are made by women for themselves, their family members, and, very often, their parents.[2] Increasingly, healthcare organizations must cater to the demands and concerns of women as dominant consumers and decision makers. These informed consumers are challenging the healthcare industry in one of the most significant sociopolitical events in modern history. Women are increasingly voting "with their feet" by leaving unsatisfactory healthcare relationships and "with their minds" by electing political candidates who are supportive of family issues, including healthcare.

Architects practicing in the industry today are met by an increasing focus on limiting the cost of construction and the cost of their services. In an effort to be responsive to the demands of their clients, some may choose the route that leads solely to greater efficiency while forgetting their responsibility to the care of their prime consumer, the patient. The emphasis of healthcare architecture today must be on improving the quality of the environment for patients and caregivers alike. Architects can support healthcare management best through efficient solutions, but not those that ignore the environment and the quality of patient-caregiver encounters that it supports.

Patients will be increasingly demanding of healthcare organizations. Those who are most responsive to patients in terms

> The emphasis of healthcare architecture today must be on improving the quality of the environment for patients and caregivers alike.

---

[1] *Trademark*, Hamilton KSA, 1996.
[2] Beatrice Black, *Marketplace*, National Public Radio, 26 January 1999.

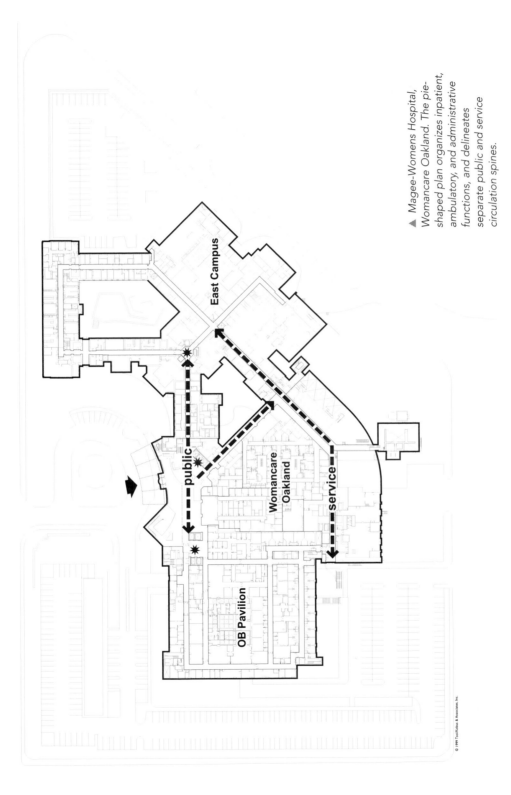

East Campus

public

Womancare
Oakland

service

OB Pavilion

▲ Magee-Womens Hospital,
Womancare Oakland. The pie-
shaped plan organizes inpatient,
ambulatory, and administrative
functions, and delineates
separate public and service
circulation spines.

© 1999 TsolKobus & Associates, Inc.

of convenience, caring encounters, service orientation, and the quality of care will do best in meeting these new demands.

Architects are regarded as talented problem solvers. The problem to be solved here is to find a way to continue delivering a high quality of care and access in a setting that is also highly supportive of human relationships during times of great anxiety and fear. With their particular skills and strengths, architects are well suited to meeting this challenge. They can help caregiving organizations to look beyond conventional healthcare settings ("the hospital") to settings that are more conveniently located, that emphasize "one-stop shopping" by providing all the care that is typically required in a consolidated setting, and that satisfy basic human needs for orientation, safety, comfort, respect, and dignity.

Good architecture in the healthcare setting starts by recognizing the unique functional needs of the healthcare environment, but it does not end there. It must also meet the special needs of the people who use such facilities in times of uncertainty, stress, and dependency on doctors and nurses. It must recognize and support patients' families and friends by providing pleasant spaces and access to information about patients' status and treatment options. Perceptual clarity must start from the moment a patient arrives on the healthcare campus to the moment of treatment and discharge:

- Wayfinding is particularly important in this unfamiliar domain.

- Separation of patients from back-of-house activities, and inpatients from outpatients, provides the necessary sense of comfort, dignity, and repose.

- Lighting is critical in an environment that all too often lacks natural light.

- Patients demand orientation to natural light, time of day, and familiar views as they move around the facility.

- Choices of materials, colors, and finishes should be conducive to a sense of quality and familiarity while providing for durability and ease of maintenance.

At its most basic level in today's turmoil, the architect's role is to help focus healthcare organizations on their customer, the patient. Orientation to the patient and the quality of the patient's encounters will ultimately lead to a higher level of satisfaction with care providers and the healthcare organization.

This book focuses on many of the current trends in architecture that are serving patients well. It is easy in times of turmoil to forget the basic instincts that lead to success. The most basic instinct in healthcare, the one overwhelming success pattern, is to focus energies on the patient and the patient's family. By following this instinct, architecture can uniquely serve the patient through its art and technical expertise by providing an environment that is fully supportive and familiar, lending respect and dignity to the patient's life-giving encounters.

Good architecture in the healthcare setting must also meet the needs of all those who use such facilities in times of uncertainty, stress, and dependency.

CHAPTER 2

ANCILLARY DEPARTMENTS

RONALD L. SKAGGS *HKS Inc.*

INTRODUCTION

The ancillary departments of a health facility serve as the backbone for delivery of inpatient and ambulatory care. These departments offer a variety of support functions ranging from treatment to information distribution.

Ancillary departments include three major categories:

- Public and administrative departments
- Diagnostic, interventional, and therapy departments
- Logistical support departments

Public and Administrative Departments

Public and administrative departments form the general office spaces of a health-care facility. Public activities are commonly located at the main entrance. This entry serves as a point of orientation for the rest of the facility. Administrative departments are typically grouped together to support operational efficiency and cross-utilization of personnel. The general office spaces include suites of offices for administration, public relations, personnel, and related functions.

Other such departments typically include the following:

- *Admitting and Discharge.* The admitting and discharge department is typically located near the main lobby, close to the business/financial services offices. At this location, patient information is processed prior to admission. Preadmission procedures, which include obtaining medical history, family information, insurance data, and other information required by the institution, are often performed within interview offices or cubicles. In many cases, pretesting and examination facilities are also located in this department.

- *Business Office/Financial Services.* The business office/financial services department houses the staff and equipment required to establish patient accounts and credit reviews. The office also processes all insurance and third-party payment requests and performs duties related to the receipt of payments and disbursements for all billings.

- *Medical Records.* The medical records department is the central area for maintaining the records and files of patient test results, diagnoses, and treatment protocols. The activities of this department are supported by systems for physician transcription, data input, and data retrieval.

- *Data Processing/Information Systems.* The data processing/information systems department is typically located close to the business/financial records and medical records office. Because this department is the center for all computerized information processing and retrieval, its design must focus on creating an environment that meets requirements for the latest electronic information technology.

- *Library/Resource Center.* As the repository of medical knowledge for

ANCILLARY DEPARTMENTS

▶ *A preadmitting area at McKay-Dee Hospital Center in Ogden, Utah.*

◀ *Combined admitting and outpatient registration at All Saints Episcopal Hospital-Cityview in Fort Worth, Texas.*

▼ *The lobby provides a point of orientation at Sharp Mary Birch Hospital for Women in San Diego, California.*

0 2' 4' 8'   16'   32'

1 WAITING	**7** WORK/OFFICE	**13** MALE DRESSING/WAITING
2 PHLEBOTOMY	**8** BLOOD DRAW	**14** TECHNICIAN READING
3 REGISTRATION	**9** SPECIMEN TOILET	**15** ECHO/ELECTROCARDIOGRAPHY EXAM
4 WORK AREA	**10** FEMALE DRESSING/WAITING	**16** COAGULATION CONSULTATION
5 RECEPTION	**11** CHEST PROCEDURE	**17** DIETITIAN OFFICE
6 WHEELCHAIR STORAGE	**12** RADIOLOGY PROCEDURE	**18** EXAM ROOM

Admitting & Outpatient Registration

the entire facility, the library/resource center must be located for easy accessibility. With the increasing emphasis on consumer understanding and participation in the care process, the department must be planned to accommodate employees, patients, and patient families, as well as medical staff.

◀ A library resource center for St. John's Regional Medical Center in Oxnard, California.

- *Public Services.* The public services department can consist of many hospital functions supporting the patient and family. Such services may include a gift shop, flower shop, volunteer and social services, counseling, and related functions.

◀ A gift shop at Mary Washington Hospital in Fredericksburg, Virginia.

- *Communications Center.* The communications center is key to the effective functioning of a healthcare facility. This department serves as the networking center for various functions, including telephone, paging, videoconferencing, telemedicine, emergency network, and related activities of intercommunication.

Diagnostic, Interventional, and Therapy Departments

The diagnostic, interventional, and therapy departments are critical to the provision of quality patient care. They are equipped to provide various diagnostic tests and evaluations and both invasive and noninvasive therapeutic procedures, often on a 24-hour basis.

◀ A conference/ educational space at St. John's Regional Medical Center in Oxnard, California.

The diagnostic, interventional, and therapy departments operate as a technical support hub to the inpatient and outpatient functions of the health facility. These departments are typically grouped together to provide integrated service.

◀ A chapel/meditation room at St. John's Regional Medical Center in Oxnard, California.

People, supplies, and diagnostic reports continuously move within and between these departments, which requires careful alignment of functions to support appropriate work flow patterns.

Because of the highly technical nature of these departments, elements should be housed in spaces similar to factory accommodations. This design uses greater floor-to-floor dimensions to incorporate the myriad utility and equipment requirements. A variety of special systems are incorporated into these departments:

- Plumbing—medical gases, special water supply, infectious waste disposal

- Electrical—equipotential grounding, emergency power, special lighting, quick-response signaling

- Heating, ventilation, and air conditioning—air purity, humidity control, special air changes

Logistical Support Departments
Logistical support departments, typically housed in loft type warehouse spaces, are necessary for supply and related functions. These departments, located away from direct nursing, clinical, diagnostic, and treatment activities, are positioned for easy material and service distribution to other departments. As a result a designer must locate these departments with access to horizontal and vertical transport systems in mind.

A variety of transport systems may be required because of the need to separate such items as medical supplies, general supplies, food trays, and movable equipment. Materials management studies should be performed to determine the kinds of transport systems (i.e., elevators, pneumatic tubes, box conveyors, and automated carts) to be included in the

facility. Consideration must also be given to methods for removing waste and soiled linen. A variety of systems are used, including gravity chutes, pneumatic chutes, and cart systems.

It is important to locate the logistical support departments next to areas designated for service truck access and waste container removal. It is best, when possible, to position the service docks out of public view.

Relationship to Other Departments
As mentioned previously, similar types of departments are ideally grouped together. Ancillary departments must be arranged for easy service to the inpatient and ancillary segments of a facility. The movement of people and goods throughout a healthcare facility can be time-consuming and expensive. Therefore, careful study is necessary to minimize distances for the movement of traffic. It is recommended that during early planning, an evaluation of departmental relationships be performed.

One approach to analyzing adjacencies is to establish a departmental matrix. Such a process can establish priorities for relationship and provide various indices and weighting factors for accomplishing appropriate departmental layouts.

General Planning Considerations
Early in the planning process, each department must be sized to accommodate the functions necessary to accomplish its objectives. Early functional planning must establish general concepts of operation, space needs, and required room relationships. As a result, a functional space program can be developed by evaluating activities, projecting work loads

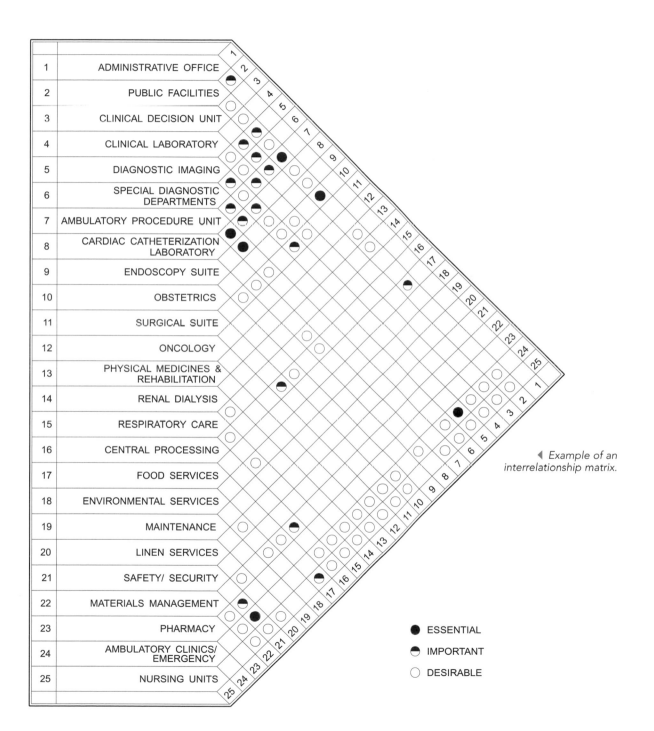

1	ADMINISTRATIVE OFFICE	
2	PUBLIC FACILITIES	
3	CLINICAL DECISION UNIT	
4	CLINICAL LABORATORY	
5	DIAGNOSTIC IMAGING	
6	SPECIAL DIAGNOSTIC DEPARTMENTS	
7	AMBULATORY PROCEDURE UNIT	
8	CARDIAC CATHETERIZATION LABORATORY	
9	ENDOSCOPY SUITE	
10	OBSTETRICS	
11	SURGICAL SUITE	
12	ONCOLOGY	
13	PHYSICAL MEDICINES & REHABILITATION	
14	RENAL DIALYSIS	
15	RESPIRATORY CARE	
16	CENTRAL PROCESSING	
17	FOOD SERVICES	
18	ENVIRONMENTAL SERVICES	
19	MAINTENANCE	
20	LINEN SERVICES	
21	SAFETY/ SECURITY	
22	MATERIALS MANAGEMENT	
23	PHARMACY	
24	AMBULATORY CLINICS/ EMERGENCY	
25	NURSING UNITS	

◀ *Example of an interrelationship matrix.*

● ESSENTIAL
◖ IMPORTANT
○ DESIRABLE

13

and assigning individual room requirements. In establishing various work loads, a variety of utilization factors must be considered in light of the operational procedures within each department. Such procedures vary from one department to another. Work loads are established by considering such factors as diagnostic tests and treatment procedures performed, patient visits, prescriptions dispensed, meals served, and pounds laundered.

After space needs are established and preliminary plans begin, care should be taken in the development of orderly circulation patterns, focusing on the separation of public traffic, service traffic, and the movement of goods. It is desirable to have clear patterns of circulation between departments as well as within each department.

A constant in the functioning of healthcare facilities is the continuing requirement for change. Departments should be planned in a manner that supports independent, open-ended growth and the location of "soft" space adjacent to high-tech functions likely to grow. In addition, the proper use of modularity, multiuse space, and changeable walls and systems can enhance a facility's ability to adapt to new technological and care requirements.

Health facilities operate within a variety of settings, ranging from small community hospitals to large academic medical centers, storefront clinics to multigroup practice ambulatory care centers, and children's hospitals to specialty rehabilitation centers. The quantity and types of ancillary departments are particular to each setting. The rest of this chapter identifies those departments most common in full-service healthcare facilities.

DIAGNOSTIC DEPARTMENTS

Clinical Decision Unit

Clinical decision units are a relatively recent development in healthcare. In an effort to minimize cost, healthcare providers are studying alternatives to limit the number of inpatient admissions. These units offer an opportunity to observe a patient to determine whether admission is necessary. Clinical decision units can also double as sites for treatment and nursing for procedures such as asthma therapy, recovery from cardiac and other interventional procedures, transfusions, enemas, and intravenous (IV) antibody therapy.

The units resemble small nursing units, with care stations and patient rooms or cubicles. To date, many states have not established licensing criteria specifically for this type of unit. If patient stays are limited to 23 hours or less, clinical decision units may be licensed as treatment units generally falling under the requirements for emergency departments. If stays are of more than 23 hours, the units must be licensed as inpatient beds and comply with the requirements for nursing units.

Because their purpose is to minimize the need for admission, these units are typically designed within inpatient hospitals. However, similar units can be used for day hospitals where patients receive nursing and treatment on an ambulatory basis.

Activities and capacities

The key activity factor or work load measure for clinical decision units is patient visits by category—observation or therapeutic procedure. The key capacity determinant is the number of patient positions or rooms. Applying the average time for a visit to the corresponding visit type indicates the amount of room time needed. This, in turn, determines the number of patient positions.

Patient and work flow

Generally, the patient and work flow in clinical decision units is similar to that in nursing units. Patients are taken to diagnostic departments for procedures, and drugs, supplies, and nourishment are brought to them on the unit. A distinguishing characteristic of these units is that patients arrive unscheduled at the hospital, typically at the emergency department. These units often operate as adjuncts and complements to emergency departments and may be under the same medical and administrative direction.

Relationships with other departments

Because of their relationship with emergency departments, clinical decision units are often directly adjacent to and accessible through the emergency entrance. Because they may also be used for scheduled therapeutic procedures, these units must be easily accessible from patient registration as well. If the units are used for recovering patients who have undergone interventional procedures, they must be accessible from the respective departments (e.g., endoscopy, cardiac catheterization laboratory, and interventional radiology).

Space summary

Patient rooms

Used for observing or nursing patients, these are typically individual rooms, although they can be cubicles.

Recommended dimensions: 12 ft × 14 ft

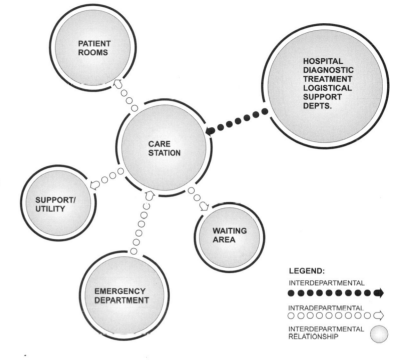

▲ *A clinical decision unit interrelationship diagram.*

Ceiling height: 8 ft is adequate, 9 ft preferable

Key design considerations:

- If licensed as inpatient accommodations, these rooms must have exterior windows. A view to the outdoors is desirable even if the unit is not so licensed.

- A patient toilet should be provided and accessible from within the room.

- Generally, visibility from the care station is desirable. Therefore, the patient toilet should be placed outboard or on the exterior.

- Family members often accompany patients in these units. The rooms should be configured and furnished to accommodate them.

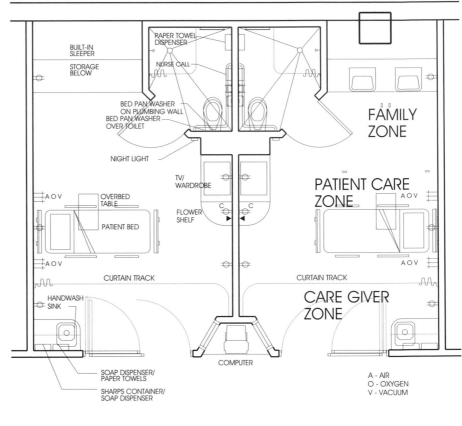

▶ *A patient room plan.*

BUILT-IN SLEEPER
STORAGE BELOW
PAPER TOWEL DISPENSER
NURSE CALL
BED PAN WASHER ON PLUMBING WALL
BED PAN WASHER OVER TOILET
NIGHT LIGHT
FAMILY ZONE
TV/ WARDROBE
FLOWER SHELF
PATIENT CARE ZONE
A O V
OVERBED TABLE
PATIENT BED
A O V
A O V
A O V
CURTAIN TRACK
CURTAIN TRACK
CARE GIVER ZONE
HANDWASH SINK
SOAP DISPENSER/ PAPER TOWELS
SHARPS CONTAINER/ SOAP DISPENSER
COMPUTER

A - AIR
O - OXYGEN
V - VACUUM

0   1'   2'   4'   8'

Special equipment: Patient bed, physiologic monitors, medical gases, and television

Individual supporting spaces: Toilet/shower

Supporting spaces
- Waiting area for family members
- Consultation room for family conferences
- Staff work/nurses station for charting and nursing activities
- Clean utility/supply area
- Soiled utility room
- Equipment storage
- Nourishment station or room
- Staff offices, lockers, lounge/conference room

Special planning and design considerations
- Unit must be on an exterior wall if patient rooms are to be licensed.
- Patients may receive family members or other guests after arriving at the

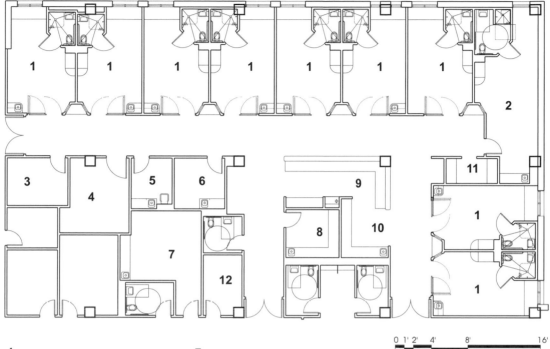

1	PATIENT ROOMS	**7**	LOUNGE
2	ISOLATION PATIENT ROOM	**8**	NOURISHMENT
3	FAMILY WAITING	**9**	CARE STATION
4	STORAGE	**10**	MEDICATION STATION
5	SOILED UTILITY	**11**	DICTATION
6	CLEAN UTILITY	**12**	CONSULTATION

▲ *A clinical decision unit floor plan at Methodist Health Center in Houston, Texas.*

unit, so ease of public access from within the hospital is important.

- A soothing, nonthreatening environment should be provided. This should include positive distractions such as views to the outdoors and artwork.

Trends
With continuing pressure for cost containment, clinical decision units will become more prevalent. They may also become more specialized; for example, a chest pain center may be established, which is a clinical decision unit focused on patients reporting some form of chest pain.

Clinical Laboratory

Functional overview
Most quantitative information about the status of the human body is acquired from studies conducted by clinical laboratory and pathology services. Clinicians use laboratory tests to make decisions about patient care. Basic lab

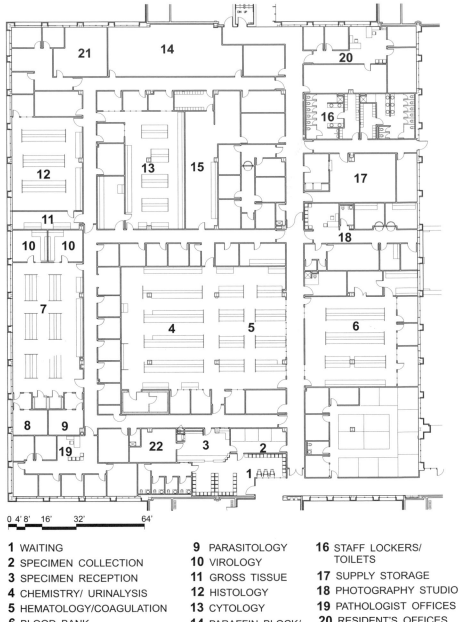

▶ Clinical laboratory floor plan at Brooke Army Medical Center in San Antonio, Texas.

0 4' 8' 16'   32'   64'

1 WAITING
2 SPECIMEN COLLECTION
3 SPECIMEN RECEPTION
4 CHEMISTRY/ URINALYSIS
5 HEMATOLOGY/COAGULATION
6 BLOOD BANK
7 MICROBIOLOGY
8 TB/MYCOLOGY

9 PARASITOLOGY
10 VIROLOGY
11 GROSS TISSUE
12 HISTOLOGY
13 CYTOLOGY
14 PARAFFIN BLOCK/ SLIDE STORAGE
15 STUDENT LAB

16 STAFF LOCKERS/ TOILETS
17 SUPPLY STORAGE
18 PHOTOGRAPHY STUDIO
19 PATHOLOGIST OFFICES
20 RESIDENT'S OFFICES
21 LAB OFFICES
22 REPORT CENTER

services provide information regarding the body's chemical makeup and balance; the presence, numbers, performance, and general activity of cells; inherent genetic characteristics; and the presence and level of bacteria and viral organisms. In addition, analyses of body tissue and cellular condition are assessed through anatomical pathology studies.

Clinical laboratory

Clinical laboratory services include tests conducted by certified medical technologists within typical lab sections:

- *Chemistry.* Consisting of general and automated chemistry, urinalysis, toxicology, and other special chemistry studies that detect or measure levels of elements, enzymes, hormones, vitamins, minerals, drugs, and so forth, within the body's systems.

- *Hematology.* Including manual, automated, and special hematology, serology, and coagulation to determine cell types, population counts, and cell behavior.

- *Blood bank.* Tissue typing and cross-matching; blood holding, preparation, and storage; and blood donor and transfusion services principally related to the collection, identification, augmentation, and re-use or exchange of blood or its components between human beings.

- *Microbiology.* Consisting of microbiology (microorganisms), virology (viruses), parasitology (parasites), mycology (fungi), and tuberculosis and other special organism studies related to the identification and quantification of organisms, natural or foreign, within the body.

- *Immunology.* Consisting of immunoassays and specialized chemistry and blood studies that focus on the characteristics and behavior of the body's immune system.

Anatomical pathology

Anatomical pathology services commonly offered within the clinical laboratory setting are performed by certified pathology technicians and physicians specialized in the field of pathology:

- *Gross tissue.* The physical examination of a large specimen of body tissue to evaluate its conditions and the presence of disease; performed only by physicians.

- *Frozen section.* A quick, preliminary, but more detailed examination of tissue and cells achieved by freezing the tissue, making a thin slice of the specimen, and studying that specimen under a microscope (usually performed for a patient undergoing surgery, during the procedure); performed only by physicians.

- *Histology.* The processing of gross tissue for study under a microscope by a physician; the processing is completed by technicians.

- *Cytology.* The processing and examination of blood or other fluid tissue for cell abnormalities; performed by both technicians (preliminary study) and physicians.

- *Autopsy/morgue.* Autopsy resources facilitate the physical examination of a corpse to identify the cause of death and to compile important postmortem data. The morgue includes this procedure room and provides capacity to temporarily hold corpses until their dispatch from the hospital.

Service locations

The basic components of a clinical laboratory are required in every acute care hospital by building code. Laboratories are frequently located in ambulatory care centers and physicians' offices. The volume of tests is a key factor to financial viability, but rapid results for the physician are of equal or greater importance.

The testing resource of laboratories is not critical to any healthcare entity's operation, except as it relates to turnaround time from specimen collection to reporting of results. The processing area of the laboratory does not have to be accessible to patients nor to occupy prime space. It is important that the collection point for specimens, however, be very convenient for ambulatory patients. Blood, urine, and certain other specimens are collected in the physician's office or a collection center. Efficiency in specimen transportation to the lab's processing area and in reporting results to the physician are critical to minimizing test turnaround time.

Many lab tests, general and specialized, may be more economically accomplished using outsourced services of a large, centralized lab. Such laboratories can perform tests at substantially lower costs. Pathology services may not always be included in smaller facilities with relationships to other institutions. Typically, the frozen section component is located adjacent to surgery for immediate access during procedures. The morgue is usually located near the service dock for discreet storage and removal of bodies.

Demand for rapid turnaround of results can justify the placement of a satellite lab resource in addition to the main laboratory. Such facilities may be next to or within emergency departments or intensive care units (adult and neonatal). A common example is blood gas analysis. If the lab is responsible for this test (sometimes performed by the respiratory therapy department), an analyzer may be located within these departments. The cost of an analyzer is relatively low, operation is simple, and instant feedback is provided. Generally, laboratories are centralized for optimum efficiency in staffing, management, quality control, and equipment utilization.

Key activity factors

Clinical laboratories are process-intensive centers. They are responsible for collecting or receiving specimens, preparing and logging them for tracking/reporting purposes, analyzing them through automated or manual procedures, and reporting the results via computer back to the physician's office or hospital unit requesting the information. The volume of procedures on a daily basis influences space demand. However, the way in which tests are accomplished is the critical space determinant. Test volume has proven to be an inappropriate measure for productivity comparison or space demand because of the variability in testing time and availability of technology.

Key capacity determinants

Laboratory capacity is determined by the speed of available technology and the number of available workstations to run tests simultaneously. The majority of tests performed in labs today are automated, requiring relatively little handling by technologists—except to initiate the testing process or to calibrate and verify properly functioning equipment. Therefore, the types and

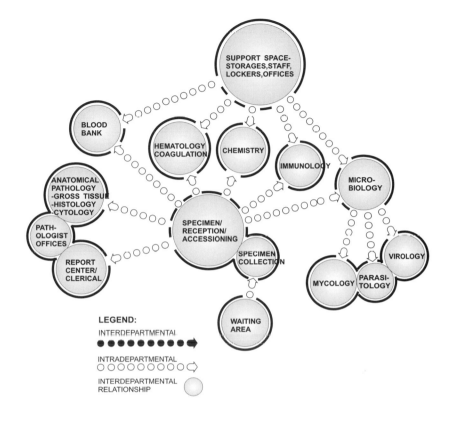

◀ *A clinical laboratory and pathology interrelationship diagram.*

numbers of testing machines within each lab section determine the capacity of the lab and the amount of space needed.

Patient and work flow

Patient flow is limited to the specimen collection area, a relatively small part of the total lab. This function, separated from the main lab processing area, should be easily accessible for ambulatory patients. The space provides for patients' reception, registration, and waiting area prior to the collection of blood, urine, or other specimens for analysis. The rest of the clinical laboratory does not occupy prime space designated for patient accessibility. However, it should have easy pathways for walking or

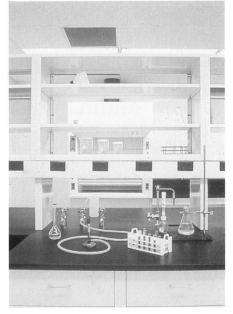

◀ *A laboratory workstation at the University of Arkansas for Medical Sciences Biomedical Research Center*

automated transport systems for the movement of specimens.

Work flow within this processing area begins in the specimen reception or "accessioning" area. It moves to various sections of the lab where tests are conducted. After they are received and logged at the accessioning area, specimens are divided, "spun down" as needed by a centrifuge, and distributed within the lab to specific spaces for testing. From the specimen reception area, they go directly to the chemistry, hematology, coagulation, immunology, blood bank, or microbiology functions for further processing, analysis, and testing.

Once a test is performed, the results are electronically reported in the report center or printed in hard copy for the physician requesting the information. Surplus specimens and pathological tissue, considered biohazardous, are collected in special containers for safe removal and disposal by waste management vendors.

Surgical specimens, which typically require a response while a procedure is under way, are examined in a frozen section lab within the surgery department. The pathologist has easy peripheral access to this area. In lieu of this design, specimens may be carried directly by courier to the gross tissue area of pathology for review.

GENERAL SPACE REQUIREMENTS, CLINICAL LABORATORIES

Workstation	Suggested Area per Station (net square feet)	Optimal Dimensions (feet)	Necessary Adjacent Support Spaces
Chemistry/Immunology/Toxicology			Refrigerated reagent storage
Countertop unit	60–100	8 x 10	Specimen set-up area
Floor unit	120–150	10 x 15	Computer/printer area
Hematology/Coagulation			Specimen set-up area
Automated station	60–100	8 x 10	
Microscope station	60–80	8 x 8	
Blood bank	60–100	8 x 10	Blood refrigerators Blood freezers
Microbiology			
Setup/prep	100–150	10 x 15	Biohazard hood
Reading	60–100	8 x 10	Incubator cabinets or room
Virology/Mycology/Tuberculosis (TB) lab	150–250	12 x 15	Biohazard hood
Gross tissue	80–120	10 x 10	(None)
Histology	100–120	10 x 10	Tissue processor area
Cytology	60–80	8 x 10	Slide storage
Autopsy	350–480	20 x 24	Changing area Body refrigerator Specimen storage room

Relationships with other departments

Most of the laboratory services that are analytical can be located away from other departments. Turnaround time for results is critical, however, and thus specimen transport is a key factor in this support service. Specimen collection is most convenient when located near outpatient registration or ambulatory surgery. In many cases, a small frozen-section lab is located within the surgical suite. The pathologist, based in the laboratory, can go to this location to quickly assess the specimen and consult with the surgeon.

Key spaces

State and local building codes typically address only the need for a laboratory resource within an acute care hospital. There are no such requirements in ambulatory care settings—only practical demand for immediate convenience. These codes should, however, always be reviewed for minimum standards necessary for plan approval.

Best practice standards within the healthcare industry, including some generations of the American Institute of Architects (AIA) *Guidelines for Design and Construction of Hospital and Health Care Facilities*, suggest guidelines for selected spaces, as shown in the table on page 22.

Key design considerations

There are numerous factors to be considered in planning the contemporary clinical laboratory; many traditional requirements have changed in recent years. The following are today's key design considerations:

- Direct access from the specimen reception center to each section of the lab is paramount for expedient work

flow. When necessary, these sections may be ranked according to volume of work flow. For example, if compromise is required because of space configuration, chemistry and hematology are most frequently located closest to the specimen reception area. Microbiology may be located farthest away from the reception area because of the lower volume of testing to be performed, and to isolate these biohazardous activities from other procedures. Pathology areas may also be farther away, as the specimens are fewer in number and may go directly from surgery or other procedure areas to the pathology lab, bypassing the reception center.

- Many workstations within the laboratory function most effectively as large open areas offering maximum flexibility. Some areas, such as microbiology, must be enclosed in separate rooms because of the potential for the spread of infectious disease or unpleasant odors. Specimen collection areas, the only areas of patient interaction, must be designed with patient accessibility, comfort, and privacy in mind.

- Clinical laboratories provide 24-hour service in hospital settings. If by design or operational decision the lab sections are large and physically far apart, a "stat lab" may be created within the lab to speed response time. The "stat lab" is designed to handle the most routine of specimen analyses from each of the lab sections. In this instance, travel distance for the minimum staff on night shifts is the prime consideration. Ideally, the

▲ *A clinical laboratory using modular casework at Texas Scottish Rite Hospital for Children in Dallas, Texas.*

physical configuration of all sections proximate to the specimen reception area can obviate the need for the potentially redundant equipment of a stat lab.

- Various support spaces for the lab sections can be expensive and can require considerable floor area. Examples include cold rooms and walk-in refrigerators, water purification equipment, incubators, storage for flammables, microscope slide storage, and paraffin block storage.
- The pathologist's office and transcription and clerical work areas are best located near the gross tissue lab, histology, and cytology, where frequent physician interaction is required.

Special equipment or furniture requirements

The modern laboratory uses highly technical equipment. Thus, there are a number of special considerations:

- Workstations must be capable of accommodating manual testing by technologists, or automated testing by bench-top or floor-standing equipment. Countertop heights vary depending on whether the technician is standing or sitting. Stations for tasks that are conducted in a sitting position include cross-matching in the blood bank, manual differential counting stations for hematology, and microscope reading stations for microbiology and cytology.

- The broad array of automated analyzers used throughout the lab often requires special plumbing, electrical, ventilation, or antivibration design measures. Chemistry and hematology analyzers require floor drains or self-contained runoff collection systems. Pathology gross tissue examination stations and histology tissue processors require considerable design attention to control and exhaust fumes properly. Virtually all of this equipment has built-in or complementary computer keyboards, monitors, and printers. These systems often require clean power via dedicated circuits. Telecommunications connections are now required for automated equipment, telephones, Internet, data transfer, and direct reporting of test results.

- Biohazard hoods for strict ventilation management of potentially infectious diseases or agents are required in microbiology, mycology, parasitology, tuberculosis, and virology labs.

- Many laboratory areas require highly purified water, which is usually supplied by a reverse osmosis system either centrally located or distributed near equipment requiring this resource.

- Many specimens and reagents require refrigeration, which should be decentralized to local storage areas close to the consuming units.

- Where there is exposure to infectious materials and chemical agents, emergency eye-washing and shower facilities within the immediate work area are essential and required by code.

- Pneumatic tube systems, typically 6 in. in diameter, are widely used for specimen transport from locations throughout a facility to the lab. Virtually all specimens can be handled by these systems, although pathology tissue specimens are still physically carried, by habit. More sophisticated transport systems may be used, but these are typically not economically feasible. Manual transport by courier or by the phlebotomist on routine schedules may also be used, but this method is diminishing as the processing areas of laboratories are located farther from prime public spaces used for patient care.

Supporting spaces

Support spaces for the direct procedure areas of the lab are varied, as follows:

- Many types of storage space within casework or in dedicated rooms are needed for chemical reagents, patient test and quality control records, bulk supplies, specimens, microscope slides, paraffin blocks, and clinical specimens used for education or research.

- Phlebotomists frequently circulate through the nursing units to collect regularly scheduled specimens. Other departments, such as emergency and surgery, send specimens to the lab as needed, using employee couriers and pneumatic tubes. The phlebotomists need a well-stocked supply storage area proximate to the specimen reception areas where they conclude their scheduled rounds.

- The lab utilizes several flammable reagents and other nonflammable substances, such as formaldehyde. These are delivered to the logistics dock and then distributed to the lab. Special storage is required for these substances in small quantities within the lab. A ventilated, rated storage room for backup stock is typically located near the dock.

- For autopsy, the deceased body is transported discreetly to the body holding area or the autopsy suite. After the autopsy, the body can be released for mortuary pickup.

Support spaces for service administration and staff are also required:

- Each section of the lab needs a quality control and section director administrative work area.

- Reception and registration areas are required within the specimen collection area.

- Because of the 24-hour utilization of areas like the stat. lab, staff support areas in close proximity to the lab work areas are required. Accommodations include a staff lounge with pantry, lockers, and toilets (separate from patient toilets).

Special planning and design considerations

Special design considerations for the clinical laboratory include the following:

- Laboratories have traditionally been organized around a repetitive array of casework configurations, which enhances flexibility. Today's casework is modular and easily moveable to facilitate quick, economical rearrangement, accommodating the latest technology. This technology may require open floor areas rather than bench space, or movable benches for frequent access to areas behind the equipment for maintenance or quality control.

- Because the use of lab bench casework is intensive, work height becomes critical, especially in light of the Americans with Disabilities Act (ADA). Casework 36 in. high is standard. However, 34 in. is required for handicapped accessibility. Modular, "active" casework systems contribute substantially to work height flexibility.

- The large amounts of carcinogenic or flammable reagents present in a lab, as well as the handling of bodily tissues and biohazardous materials, invokes regulation of laboratory design and operation by agencies such as the Occupational Safety and Health Administration (OSHA) and the National Fire Protection Association (NFPA).

- Chemical-resistant and stain-resistant materials should be used for laboratory worktops and casework finishes. Bacteria-resistant, cleanable building finishes should be used in all areas. In areas of gross tissue handling, such as gross tissue stations and the frozen section lab, stainless steel is often used to enhance cleanability and durability.

Trends

Analyzers and processors are becoming entirely computerized for handling specimens and reporting lab results. A natural extension of this progression would indicate that robotics are a probability in the lab of the future. The system developmental cost will allow the current trend—centralized laboratory services, located in a less expensive, nonhospital setting, serving more than one facility—to continue. Point-of-care testing, individual tests performed by the caregiver at bedside or in the examining room, will become affordable and, ultimately, will replace many of today's routine laboratory tests performed in large processing centers. Progress in genetic mapping and gene therapy research will, however, broaden the current activities of the clinical laboratory and pathology to support the efforts of medical science to predict—and then to manage or prevent—disease, much as we seek to identify and cure disease today.

Diagnostic Imaging

In the last two decades, the pace of advancement in imaging technology has drastically accelerated. This is due to the development of digitized information technology—the recording of images via electronic rather than film media. The first development with widespread clinical applications was computerized axial tomography, or the CT scan.

Developments in digital technology will continue, making imaging more accessible and cost-effective. There are various ways in which a signal is created; for example, images are created with the use of isotopes generated by a cyclotron in positron emission transmission. Magnetic resonance imaging (MRI) also uses digital imaging technology. Not only does this afford a better way of imaging soft tissue, which does not have to be made radio-opaque, it portends the development of spectroscopic techniques allowing chemical diagnosis of the body without taking specimens.

Context

Imaging facilities can be located in many places: the traditional hospital radiology department, the ambulatory care center, freestanding imaging centers. In smaller facilities, one department typically contains all modalities. In larger facilities, inpatient and outpatient modalities may be separated. For example, there may be a separate nuclear medicine department or MRI facility. In some instances, imaging modalities can be collocated with other diagnostic/treatment facilities to create healthcare centers of excellence (various technologies to focus on a specific organ or patient type), such as mammography and ultrasonography in a women's center.

Many modalities can also be provided through portable devices. This allows procedures to be performed at the point of care in a patient's bedroom, in an examination room, or in other treatment areas, such as the operating room.

Patient and work flow

Patients may receive more than one procedure per visit, so it is important to quantify the number and the average duration of procedures a patient undergoes.

Patients can arrive at an imaging facility from a number of sources. Wheelchair or stretcher-borne patients may come from inpatient units or other treatment areas, such as emergency. Ambulatory patients may arrive—scheduled or without appointments—at a reception desk. Typically, departments are configured to separate the flow of these two types of patients.

Another key consideration in patient flow is the requirement for changing— that is, donning a hospital gown in preparation for a procedure. Historically, patients were separated by gender and waited, gowned, in waiting areas. More recent departmental designs provide individual dressing rooms adjacent to the procedure room, where patients can change and wait with greater privacy.

The flow of patients through the department intersects with the process of image generation, interpretation, and results reporting. Historically, this was a sequential process that involved

1. exposing the film, using the appropriate modality,

2. developing and checking the quality of the film image,

3. repeating the exposure if necessary,

4. viewing and interpretation by a radiologist,

5. dictation and transcription of the interpretation and forwarding the report to the requesting physician or surgeon,

6. filing both the film and the written report.

This process required the radiologist's location to be central to the patient and work flow in order to expedite the interpretation of the film. With the development of digitized image storage systems, this need has dwindled.

Relationships with other departments

The imaging department interacts with a large number of other departments. Both outpatients and inpatients can be referred to imaging for diagnostic studies; however, certain departments have stronger relationships with imaging. The emergency department, for example, is

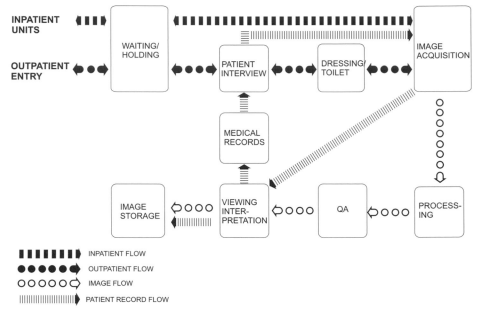

INPATIENT
UNITS

OUTPATIENT
ENTRY

WAITING/
HOLDING

PATIENT
INTERVIEW

DRESSING/
TOILET

IMAGE
ACQUISITION

MEDICAL
RECORDS

IMAGE
STORAGE

VIEWING
INTER-
PRETATION

QA

PROCESS-
ING

▮▮▮▮▮▮▮▮▶ INPATIENT FLOW

●●●●●●▶ OUTPATIENT FLOW

○○○○○⇦ IMAGE FLOW

||||||||||||||||||||||▶ PATIENT RECORD FLOW

▶ *An imaging department's patient and work flow diagram.*

frequently positioned adjacent to imaging because of the large proportion of emergency patients requiring prompt radiological studies.

Other special situations include casting facilities, women's diagnostic centers, and nuclear cardiology. Casting facilities, for resetting broken bones, may be placed in emergency departments or in speciality clinics. These facilities require radiography to ensure that broken bones have been set properly. This is usually achieved by providing radiographic capabilities in or adjacent to cast rooms. Otherwise, the casting area should be next to imaging for confirming the appropriateness of bone reduction.

Women's diagnostic centers require mammography, ultrasonography, and bone densitometry to test for

osteoporosis. Satellite imaging facilities are often incorporated within these centers. Alternatively, women's imaging may be incorporated as a "subdepartment" of imaging, with a separate entrance and waiting area.

Nuclear cardiology is a unique crossover of services providing cardiologic diagnosis via imaging technology. The process involves introducing a radioactive medium into the vascular system. The effectiveness of the patient's cardiovascular system is then observed by monitoring the movement of the medium through the body while the patient is "stressed" through exercise. Because this service treats cardiology patients, the usual preference is to perform such studies in cardiodiagnostic areas (e.g., in a noninvasive cardiac laboratory).

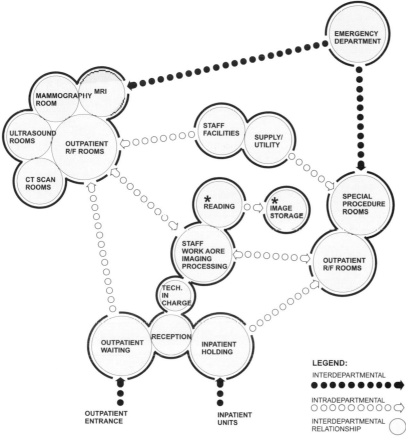

LEGEND:

INTERDEPARTMENTAL
●●●●●●●●➤

INTRADEPARTMENTAL
○○○○○○○○○⇨

INTERDEPARTMENTAL
RELATIONSHIP ◯

* WITH DIGITAL ARCHIVING, READING AND IMAGE STORAGE MAY BE REMOTE

◀ *An imaging department's interrelationship diagram.*

Space summary

Radiography room

Radiography is the simplest form of radiology, relying on direct exposure of film (or a digital image processor) with an X-ray-emitting device called a tube. This is most useful for creating images of X-ray absorbing tissues such as bones. A variation of radiography is tomography, which uses a rotating tube source and film carrier to create a two-dimensional image of a "slice" of the body. Although the equipment is slightly different, the room requirements and considerations are essentially the same for both techniques. All types of radiography rooms require lead-lined walls.

Recommended dimensions: 17 ft x 15 ft; making the room 20 ft x 16 ft renders it capable of conversion to a radiography/fluoroscopy room, should that later become desirable.

Ceiling height: 9 ft 6 in.

Key design considerations:
- Configure the space to allow a stretcher to be maneuvered into the room with minimum turns, typically by placing the axis of the X-ray table perpendicular to the wall with the door by which the patient will enter the room.
- Place the control console opposite the door with direct access to the vertical work core.

Special equipment: Table and tube, wall bucky (a device that holds film in a position during exposure), control console, sink and casework, and transformer and power cabinet (the latter may be placed outside the room).

Individual supporting spaces: None.

General fluoroscopy room

Fluoroscopy makes use of radio-opaque media that may be introduced into the body to create images of tissue that would not otherwise show up well on an X-ray. Because the radio-opaque material is typically barium introduced through the mouth or the rectum, it is important to have a toilet room directly accessible from the procedure room.

Recommended dimensions: 20 ft x 16 ft

Ceiling height: 9 ft 6 in.

Key design considerations:
- Configure the space to allow a stretcher to be maneuvered into the room with minimum turns, typically by placing the axis of the X-ray table perpendicular to the wall with the door by which the patient will enter the room.
- Place the control console opposite the door with direct access to the work core.

- These rooms often serve as radiography rooms as well.
- Attach the toilet room directly to the fluoroscopy room.
- Barium may be prepared in the procedure room or a nearby "kitchen."

Special equipment: Fluoroscopic X-ray tube and table, image intensifier, cine or "spot" film camera, video monitor, wall bucky, control console, sink and casework, and transformer and power cabinet (the latter may be placed outside the room).

Individual supporting spaces: Patient toilet, barium preparation area.

Chest room

Chest X-rays typically constitute the largest single category of diagnostic procedures. They are often performed as a screening tool in conjunction with hospital admission or invasive procedures that will require general anesthesia and suppression of respiration. Many radiography or radiography/fluoroscopy rooms are equipped with wall buckies for chest imaging. However, because chest imaging can constitute a high proportion of this department's activity, a large department can justify dedicating a room or rooms solely to chest imaging. Because such rooms are designed specifically for this purpose, they are typically more operationally efficient than multipurpose rooms. Even greater efficiencies can be achieved by incorporating film processing with equipment that automatically feeds directly into the film processor.

Recommended dimensions: 12 ft x 11 ft (without in-room processing), 16 ft x 14 ft (with in-room processing)

Ceiling height: 9ft 6in.

Key design considerations:

- To maximize efficiency, the equipment control console is typically incorporated directly into the room.

- The focal length of the tube assembly is fixed and must be maintained.

- If in-room processing is utilized, chemicals and equipment must be accommodated outside the patient area.

- In larger rooms, it is possible that a stretcher-borne patient will be X-rayed. Thus, the room should have a door large enough to accommodate a stretcher and be configured to allow maneuvering of the stretcher.

Special equipment: Tube assembly, changer and stand, console control and transformer in room without processing; the same equipment, plus auto film transport, auto film processor, silver recovery, and chemical manifold in room with processing.

Individual supporting spaces: None.

Mammography room

Mammography is a specific type of radiography that employs low-level radiation to identify tumoral calcifications and to characterize palpable lumps and unpalpable cysts or lumps in breast tissue. The mammography room is single-purpose room with a X-ray unit. Using a specialized type of mammography, the stereotactic room provides the radiologist with a three-dimensional view of the breast for localizing neoplasms for biopsy.

Recommended dimensions: 10 ft x 12 ft for an upright unit, 18 ft x 12 ft for a prone or stereotactic unit

Ceiling height: 8 ft

Key design considerations:

- As this is a smaller room and the patient will be disrobed, reverse swinging doors and/or curtains are used to prevent exposure of the patient.

Special equipment: Mammography unit, film illuminators, and sink in a mammography room; stereotactic biopsy table, operator's console and digitizer in a stereotactic room.

Individual supporting spaces: None.

Ultrasound room

Ultrasound or sonography operates on the principles of sonar and records size and shape by tracking reflected sound waves. Typically, a hand-held transducer emits regular pulses of high-frequency sound and translates the received "echoes" into images. Because tissue density affects sound reflectivity, the returned sound wave's amplitude allows graphic depiction of different tissues. This procedure is especially beneficial when the use of ionizing rays could be harmful to tissue, such as when a fetus is present.

Recommended dimensions: 11 ft x 14 ft

Ceiling height: 8 ft

Key design considerations: Because this is a smaller room and the patient may be disrobed, reverse swinging doors and/or curtains are used to prevent exposure of the patient.

Special equipment: Ultrasound unit (console typically placed to the patient's right side), stretcher, film illuminators.

Individual supporting spaces: None.

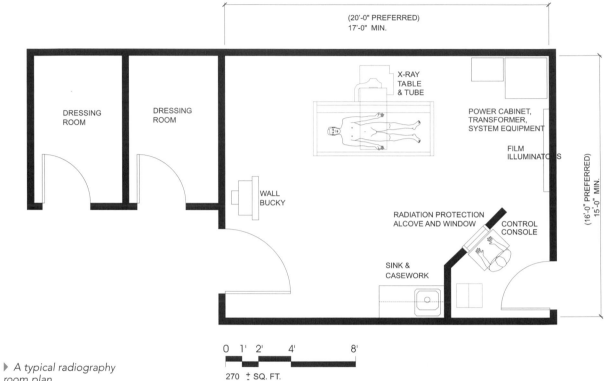

(20'-0" PREFERRED)
17'-0" MIN.

DRESSING ROOM

DRESSING ROOM

X-RAY TABLE & TUBE

POWER CABINET, TRANSFORMER, SYSTEM EQUIPMENT

FILM ILLUMINATORS

WALL BUCKY

RADIATION PROTECTION ALCOVE AND WINDOW

CONTROL CONSOLE

SINK & CASEWORK

(16'-0" PREFERRED) 15'-0" MIN.

0 1' 2'   4'   8'

270 ± SQ. FT.

▶ A typical radiography room plan

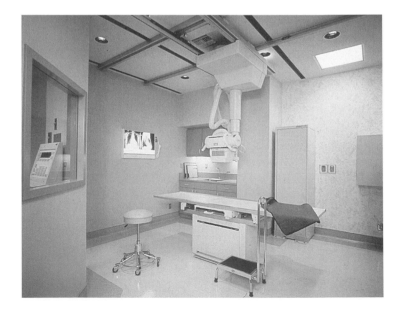

▶ A radiography room at Sharp Mary Birch Hospital for Women in San Diego, California.

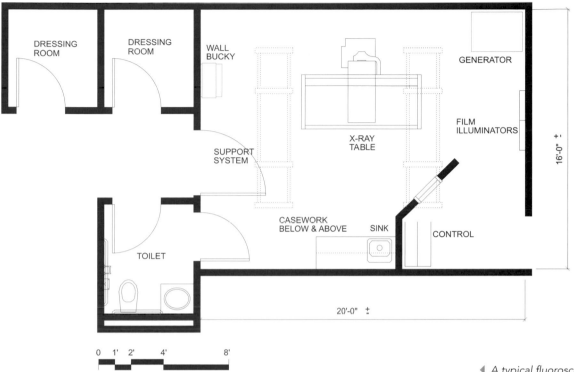

DRESSING ROOM

DRESSING ROOM

WALL BUCKY

GENERATOR

FILM ILLUMINATORS

SUPPORT SYSTEM

X-RAY TABLE

CASEWORK BELOW & ABOVE

SINK

CONTROL

TOILET

16'-0" ±

20'-0" ±

0 1' 2' 4' 8'

320 ± SQ. FT.

◀ A typical fluoroscopy room plan.

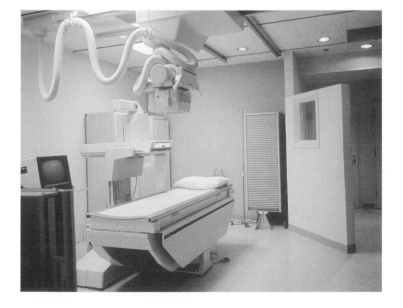

◀ A fluoroscopy room at All Saints Episcopal Hospital-Cityview in Fort Worth, Texas.

33

ANCILLARY DEPARTMENTS

▶ *A typical chest room plan.*

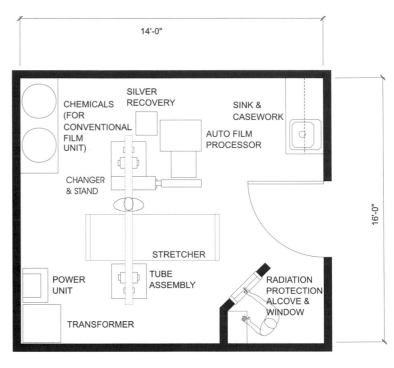

14'-0"

CHEMICALS (FOR CONVENTIONAL FILM UNIT)

SILVER RECOVERY

SINK & CASEWORK

AUTO FILM PROCESSOR

CHANGER & STAND

STRETCHER

POWER UNIT

TUBE ASSEMBLY

RADIATION PROTECTION ALCOVE & WINDOW

TRANSFORMER

16'-0"

* 11'-0" x 12'-0" WITHOUT FILM PROCESSOR

0   1'   2'   4'   8'

225 ± SQ. FT.

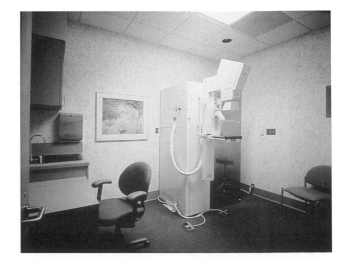

▶ *A mammography room at Sharp Mary Birch Hospital for Women in San Diego, California.*

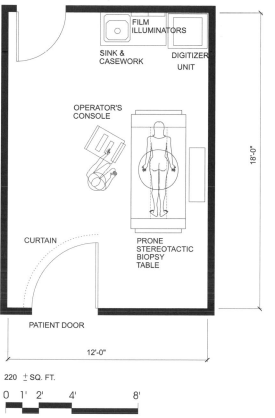

WORK CORE

STAFF DOOR (OPTIONAL)

FILM ILLUMINATORS

SINK & CASEWORK

DIGITIZER UNIT

OPERATOR'S CONSOLE

18'-0"

PRONE STEREOTACTIC BIOPSY TABLE

CURTAIN

PATIENT DOOR

12'-0"

220 ± SQ. FT.

0 1' 2'   4'   8'

◀ *A typical stereotactic (women's diagnostic imaging) room plan.*

▼ *A typical mammography room plan.*

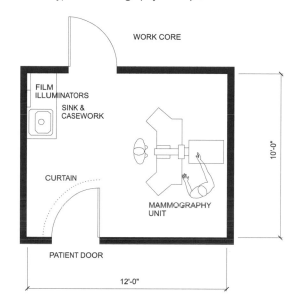

WORK CORE

FILM ILLUMINATORS

SINK & CASEWORK

10'-0"

CURTAIN

MAMMOGRAPHY UNIT

PATIENT DOOR

12'-0"

120 ± SQ. FT.

CT scanning room

A computed tomography (CT) room provides an X-ray source that rotates rapidly around a patient, generating digital data.

Recommended dimensions: 16 ft x 19 ft for a procedure room, 10 ft x 12 ft for a control room, and 7 ft x 10 ft for an equipment room.

Ceiling height: 9 ft 6 in.

Key design considerations:

• The patient access door should be positioned to minimize stretcher turning because of the length of the equipment. At the same time, the view from the control room of the patient on the table while positioned in the opening of the unit must be at least partially preserved. At times, a video camera is used to supplement this capability.

Special equipment: CT gantry and table in the procedure room. The control room includes operator's console, video monitor, injector control, laser imager, and physician's viewing or diagnostic

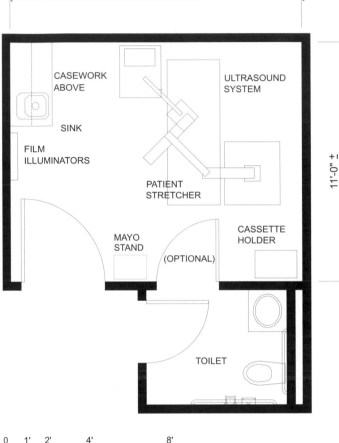

14'-0" ±

CASEWORK ABOVE

ULTRASOUND SYSTEM

SINK

FILM ILLUMINATORS

PATIENT STRETCHER

11'-0" ±

MAYO STAND

CASSETTE HOLDER

(OPTIONAL)

TOILET

0 1' 2' 4' 8'

160 ± SQ. FT.

▲ A typical ultrasound room plan.

station. (The last two items may be placed remotely in a multiunit suite.) An equipment room houses the power and computer equipment.

Individual supporting spaces: Control and equipment rooms. These may serve more than one procedure room.

MRI scanning room

Magnetic resonance imaging (MRI) is performed by placing the patient in a powerful magnetic field that aligns the magnetic spin of atomic nuclei. Radio frequency energy is introduced, which disturbs the alignment of the nuclei. Different atoms respond at different radio frequencies, thus providing a distinction between tissue types. This powerful tool does not utilize ionizing rays and can create detailed two-and three-dimensional images of both hard and soft tissue.

Recommended dimensions: Varies with strength of magnet; generally, about 20 ft x 26 ft for procedure room with a midstrength magnet; along with a 10 ft x 12 ft control room and an 8 ft x 18 ft adjacent equipment/computer room. With lower-strength magnets, the room can be as small as 12 ft x 16 ft with a 9 ft x 12 ft equipment room and the control station in the open. (Refer to manufacturer's specifications for specific model.)

Ceiling height: Varies.

Key design considerations:

• The MRI magnet creates a field whose strength diminishes with distance. Magnetic field strength is expressed in units of measure called *gauss.* More recent generations of MRI units contain the 5-gauss line within the procedure room itself.

• As MRIs use radio frequencies to generate images, they are susceptible to electromagnetic interference from

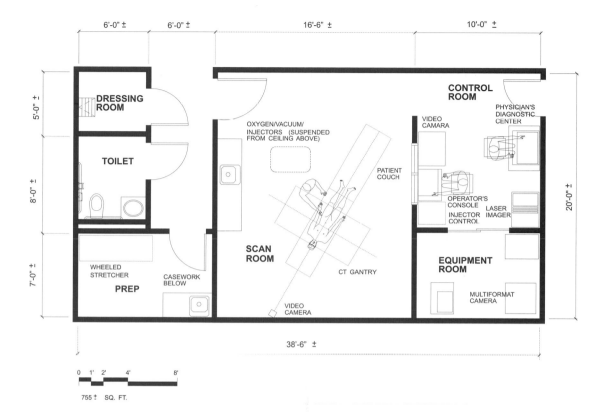

6'-0" ± 6'-0" ± 16'-6" ± 10'-0" ±

5'-0" ±

DRESSING ROOM

CONTROL ROOM

PHYSICIAN'S DIAGNOSTIC CENTER

VIDEO CAMARA

TOILET

OXYGEN/VACUUM/ INJECTORS (SUSPENDED FROM CEILING ABOVE)

PATIENT COUCH

8'-0" ±

OPERATOR'S CONSOLE

INJECTOR CONTROL

LASER IMAGER

20'-0" ±

SCAN ROOM

WHEELED STRETCHER

CASEWORK BELOW

PREP

CT GANTRY

7'-0" ±

VIDEO CAMERA

EQUIPMENT ROOM

MULTIFORMAT CAMERA

38'-6" ±

0 1' 2' 4' 8'

755 ± SQ. FT.

outside sources. To shield the room it is often wrapped with a copper fabric.

• Because the patient is placed into a unit approximately 8 ft in length and 2½ ft in diameter, claustrophobia can be a problem. New-generation magnets have mitigated this problem with ultralow field strength magnets designed with open architecture. Still, procedure room interior design should take into consideration exterior lighting (or the implication of it) and other devices to address this issue.

Special equipment: MRI unit, patient couch, and coil storage in procedure room. Control room includes operator's console and video monitor. Equipment room houses the power and computer equipment.

▲ A typical CT scanning room plan.

◀ A CT scanning room at McAllen Regional Medical Center in McAllen, Texas.

37

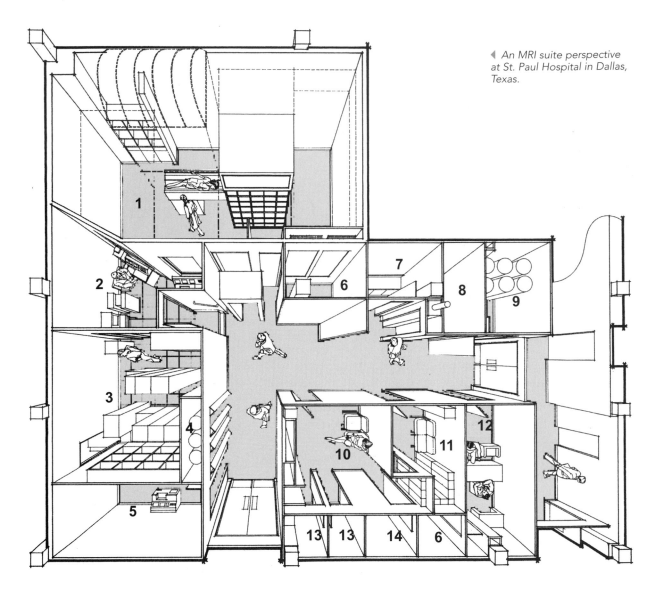

An MRI suite perspective at St. Paul Hospital in Dallas, Texas.

1	SCAN ROOM	8	ELECTRICAL ROOM
2	CONTROL	9	GAS STORAGE
3	COMPUTER ROOM	10	WAITING
4	HALON STORAGE	11	EMPLOYEE LOUNGE
5	DOCTORS READING	12	PHYSICST OFFICE
6	STORAGE	13	DRESSING
7	DARK ROOM	14	TOILET

Individual supporting spaces: Control and equipment rooms. These may serve more than one procedure room.

Nuclear medicine room

Unlike radiography, which transmits radiation in the form of X-rays, nuclear medicine introduces a low-strength, short-lived, radiation-emitting isotope into the body. The emissions are captured by a camera and translated into images. By introducing the isotope or radio-pharmaceutical into specific tissues and organs, radiologists can capture images that would otherwise be unattainable. A recently developed type of nuclear medicine camera—single photon emission computed tomography, or SPECT—has gained wide acceptance and application. It combines a nuclear medicine or gamma camera with digital image acquisition and interpretation capabilities to generate tomographic portrayals of blood flow to the brain and heart.

Recommended dimensions: 18 ft x 16 ft for a single camera room. Because nuclear medicine does not involve the use of X-rays, multiple cameras may be placed in a single room with adequate space.

Ceiling height: 9 ft

Key design considerations:

• Because nuclear medicine involves the use of radioactive materials, special provisions must be made for their containment and disposal. Most of these are injectable substances. However, some are gaseous pharmaceuticals, such as xenon gas for ventilation studies, which must be specially contained and exhausted.

Special equipment: Control console, computer workstation, collimator, collimator stand, whole body scintillation camera and table, and xenon delivery system.

Individual supporting spaces:

• A hot lab where radiopharmaceuticals are prepared, equipped with cabinets and work counter, lead-lined containers for storing and working with radioactive substances, lead-lined refrigerator, 100 percent exhaust radioisotope hood, and approved system for radioactive waste collection and disposal.

• Dose room, where patients are injected with radiopharmaceuticals. The inclusion of this room enhances procedure room productivity.

Positron emission tomography scanning room

In the positron emission tomography (PET) scanning room, physicians introduce radioisotopes by injection or inhalation. The isotope attaches to the body's own molecules, becoming a tracer

◄ *An MRI scanning room at MD Anderson Cancer Center in Houston, Texas.*

▶ *A typical nuclear medicine room plan.*

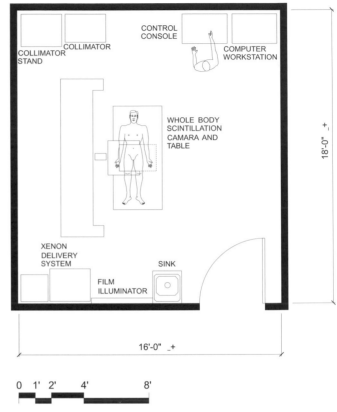

▼ *A nuclear medicine full-body scanner at McAllen Regional Medical Center in McAllen, Texas.*

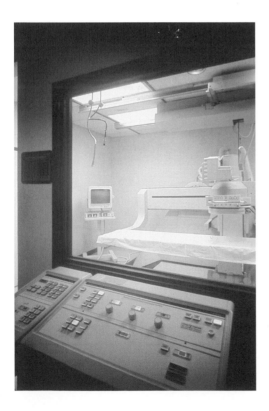

as it moves throughout the body. Typically, the isotope is very short-lived and must be generated on-site with a cyclotron. This makes PET an expensive, but effective, diagnostic tool.

Recommended dimensions: 15 ft × 20 ft for scanner room alone

Ceiling height: 10 ft

Key design considerations:

- Ideally, the scanning room is placed adjacent to the radiochemistry lab, which itself must be adjacent the cyclotron. When this is not possible, a pneumatic tube system can be used to deliver the radiopharmaceutical to the clinical lab.

Special equipment: Scanner and patient couch, computer.

Individual supporting spaces:

- Cyclotron room of 500 sq ft with 10 ft ceiling. Because of the weight of these units (approximately 120,000 lb), a grade level location should be sought.

- Radiochemistry lab of 600 sq ft where the actual pharmaceuticals are prepared. Ideally, it is located adjacent to the cyclotron room.

- A control room, where computer equipment for data acquisition and processing is housed.

- Patient preparation rooms with stretchers or chairs.

Special radiography/fluoroscopy procedure rooms

Special radiography/fluoroscopy procedures include techniques that employ radiographic or fluoroscopic imaging equipment for guidance during complex exploratory and interventional procedures.

Although the procedures performed in these rooms may vary, they have in common the introduction of a catheter and the use of large and complex equipment, including one or two fluoroscopic C-arms. Because the introduction of a catheter invades the body, some minimally sterile techniques must be observed.

Recommended dimensions: 28 ft x 22 ft for the procedure room alone

Ceiling height: 10 ft

Key design considerations:

- The equipment should be arranged to allow visibility of the patient's head from the control monitor.

- Many procedures occur while the patient is awake and acutely aware of his or her surroundings. Therefore, measures should be taken to create a soothing environment.

- Because the procedures require a semisterile environment, extraneous traffic should be limited.

Special equipment:
Radiographic/fluoroscopic arm(s), one or two, depending on whether the unit has biplane capabilities; video monitors, patient table, injector, surgical lights and back tables, and catheter storage.

Individual supporting spaces:

- Control room 22 ft x 12 ft, containing control console, multiformat camera or laser imager, scrub sink, and storage cabinets.

- Equipment room 10 ft x 22 ft, housing electronics cabinets.

- Patient preparation and recovery area.

- Staff gowning and changing facilities.

Supporting spaces

The following list summarizes supporting spaces typically included in diagnostic imaging departments:

- Waiting/reception area
- Gowned waiting areas for departments
- Dressing areas for gowned waiting or individual procedure rooms
- Toilet rooms for patients
- Darkroom for processing conventional films
- Daylight processing area
- Digital image processing area
- Light room/quality assurance area
- Image reading or interpretation area
- Viewing/consultation areas
- Film files area
- Clean supply room
- Soiled utility room
- Staff locker/lounge/toilets
- Storage alcoves

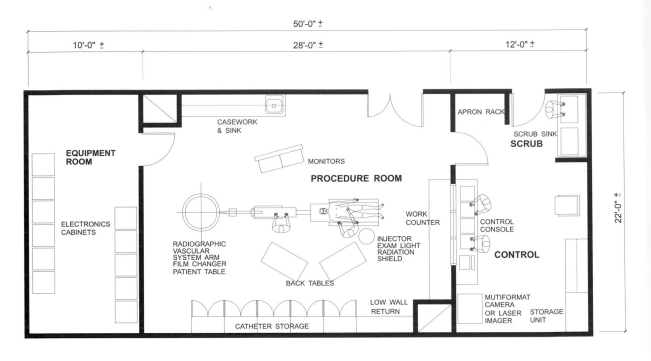

50'-0" ±

10'-0" ±   28'-0" ±   12'-0" ±

22'-0" ±

EQUIPMENT ROOM

CASEWORK & SINK

MONITORS

PROCEDURE ROOM

ELECTRONICS CABINETS

RADIOGRAPHIC VASCULAR SYSTEM ARM FILM CHANGER PATIENT TABLE

WORK COUNTER

INJECTOR EXAM LIGHT RADIATION SHIELD

BACK TABLES

LOW WALL RETURN

CATHETER STORAGE

APRON RACK

SCRUB SINK
SCRUB

CONTROL CONSOLE

CONTROL

MUTIFORMAT CAMERA OR LASER IMAGER

STORAGE UNIT

0 1' 2'   4'   8'   16'

1120 ±   SQ. FT.

▲ A typical special procedure room.

▶ A special procedure angiography room at Medical Center East in Birmingham, Alabama.

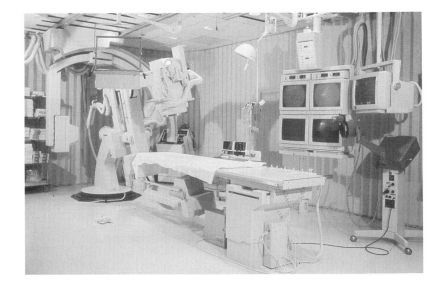

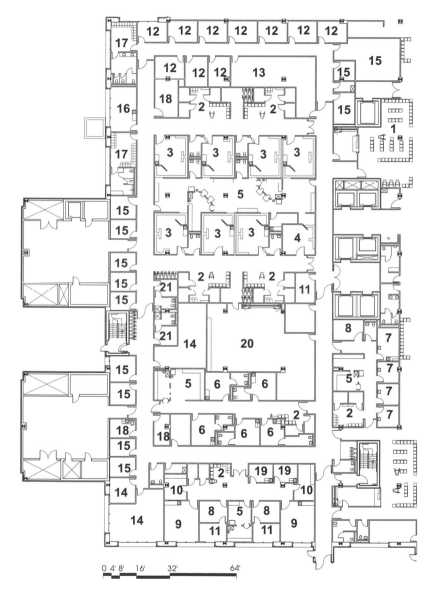

1   WAITING/ RECEPTION
2   DRESSING/SUB-WAITING
3   RADIOGRAPHY/FLUOROSCOPY
    PROCEDURE ROOM
4   CHEST ROOM
5   QC/WORK CORE/PROCESSING
6   ULTRASOUND ROOM
7   MAMMOGRAPHY ROOM
8   VIEWING/READING
9   CT SCANNING ROOM
10 CONTROL CONSOLE
11 COMPUTER/EQUIPMENT
12 RADIOLOGIST OFFICES
13 VIEWING/CONSULTATION
14 RESIDENT WORK AREA
15 ADMIN/ CLERICAL
16 STAFF LOUNGE
17 STAFF LOCKERS/TOILETS
18 STORAGE/UTILITIES
19 PREP/HOLD
20 FILM /FILE/WORK
21 SLEEP ROOM

◀ An imaging department
floor plan at Fitzsimons
Army Medical Center in
Aurora, Colorado.

Work core design

Historically, films have moved from the procedure rooms to a processing, checking, and assembly area that serves several rooms. Although conventional film processing is less prevalent, this "work core" design is still one of the most staff-efficient configurations for a department. Typically, procedure rooms encircle a work core, with staff access from within the core and patient access from the perimeter.

In larger departments, like modalities are grouped around these cores to create pods or clusters. For example, radiography and radiography/fluoroscopy rooms are typically grouped.

Mammography and ultrasound may be grouped to serve women patients. Most departments are made up of groups of clusters aggregated around common or complementary modalities.

Department organization

The pods or clusters organized around work cores are the clinical heart of the department. Typically, they are interposed between the public access areas—reception and waiting—and the staff areas—personnel facilities, storage and utility rooms, radiologist offices, and reading areas. It is important to organize the department to allow future expansion in key corridors. If any spaces are placed in the path of this expansion, they should be "soft" or easily relocated areas.

Departmental organization must recognize the potential use of mobile technology. This usually requires providing a sub-waiting area with access to the trailer in which the mobile device is contained. Depending on the climate, access may be via a covered, open-air, or pneumatically enclosed structure.

Interior design considerations

An imaging department requires high-technology equipment for diagnosing and treating individuals who may already be in a heightened state of anxiety. Thus, it is most important to create environments that are friendly and nonthreatening. In addition to the appropriate furniture, fabrics, and colors, positive distractions may be included, such as artwork, views to the outdoors, and aquariums, to relieve stress and anxiety.

Lighting is also used to create a more soothing environment. Particularly important is the use of reflected lighting in areas where patients will be lying on their backs on stretchers or procedure tables.

Trends

Imaging is clearly one of the areas most affected by developing technology, particularly digitally based equipment.

Special Diagnostic Departments

Functional overview

Special diagnostics services typically include noninvasive testing of the human body's cardiovascular or neurological performance. The tests principally use electronic, sonographic, or scintillation counter technology to monitor the body's anatomy or physiological activity. These procedures produce measurements that are recorded over time in hard copy or digital storage media for physician review and reference. Most measurements occur over periods of 5 to 45 minutes, although durations of 24 hours are useful in some studies.

Noninvasive diagnostic testing of the cardiovascular systems includes the following:

- *Electrocardiography (ECG).*
  Observation of cardiac performance

◀ *A radiology waiting area at Bristol Regional Medical Center in Bristol, Tennessee.*

▼ *A special diagnostic floor plan at Mercy Regional Medical Center in Laredo, Texas.*

0 2' 4' 8'   16'   32'

1	WAITING	7	HOLDING/MONITORING	13	SUPPORT SPACE
2	TECH WORK AREA	8	INPATIENT HOLDING(SHARED)	14	PATIENT PREP
3	ELECTROCARDIOGRAPHY	9	ELECTROENCEPHALOGRAPHY		
4	ECHO CARDIOGRAPHY	10	SLEEP STUDIES		
5	STRESS TESTING LAB	11	PATIENT/STAFF TOILET		
6	PERIPHERAL VASCULAR LAB	12	PHYSICIAN READING/DIC.		

through electronic physiological monitoring.

- *Echocardiography (Echo ECG).* Observation of cardiac performance through Doppler ultrasonography monitoring coupled with physiological monitoring. Transthoracic echocardiography is the basic study, and transesophageal echocardiography (TEE) is a common procedure using the same technology.

- *Exercise stress testing.* Observation of cardiac performance through physiological monitoring while the patient is subjected to varying levels of exercise demand by treadmill or exercycle. Tilt tables may also be provided in this area for identifying reflex-induced problems.

- *Nuclear scans.* Observation of cardiovascular performance through physiological monitoring and gamma camera or SPECT (single photon emission computerized tomography) camera imaging of absorbed substances tagged with radioactive isotopes. Patients are typically subjected to varying levels of exercise demand via treadmill or exercycle during these studies. Nuclear scans combined with computerized tomography, known as PET scanning (positron emission tomography), are also useful but remain cost-prohibitive in most cases. Thus, this technology is generally found only in teaching institutions to date.

- *Holter monitoring.* An ambulatory ECG recorded continuously over a 24-hour period via portable magnetic tape media to monitor electro-physiological data related to cardiac behavior and performance.

- *Pacemaker verification.* Periodic and routine testing of pacemaker devices inserted to assist in regularizing the behavior of the heart.

- *Peripheral vascular studies (PV).* Noninvasive testing of the arteries, veins, and lymphatic system in the body extremities, using Doppler ultrasonography.

Noninvasive diagnostic testing of the neurological system utilizes the following studies:

- *Electroencephalography (EEG).* Observation of brain activity through electronic physiological monitoring.

- *Sleep studies.* Extended observation via camera and microphone, along with electronic physiological monitoring via EEG and EKG, through normal (8-hour) or short-term periods of sleep.

Service locations

Special diagnostic services are typically found in hospital settings within departments including cardiology, cardiovascular, cardiopulmonary, neurodiagnostic, or electrodiagnostic services. These services are often centralized for inpatients and outpatients, although most inpatient ECG and EEG studies are conducted at the patient's bedside. Stress testing, echo ECG, peripheral vascular (PV) studies, and isotope scans are usually centralized owing to equipment requirements. Outpatient ECGs are completed mainly in physicians' offices, except when required for hospital preadmission testing records. Holter monitoring, pacemaker verification, and sleep studies are entirely outpatient services.

TYPICAL WORK LOAD PARAMETERS, SPECIAL DIAGNOSTICS					
Procedure Type	Percentage of Total Volume	Average Length of Procedure	Outpatient Percentage of Volume	Inpatient Percentage of Volume	Inpatient Procedure Location
Electrocardiogram (ECG/EKG)	20	15 min	30	70	Patient room
Echocardiogram (EECG)	15	45 min	60	40	In dept.
Nuclear scan	10	45 min	70	30	In dept.
Exercise stress test	15	45 min	90	10	In dept.
Holter monitoring	5	15 min	100	0	N.A.
Pacemaker verification	5	15 min	100	0	N.A.
Peripheral vascular study	15	60 min	80	20	In dept.
Electroencephalography (EEG)	10	60 min	80	20	In dept.
Sleep study	5	8 hr	100	0	In dept.

Key activity factors

Planning for special diagnostics is based on projected work load volumes for inpatients and outpatients. The work loads are categorized by average procedure time and distribution between inpatient and outpatient volumes (see table above). The percentage of inpatient services is important, because many procedures are performed in the inpatient's room, thus reducing demand for diagnostic space within the central area of the service.

Key capacity determinants

The variety of special diagnostic services requires many distinct procedure rooms to separate functionally incompatible activities, facilitate efficient work flow, and avoid excessive waiting time for patients. Some procedures, such as exercise stress testing, require strenuous physical activity by the patient. Doppler equipment used in echocardiography studies may generate noise. Risk of exposure to radioactive materials used in nuclear scans must be carefully controlled. Sleep and EEG studies require quiet areas without

significant audio stimuli. The number of these rooms required is based on an 8 hours per day, 5 or 6 days per week (excluding holidays) schedule. The service is available on a 24-hour basis in the acute care setting, but principally for emergency needs after regular hours.

Patient and work flow

Easy patient access to special diagnostic procedure rooms is paramount. These rooms are designed for outpatient convenience. Scheduled appointments dictate that adequate parking, clear ambulatory care entrance points, and simple way finding to the reception and waiting areas be available. Ambulatory patients should have direct access between the waiting area and procedure rooms without passing through staff or physician work areas. Easy transfer of inpatients, as required, to procedure rooms is also a factor in design. Clear access to inpatient areas that keeps patients or staff from passing through public spaces is preferable.

The technician staff requires workroom space close to the procedure areas, to

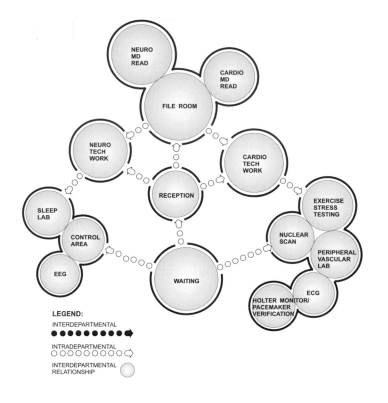

NEURO
MD
READ

CARDIO
MD
READ

FILE ROOM

NEURO
TECH
WORK

CARDIO
TECH
WORK

RECEPTION

EXERCISE
STRESS
TESTING

SLEEP
LAB

CONTROL
AREA

NUCLEAR
SCAN

PERIPHERAL
VASCULAR
LAB

EEG

WAITING

ECG

HOLTER MONITOR/
PACEMAKER
VERIFICATION

LEGEND:
INTERDEPARTMENTAL
●●●●●●●●➤
INTRADEPARTMENTAL
○○○○○○○○○○➤
INTERDEPARTMENTAL
RELATIONSHIP ⬤

▲ *A special diagnostic
department interrelationship
diagram.*

Relationships with other departments
Special diagnostics is predominantly an outpatient service. It should be easily accessible and preferably visible from the facility's ambulatory care entrance. The use of nuclear medicine technology in association with exercise stress testing for cardiovascular studies influences the location of this service. During some tests, patients are moved from the stress testing area to the scanning camera. Scanning cameras (gamma or SPECT) may be located within the special diagnostics patient care area where procedure volumes justify this expensive technology. Special diagnostics services can also be located next to the nuclear medicine section of imaging services. In this location, all types of radioactive testing are performed, thus optimizing the use of the equipment.

The special diagnostics service houses the noninvasive diagnostic procedures offered within the product line of cardiovascular services. The invasive diagnostic or therapeutic portion of this product line is the cardiac catheterization laboratory (cath lab). The cath lab has distinct relationships to surgery, the inpatient critical care areas, and the emergency department. For efficiency, technicians in special diagnostics or cardiac catheterization are typically assigned to one or the other area permanently. However, a cardiologist may work in both areas, usually on a scheduled basis, and administrative staff support both areas. This relationship suggests value in locating special diagnostics near the cath lab.

Many special diagnostics procedures for inpatients are conducted in the patients' rooms by service technicians. These procedures usually require transporting

allow charting between cases without excessive travel. Once each test is complete, the results—via hard-copy paper strip, videotape, or electronic file—are moved to nearby physician reading areas for ECG, Echo/PV, and EEG review. Reports are dictated in this area. The reports are then transcribed in the department or off-site and stored in a record-keeping area.

Staff and physicians should be able to come and go from the department without passing through public areas. Proximity or a conveniently direct pathway to the cardiac catheterization lab is beneficial to allow cardiologists to travel quickly between that area and the the special diagnostics department.

GENERAL SPACE REQUIREMENTS, SPECIAL DIAGNOSTICS

Room	Suggested Area (square feet)	Optimal Dimensions (feet)	Necessary Adjacent Support Spaces
Electrocardiography (ECG)	80–100	10 x 10	
Echocardiography (EECG)	120–150	10 x 15	
Nuclear scan room (optional)	280–320	16 x 20	Hot lab (radioactive material)
Exercise stress testing lab	150–180	12 x 15	Dressing/prep area
Holter monitoring room	80–100	8 x 10	
Pacemaker verification room	80–100	8 x 10	
Peripheral vascular lab	180–200	12 x 15	
Electroencephalography (EEG)	150–180	12 x 15	Control/observation room
Sleep lab	180–200	12 x 15	Control/observation room

portable equipment such as an EKG machine or an ultrasound unit. Easy access to and from the inpatient areas optimizes staff time. Wheelchairs or stretchers transport inpatients undergoing procedures in the special diagnostics area. This necessitates simple pathways of connection, vertically or horizontally, between these areas. Transport via pathways that are separate from public and outpatient areas is fundamental to successful planning.

The inpatient areas attended most frequently by special diagnostics staff are the intensive care unit (ICU), coronory care unit (CCU), step-down units, and medical units. Technicians also visit other inpatient care units in the facility accord-ing to a schedule or for emergencies.

Key spaces

State and local building codes rarely address the specific size of the various rooms within special diagnostics areas. Sometimes minimum generic examination room sizes may apply. However, these codes should always be reviewed for plan approval standards.

Best practice standards within the healthcare industry, including some generations of the AIA *Guidelines for Design and Construction of Hospital and Health Care Facilities*, suggest guidelines for selected procedure spaces, as shown in the table above.

Key design considerations

The design of the special diagnostics area should address the following considerations:

- Special diagnostics is a consolidation of traditional cardiology, neurology, and, possibly, nuclear medicine studies. The consolidation facilitates centralized convenience for patient use, the sharing of support spaces, and cross-training of staff for more economical operations. The needs of these distinct areas must be addressed with a focus on the sharing of resources without compromising efficiency.

- Testing areas should be centralized for convenient access from outpatient waiting areas.

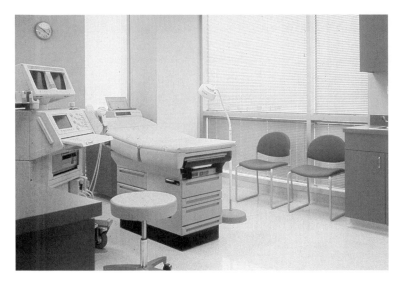

▲ An echocardiography room at Bayfront Medical Center in St. Petersburg, Florida.

simplify the patient care process and to minimize the specialized expertise required of staff will stimulate the development of smaller, more portable, and more rapid measurement devices capable of use at the point of care. Where such devices still require centralized use because of cost or lack of portability, the establishment of quick diagnostic centers will absorb many of these services into convenient areas of care where common testing required for outpatients and preadmission testing of inpatients are colocated.

INTERVENTIONAL DEPARTMENTS

Ambulatory Procedure Unit

Functional overview
Ambulatory surgery, also called "outpatient surgery," "day surgery," "in-and-out surgery," "come-and-go surgery," and "same-day surgery," refers to surgical procedures that require the technical support of a dedicated operating room and specially trained staff. However, these procedures do not require the full support of a hospital setting or an overnight stay. The ambulatory procedure unit (APU) provides a multifunction service that includes ambulatory (outpatient) surgery procedures, endoscopy surgery and special procedure recovery (cardiac catheterization, etc.), and observation beds. Among the procedures and services included in an APU are the following:

Blood transfusions

Clinical investigations

Cosmetic and plastic surgery

Cystoscopy

Diabetic clinics

- Inpatient access to testing areas must be available without transport through public areas.
- Centralized staff work areas, where charting is performed outside testing rooms, provide for quick room turnaround. These work areas must be close to the procedure space to minimize travel distance.
- Physician reading areas must be nearby, but separated for ECG (hard-copy review), echo EKG and peripheral vascular (video monitor review), and EEG (hard copy review) functions.
- A central location is required for observation of multiple EEG, sleep lab, and multiple stress testing stations.

Trends
The healthcare technology industry will continue to explore alternative imaging and physiological testing modalities that are faster, less intrusive, and more reliable than currently used tools. Efforts to

Endoscopy

Gastroenterology

General surgery

Gynecology

Neurosurgery

Ophthalmology

Oral surgery and dentistry

Orthopedics

Otolaryngology

Pain management

Pediatric dentistry

Pediatric surgery

Phototherapy

Physician clinics

Plasmapheresis

Plastic surgery

Podiatry

Vascular surgery

Wound care

The components of an ambulatory procedure unit include the following:

Ambulatory (outpatient) surgery. An ambulatory procedure patient is an outpatient undergoing an operative procedure. Such procedures are performed in an ambulatory surgery suite, in other designated areas of the hospital (e.g., cardiac catheterization lab, endoscopy suite), or in the hospital's freestanding surgical center. Outpatients are received the day of surgery. The patients are prepared for surgery, undergo the procedure, complete the recovery process, and are discharged the day (with 23 hours) of surgery. The ambulatory surgery area includes outpatient reception, surgery preparation and (possibly) dedicated outpatient operating rooms, postanesthesia care unit (PACU or Phase I), and a final (Phase II) stage of recovery.

Endoscopy surgery. Endoscopy surgery is performed on an outpatient basis, without admission to the hospital. Surgery types include respiratory, urinary, and digestive system diagnostic endoscopy. An endoscope (an optical instrument with a lighted tip) is inserted into the organ, which allows visual examination of the cavity.

Special procedure recovery. Endoscopy surgery, cath lab, and similar procedures require a recovery period of less than 24 hours.

Observation unit. An observation unit provides an outpatient with a bed and periodic monitoring by the hospital's nursing or other staff.

Operational considerations

Calculating the total number of patients seen in a given period of time, measured against patient bed capacity, is a means of determining the size of the APU. This analysis can be based on an hourly or daily activity level. Key work areas include preoperative patient examination rooms and postoperative patient recovery areas.

Outpatients should conveniently arrive at a reception/waiting area. After a patient is admitted, he or she is escorted to an examination room or a changing area. A physician then consults with the patient in a private examination room. Once approval is received, the patient is prepared and transported to the procedure/surgery room for the operation. Depending on the complexity of the procedure, the patient may recover in the postanesthesia recovery unit (PACU) and then be transported to the

ANCILLARY DEPARTMENTS

▶ *An interrelationship diagram of an ambulatory procedure unit.*

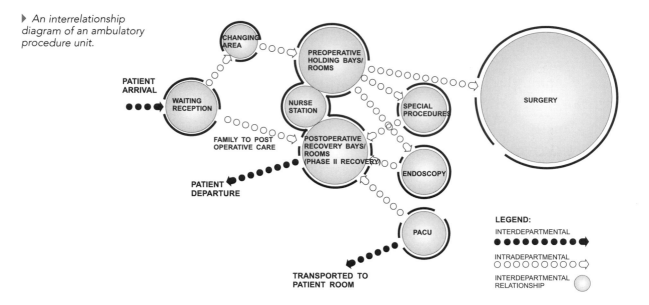

PATIENT ARRIVAL

CHANGING AREA

WAITING RECEPTION

PREOPERATIVE HOLDING BAYS/ ROOMS

NURSE STATION

SPECIAL PROCEDURES

SURGERY

FAMILY TO POST OPERATIVE CARE

POSTOPERATIVE RECOVERY BAYS/ ROOMS (PHASE II RECOVERY)

ENDOSCOPY

PATIENT DEPARTURE

PACU

TRANSPORTED TO PATIENT ROOM

LEGEND:

INTERDEPARTMENTAL

INTRADEPARTMENTAL

INTERDEPARTMENTAL RELATIONSHIP

postoperative care area (Phase II recovery), or the patient may be directly transported to the postoperative care area (often joined by a family member). The patient is discharged following recovery. The key to this process is maintaining a one-way flow for patients moving through the department. Physicians should also have convenient access to recovering patients and to family consultation rooms.

Logistical support is required from central sterile supply and linen, pharmacy, laboratory, materials management, and environmental services. The central sterile processing area should be adjacent, horizontally or vertically, to surgery. This allows convenient transport of sterile supplies and instruments. The pharmacy area must have easy access to medications. Laboratory areas require a satellite location in surgery for processing and interpretation of frozen sections and specimen transport.

Space summary

An APU has two primary areas, preoperative and postoperative. These areas include either a room or a bay for each patient, as follows:

Preoperative examination rooms / bays—120 net sq ft: 10 ft x 12 ft

Postoperative recovery rooms / bays— 120 net sq ft: 10 ft x 12 ft

The spaces typically included in an APU are as follows:

Preoperative area

Changing/locker area

Patient rooms/bays

Patient lockers

Postoperative areas

Open stalls

Private rooms

Patient lockers

Nourishment area

Support areas

Clean supply

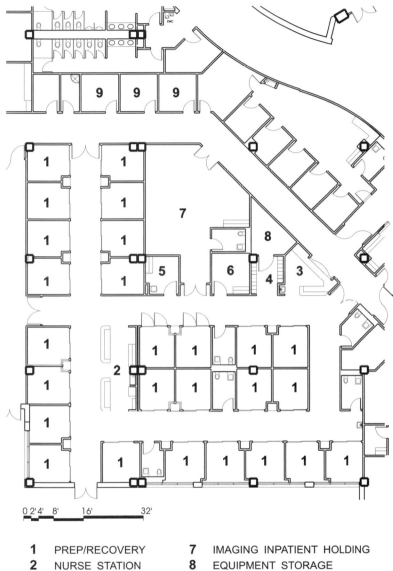

◀ A floor plan of an ambulatory procedure unit at Washington Regional Medical Center in Fayetteville, Arkansas.

0 2' 4' 8' 16' 32'

1	PREP/RECOVERY	**7**	IMAGING INPATIENT HOLDING
2	NURSE STATION	**8**	EQUIPMENT STORAGE
3	WORK/ RECEPTION	**9**	CONSULT
4	PATIENT LOCKER		
5	SOILED ROOM		
6	CLEAN ROOM		

Equipment storage

Housekeeping/trash/recycling room

Nurses' station

Physician dictation area

Soiled utility

Staff toilet

Wheelchair/stretcher alcove

Supply and cleanup areas

Storage areas

Office areas (as needed)

The APU should be collocated with inpatient surgery to share instruments and staff. A developing trend is to include invasive imaging and pain management in the APU setting.

Cardiac Catheterization Laboratory

Functional overview

Cardiac catheterization determines the feasibility of mechanical intervention in patients with coronary artery disease, congenital anomalies, heart failure, acute heart attack (myocardial infarction, or MI), or conduction disturbances. Anatomical information about the heart chambers, coronary arteries, heart valves, great vessels, and myocardium (tissue surrounding the heart) is provided. Measurement of intracardiac electrical activity, as well as tissue biopsy, can also be performed in the cath lab.

Imaging occurs by fluoroscopy and X-ray angiograms using a catheter to introduce radio-opaque dye into the vessel or heart chamber. Images are stored on digital media and plane film for video and hard copy for review. In the past, catheterization imaging used 35 mm cine films. Thus, it may be necessary to review records of patients with a history of cardiac and vascular problems using this medium.

Diagnostic catheterization is used to identify cardiac and vascular problems for determining the best course of patient therapy. Diagnostic procedures include the following:

- *Heart catheterization.* The real-time imaging of the anatomy of heart chambers and great vessel

- *Electrophysiology studies.* Invasive procedures that use programmed stimulation techniques to simulate or trigger electrical responses in the heart for diagnostic purposes

Therapeutic catheterization is used to improve blood flow or cardiac performance. Therapeutic procedures include the following:

- *Balloon angioplasty.* Revascularization of coronary arteries narrowed by atherosclerosis by expanding a tiny balloon against the vessel walls to compress the substances blocking the passageway; also known as PTCA, or percutaneous transluminal coronary angioplasty. Along with thrombolytic therapy, PTCA is a major alternative to coronary artery bypass in the treatment of heart attacks.

- *Stint insertion.* An additional measure to balloon angioplasty. A tiny tube is inserted into the vessel cleared by balloon angioplasty to minimize the need for repeated revascularization procedures.

- *Pacemaker insertion.* The insertion of a battery-operated electronic device into the body, attached to the heart muscle, which emits electrical impulses to regulate heart beat, defibrillate, or otherwise manage the heart's electrical behavior.

0 4' 8' 16'   32'   64'

1 WAITING

2 RECOVERY

3 CLEAN UTILITY

4 SOILED UTILITY

5 ENGINEER STORAGE

6 ELECTRONICS ROOM

7 CATH LAB

8 RESPIRATORY THERAPY CLEAN UP

9 RESPIRATORY THERAPY/SUPPLY/ STORAGE

10 CLEAN SUPPLY

11 CONTROL

12 PROCEDURE ROOM

13 NURSE STATION

14 PULMONARY FUNCTION LAB

15 ECHO/ELECTROCARDIOGRAPHY WORK ROOM

16 READ

17 RECEPTION

18 FILM ROOM

Service locations

Today, 40 to 60 percent of cath lab procedures are performed on an outpatient basis. Procedure risks, emergency and critical inpatient care needs, and imaging systems costs demand that these labs be located in hospital settings. A cath lab may be located in an ambulatory care setting; however, this is the exception and not the rule.

Key activity factors

Cath lab planning is based on projected work load volumes for inpatients and outpatients. These work loads are aggregated into average procedure times and distribution between inpatient and outpatient volumes (see table on page 56). Patient recovery is a major factor in space demand—inpatients recover for a relatively short period of time in the cath

	TYPICAL WORK LOAD PARAMETERS, CATHETERIZATION LABORATORIES			
Procedure Type	Percentage of Total Volume	Average Length of Procedure	Outpatient Percentage of Volume	Inpatient Percentage of Volume
Diagnostic cath study—monoplane	40	45 min	60	40
Diagnostic cath study—biplane	N.A.	20 min	30	70
Electrophysiological study	5	90 min	10	90
Pacemaker insertion	10	20 min	10	90
Balloon angioplasty	30	45 min	60	40
Stint insertion	15	60 min	60	40
Patient prep	–	45 min	60	40
Patient recovery—inpatient	–	90 min	–	–
Patient recovery—outpatient	–	6 hours	–	–

lab before returning to their rooms. On the other hand, outpatients in the cath lab require the longest recovery time of any patients undergoing invasive procedures.

Key capacity determinants

The heart catheterization and patient prep/recovery stations determine capacity and space demand. Diagnostic and therapeutic services are provided in the same procedure rooms. Electrophysiology (EP) studies can also be performed if the rooms are large enough to contain additional equipment. EP labs frequently accommodate other catheterization procedures, such as pacemaker implants.

Space for patient preparation and recovery is a lay factor. All outpatients are prepared in this area and require 5 to 6 hours of recovery. Inpatients require 60 to 90 minutes of recovery before returning to their rooms. The number of procedures and patient holding spaces is based on an 8 hour per day, 5 or 6 day per week (excluding holidays) schedule. The service is available 24 hours per day on an emergency basis.

Special diagnostics also requires work areas for test review and interpretation by physicians, charting by staff technicians, and record keeping. The specialization of physicians and technicians sharing this service center tends to dictate separate work areas for ECG, echo ECG/peripheral vascular, and neurodiagnostic services. These areas can occupy a substantial portion of the overall service space.

Patient and work flow

Cath lab work is a combined in-flow of scheduled outpatients and inpatients, as well as emergency cases. All must access the service via the prep/recovery area. Outpatients must change and store their clothing in lockers. Such activity can occur in the prep/recovery space if privacy is adequate. Inpatients and outpatients are also prepped in this area by nurse caregivers before the procedure is performed.

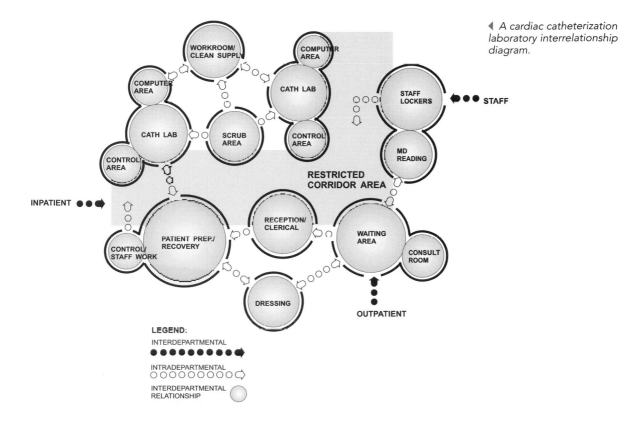

◀ *A cardiac catheterization laboratory interrelationship diagram.*

LEGEND:
INTERDEPARTMENTAL
●●●●●●●●➡
INTRADEPARTMENTAL
○○○○○○○○○▷
INTERDEPARTMENTAL
RELATIONSHIP ⬤

The patient is then moved by stretcher into the cath lab for the procedure. Procedure times can vary, owing to unforeseen complications. Therefore, convenient access to the surgery suite is important. Following the procedure, the patient is returned to the recovery area for a period of observation (which can vary in length) by caregivers. Inpatients are returned to their rooms, emergency patients are admitted to a room, and outpatients are transported via wheelchair to a patient pickup point for discharge.

Clinical staff work occurs in two primary work zones—the cath lab suite and the prep/recovery area. The cath lab suite is a controlled environment requiring scrub attire and cover gowns for staff during the procedure. Access to this area is controlled. Using locker areas as pass-through vestibules into the procedure areas forces staff to observe proper sterile techniques.

The controlled lab area typically has a work core connected to each cath lab. This setup allows catheters and supplies to be centralized outside the labs. Access to the work core is possible without passing through the labs. Each lab has a dedicated control room with immediate image review capability and a computer equipment room. If the design permits, shared access to a cleanup utility room is provided for the labs.

The prep/recovery area is typically located outside the sterile controlled lab core to facilitate access by visitors to the patient before and after the procedure. The prep/recovery area is directly linked to the procedure rooms via a patient corridor, typically separate from the staff work core. Minimum travel distance for postprocedure transfer of patients to recovery is critical.

Other clinical and administrative work also occurs outside the controlled area of the lab and patient holding areas. Physician interpretation and dictation are performed in reading rooms equipped with the appropriate technology to review current work, as well as historical patient information, in digital, video, or 35 mm film (no longer used in contemporary cath labs) format. Consulting rooms should be located near the waiting room to allow private discussion between the physician, the patient, and the family.

Administrative support areas do not require a unique work flow design, because most record keeping and information transfer occurs within the clinical work areas. Reception and management of arriving patients and their waiting visitors is the principal need. However, staff will require separate male and female locker and toilet facilities, along with a staff lounge and pantry.

Relationships with other departments

The ability to rapidly move inpatients from critical care units (CCU in particular) and unscheduled patients from the emergency department to the cath lab is of the highest priority. Accessibility for ambulatory patients from the outpatient entrance of the facility is equally important. In emergencies, direct movement of patients from the cath lab to surgery, without passing through public areas, should be possible. However, this relationship does not dictate that an immediate adjacency be created.

In many recently designed facilities, an effort to consolidate all patients having invasive procedures in one centralized prep/recovery area has been planned. This configuration facilitates the flexible use of space between prep and recovery needs. It also serves clinic service needs relative to varying patient volumes during the week. It affords, in some instances, an opportunity to reduce staffing requirements based on shared, overlapping resources. This concept suggests that the location of the cath lab may be coordinated with other invasive procedure services that use the area (e.g., angiography or interventional radiology, surgery, and endoscopy).

Invasive procedures conducted by cardiologists as a medical subspecialty are performed in the cath lab. The noninvasive procedures area is located within the special diagnostics service. Many factors come to bear in planning that necessitate separation of these two areas. Special diagnostics must be highly accessible to ambulatory patients because of the substantial numbers of these patients. The cath lab has to be located near critical and acute service areas of the hospital. Functionally, the activities are distinct and separable with respect to staff capabilities. The possible benefits of collocation include shared administrative staff and collaboration of the collective cardiology team members. In any instance, patient flow to the distinct procedure areas must not be compromised.

Key spaces

State and local building codes often mandate a minimum size for cath labs. Many codes dictate the size of patient recovery space and support spaces, particularly relative to creating a controlled sterile environment by requiring dedicated changing areas for staff. These codes should always be reviewed for the minimum standards necessary for plan approval. Historically, technology changes in the cath labs have proven that code minimums are sometimes too small to accommodate future system demands. Flexibility requires that rooms be larger than the minimum standard. Furthermore, the codes do not address electrophysiology (EP) lab minimum sizes. Typically they are larger than the basic diagnostic cath lab.

Best practice standards within the healthcare industry, including some generations of the AIA's *Guidelines for Design and Construction of Hospital and Health Care Facilities,* suggest guidelines for selected procedure spaces (see the table below).

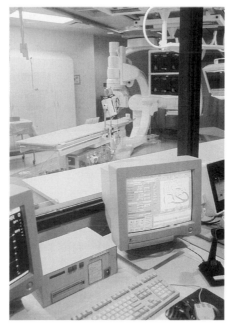

◀ *A cardiac catheterization laboratory at Valley Children's Hospital in Madera, California.*

Key design considerations

The design of the cardiac cath lab suite should address the following considerations:

- Access to the cath lab is needed by scheduled ambulatory patients and emergency inpatients—the

GENERAL SPACE REQUIREMENTS, CATHETERIZATION LABORATORIES			
Room	Suggested Area (square feet)	Optimal Dimensions (feet)	Necessary Adjacent Support Spaces
Cath lab—monoplane	600–700	24 x 28	Control room Computer room Utility room Supply core
Cath lab—biplane	600–700	24 x 30	(same)
EP lab	750–900	26 x 30	(same)
Control room	120–150	10 x 15	
Computer rroom	100–120	8 x 15	May be within lab— preferably separate
Patient prep/recovery space	80–120	140 x 10	Dressing/prep area/toilets

path of travel should be separate for each.

- A centralized arrangement of patient holding spaces or rooms usable for preprocedure prep, as well as postprocedure recovery, facilitates greater efficiency in the use of staff and physical space. Consolidation of this area with the prep/recovery areas of other invasive procedure services should be considered when possible (surgery, cath lab, angiography, interventional radiology).

- A clean procedure area separate from public and casual staff traffic must be created. Access to this area requires the design of staff lockers as pass-through vestibules separating the public areas from the procedure areas. Prep and recovery should be outside this zone but directly accessible to the procedure rooms without traversing staff work areas. Staff should be able to move between procedure rooms and immediate support areas without encountering patient or public traffic.

- The support core of supplies and cleanup for the procedure rooms should be combined as a central shared space when possible.

- The patient is alert through the entire course of prep and recovery—sedation usually occurs in the procedure room and wears off relatively quickly. A pleasant, relaxing environment that puts the patient at ease is highly preferable to the traditional clinical atmosphere.

Special equipment or furniture requirements

An extensive amount of special equipment is used in the cath lab. In summary, such equipment includes the following:

- *Imaging systems.* In each cath lab, the basic catheterization equipment is typically supplied as an integrated system by a single vendor. The system includes components such as real-time imaging via image intensifiers on C-arms, video processors, monitors, tubes and recording system, plane film exposure system, procedure table floor with automated movement capability, remote control capability, and a central control console for the remote control room. This equipment may be ceiling- or floor-mounted, including ceiling tracks that allow variable location of the components. Less is more when it comes to equipment occupying floor space and encumbering free movement in case of emergency. Special electronic racks and cabinetry are a part of the system. Some of these items are located within the cath lab and some are in an adjacent computer room. Cath labs are typically monoplane, meaning that one image at a time (although continuous) is produced in a single plane through the body. Biplane systems are available that can deliver two image planes simultaneously. The advantage is reduced time for producing the set of images in multiple planes that are necessary to make a diagnosis. Use of this technology is popular for pediatric patients and some adult patients when expediency of results is required. Biplane technology, however, is much more expensive and is thus used less frequently for routine work other than in centers with large pediatric services.

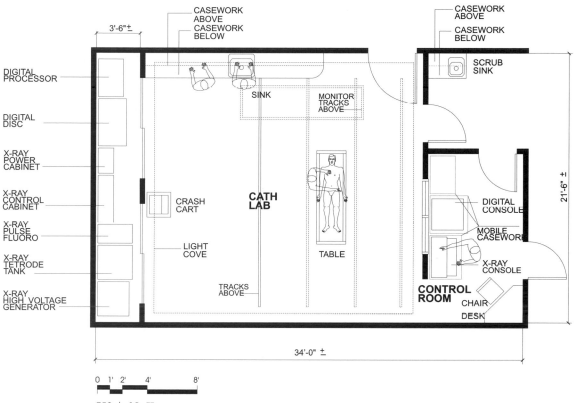

CASEWORK ABOVE
CASEWORK BELOW

CASEWORK ABOVE
CASEWORK BELOW

SCRUB SINK

3'-6"±

DIGITAL PROCESSOR

DIGITAL DISC

X-RAY POWER CABINET

X-RAY CONTROL CABINET

X-RAY PULSE FLUORO

X-RAY TETRODE TANK

X-RAY HIGH VOLTAGE GENERATOR

SINK

MONITOR TRACKS ABOVE

CRASH CART

CATH LAB

LIGHT COVE

TABLE

TRACKS ABOVE

DIGITAL CONSOLE

MOBILE CASEWORK

X-RAY CONSOLE

CONTROL ROOM

CHAIR

DESK

21'-6"±

34'-0" ±

0 1' 2'   4'   8'

750 ± SQ. FT.

- *Computerized image processing systems.* Additional electronics racks and computer components for processing and distributing images are located in a computer room, typically located adjacent to the cath lab.

- *Electronic stimulus systems.* Electrophysiology labs require more elaborate electronics systems to stimulate responses from the heart or simulate physiological circumstances of an electrical nature to be studied via a catheterization procedure. EP studies are not performed in diagnostic cath labs; performance of these procedures is dependent on the

practices of the cardiology staff utilizing a particular facility.

- *Physiological monitoring systems.* A critical component of the procedure room, as well as each patient prep/recovery space or room, is the physiological monitoring system. The system tracks basic vital signs and specialized data essential to knowing a patient's status at all times. A centralized monitor for all recovering patients is located in the recovery room. Additional monitors are located in the control room of each cath lab, driven by the primary multiple monitors mounted on ceiling tracks.

▲ A typical catheterization laboratory floor plan.

- *Image reading systems.* Video monitors, computers, cut file viewing, and laser printing capability are provided in the physician reading rooms. Because older records of patients may be on 35 mm cine film, a viewer may be provided. However, many of these records are being transferred to video format to cut back on additional equipment.
- *Image media storage.* Computer files, film, and videotape are potential storage systems for cath procedures. Currently, all of these images are recorded digitally in storage disk or compact disk format.
- *Catheter storage.* Catheter storage requires special racks or wide, flat drawers for convenient access. A broad array of catheter types and sizes must be maintained in an orderly fashion to facilitate finding the right tool quickly during a procedure.

Support space for the patient care areas includes the following:

- Preprocedure prep areas, including dressing, locker, and toilet facilities leading into the prep/recovery room
- Space in prep/recovery areas for medications, clean supply holding, clean and soiled utility room, nourishments, and equipment holding
- Cath lab control room, computer room, clean workroom, and supply room for catheters, medical-surgical supplies, and linens
- Image-viewing room for physicians to review and report on a case after the procedure is complete
- Image processing and storage areas, including picture archival

communication system (PACS), laser printer, darkroom for spot film, cine film or videotape storage racks
- Patient holding alcove if the prep/recovery room is too far from the procedure room; good design will avoid this necessity, as it complicates staffing and can result in poor continuity of patient surveillance
- Soiled utility linen holding room/housekeeping

Support space for service administration and staff includes the following:

- Reception/registration/scheduling work areas
- Waiting area with consulting room for physicians
- Offices for the administrative director
- Clerical workstations
- Record storage areas (hard copy files, three to seven years)
- Staff lounge with pantry
- Male and female locker rooms and toilets (separate from patient toilets)

Special planning and design considerations

Special design considerations for the cath lab include the following:

- Cath labs use X-ray technology. It must be shielded for the protection of anyone outside the procedure room. Lead-lined walls and doors are required. Lead-infused windows, allowing a view from the control area, and maze designs are also required.
- Direct design and/or protective materials must stop lines of radiation exposure.
- "Universal radiographic room design" is a useful concept for the cath lab,

where systems may be upgraded or replaced as often as every five years. Because the systems may be ceiling and/or floor mounted and some components may be wall mounted, a structural system in the ceiling and walls may be designed to facilitate easy installation and change of systems. This design essentially allows for the variation of connection points in the different structures of the major vendors of these imaging systems. Floor and wall ducts may also be installed to facilitate management of the cables and electronic wiring between the components. In most cases, the floor slab will be affected by installation of a pedastal for the table—either through a topping slab of the equipment after installation or coring and drilling a position for a new system for which the room was not originally designed. To avoid this problem and minimize equipment encumbrances on the floor, some systems are designed to be entirely suspended from the ceiling.

- Electrophysiological studies are more extensive invasive procedures. Some cardiologists believe that the studies should be performed in a more controlled environment than a typical cath lab. Air flow and exchange may be designed to meet more rigorous standards, approaching those established for operating room designs. These measures are taken to improve sterile technique for long invasive procedures. As yet, building codes have not specifically addressed this concept as a requirement.

- Structural requirements must accommodate substantial weight above the ceiling of the procedure rooms for the suspension of equipment.

- Mechanical system design requirements are numerous, owing to the "clean" environment demanded in the procedure rooms and the extensive array of electronic equipment present in many of the rooms.

- Special electrical demands include power filtering and stabilization, generators for the imaging systems, substantial voice/data linkages, physiological monitoring and recording, alarm systems, intercom systems, interlocks between imaging systems and doors, variable-level lighting, and illumination design around a cadre of ceiling-mounted equipment components.

- Because of the images produced principally on video monitors in the cath lab, variable light control is required in the procedure rooms and control room.

- Bacteria-resistant, cleanable building finishes are required, with hard ceiling construction in the procedure rooms.

- Building codes are typically more specific for this area.

Trends

Cath lab procedures are increasingly shifting toward outpatient care. Thus, the need for timely recovery of patients for discharge is increasing. Design features and elements that foster "patient-focused care" contribute to the use of catheterization as an interventional, therapeutic agent that may serve as a lower-risk and less costly alternative to cardiovascular surgery. However, the use of catheterization as a diagnostic tool may decline as noninvasive imaging alternatives are developed and applied.

Endoscopy Suite

Functional overview

When referred to as a service or department of a healthcare facility, endoscopy is defined as the study of the digestive system or gastrointestinal (GI) tract of the body. It principally employs a specialized medical instrument known as an endoscope to search for and treat bleeding, inflamed, or abnormal tissue. The endoscope is a slender, flexible tube equipped with lenses and a light source. Fiber-optic technology transmits light into the body cavity and returns real-time images via lenses and video technology for viewing on a video monitor. This instrument also has a channel through which tiny instruments, such as forceps, scissors, and suction devices, may be introduced to the site of study for manipulation, biopsy, or removal of suspect tissue. Removal of abnormal tissue growth (such as polyps) is common.

Diagnostic studies of the gastrointestinal system may also involve the supplemental use of fluoroscopic imaging and, occasionally, other motility-related laboratory studies. These procedures may be conducted within the endoscopy suite. They are often supported by equipment in the imaging or clinical laboratory, where supplemental equipment can be more efficiently used for other procedures beyond GI studies.

Endoscopy as a diagnostic and therapeutic technology extends beyond the endoscopy suite. Other applications of endoscopes include bronchoscopy (lungs), laparoscopy (abdomen), laryngoscopy (vocal chords), colonoscopy (colon), and arthroscopy (joints). Of these applications, bronchoscopy is most often included in the endoscopy suite, in as much as it is an internal medicine subspecialty and requires support facilities akin to those used in endoscopy.

Generally, services are defined in four broad categories:

- *Upper GI studies* consist of procedures conducted by introduction of an endoscope into the body via the mouth. Visual examination of the upper components of the alimentary canal, including the throat, esophagus, stomach, and gall bladder, is made possible. Biopsies and other interventional procedures may be performed via the endoscope.

- *Lower GI studies* consist of procedures conducted by introducing an endoscope into the body. A visual examination of the lower components of the alimentary canal includes the rectum, colon, and small intestine. Special endoscopes are employed, such as sigmoidoscopes for rectal studies and colonoscopes for colon/small bowel studies. Biopsies and other interventional procedures may be performed through the endoscope.

- *ERCP studies* consist of endoscopic retrograde cholangiopancreatography studies (ERCPs), which are visual studies of the pancreas and biliary duct anatomy. This technique utilizes upper endoscopy to visualize the alimentary canal, simultaneously with radiographic fluoroscopy images to visualize the pancreatic bile ducts. Biopsies and other interventional

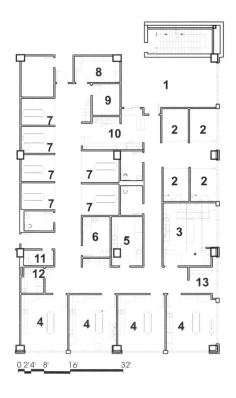

1 WAITING
2 PRE-OPERATION
3 FLUOROSCOPY
4 ENDOSCOPY
5 SCOPE WASH
6 LOUNGE
7 RECOVERY
8 CLEAN SUPPLY
9 OFFICE
10 NURSE STATION/MED./NOUR.
11 HOUSEKEEPING
12 SOILED UTILITY
13 DICTATION

◀ A floor plan of an endoscopy suite at M. D. Anderson Cancer Center in Houston, Texas.

procedures may be performed via the endoscope. This procedure requires access to radiographic/fluoroscopic equipment.

• *Bronchoscopy studies* consist of procedures conducted by introduction of a special endoscope—the bronchoscope—into the body's pulmonary breathing system via the mouth. Visual examination of the upper airway, lungs, and tracheobronchial tree is used to allow examination of tissue details. Sampling of respiratory tract secretions, tissue biopsies, and other interventional procedures may be performed through the bronchoscope.

Service locations

Endoscopy is a service that may have many locations. Endoscopy is always available in the acute care hospital setting, because the service must be available for inpatients and emergencies. Smaller facilities may provide the procedure within an operating room. The trend is to create a separate endoscopy suite that does not require the same level of sterile technique as required in a surgical suite. However, the largest and growing portion of this service is provided on an outpatient basis. Endoscopy is sometimes located in an ambulatory care setting, including freestanding digestive health centers operated by GI physicians. Because of the staffing requirements for

TYPICAL WORK LOAD PARAMETERS, ENDOSCOPY					
Procedure Type	Percentage of Total Volume	Average Length of Procedure	Outpatient Percentage of Volume	Inpatient Percentage of Volume	Inpatient Procedure Location
Upper GI study	40	45 min	70	30	Patient room
Lower GI study	38	45 min	70	30	In dept.
ERCP study	10	60 min	70	30	In dept.
Bronchoscopy	10	15 min	50	50	In dept.
Motility study	2	15 min	90	10	N.A.

patient prep and recovery, this service is rarely found in an individual practitioner's office. Instead, such services are employed in a center where several physicians share resources. For this reason, endoscopy is often centralized at a hospital, where space and staff may be shared most effectively between inpatient and outpatient services.

Key activity factors

The plan for an endoscopy suite is based on projected work load volumes for inpatients and outpatients. These work loads are aggregated into a number of categories, average procedure times, and distribution between inpatient and outpatient volumes, as shown in the table above.

Key capacity determinants

Operating protocol and physician practice patterns are the principal determinants of capacity and space requirements for endoscopy. Hours of day and days of the week available for procedure scheduling dictate the number of procedure and prep/recovery spaces needed. Endoscopy rooms are interchangeable between upper and lower GI studies. Infection control in bronchoscopy rooms is accomplished by not combining respiratory/GI patients

and procedures in the same room.

Common practice for physicians is to schedule all procedures in the morning and conduct clinic or hospital rounds in the afternoon. The result of this practice is that procedure rooms are heavily utilized for four to six hours per day and empty for the rest of the time. Endoscopy procedures require little support space other than the patient reception, preparation, and recovery areas. Toilets should be available in the recovery room, as well as directly accessible from one or more of the procedure rooms (for lower GI studies).

A staff work core, accessible to the procedure rooms and prep/recovery area, is necessary. Elements of this core begin with a separate, well-ventilated room. The room is essential for the cleanup and reprocessing of endoscopes. Provisions must be made for charting by nurses, visual monitoring of patients, and storage of patient care medications, supplies, linens, and nourishments. Physicians need a workroom area for dictation. A consultation room associated with the patient waiting area is beneficial. An office for the nurse manager, reception/clerical support, and records staff is also needed. Staff facilities including lockers, lounge, and toilets should be provided.

Patient and work flow

Easy access for outpatients to the endoscopy reception and waiting area is a priority. This provides a direct connection to the prep/recovery area for outpatients. Inpatients, if included, should be able to enter this patient holding area without passing through outpatient traffic and waiting areas.

The patient prep/recovery area is a single area where nursing staff can address both preprocedure preparation and postprocedure recovery. This configuration supports optimal utilization of staff resources and "swing use" of patient beds for either purpose, depending on the demand. Immediate proximity of this area to the procedure rooms is essential for minimum patient transport time. Depending on sedation requirements, some patients may walk from the prep area to the procedure room, whereas others may be moved via stretcher. Outpatients enter the prep/recovery space through an area designated for dressing, lockers, and toilets. Respect for the patients' privacy is an important consideration at the procedure area's entry point.

Patient movement back and forth from the recovery area should be direct and private. Staff movement begins with patient contact and transfer from the waiting area to prep/recovery, then continues to the procedure room and back. Staff must also move scopes to and from the procedure rooms for preprocedure setup and postprocedure cleanup/reprocessing. The scope cleanup room may be centralized for all procedure rooms or located between two or three rooms for direct access without staff's having to enter the corridor. The latter configuration offers greater convenience

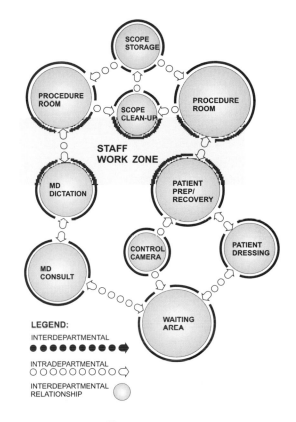

▲ An interrelationship diagram of an endoscopy suite.

but may require more staff time or equipment and space duplication. A workroom for physician dictation near but outside the procedure rooms is necessary to facilitate rapid room turnaround. Access from this workroom to a consultation room near the waiting area is helpful.

Finally, access from the inpatient care units of an acute care facility should be convenient and direct. Patients in these units should be capable of entering the procedure area without passing through public areas or the prep/recovery area.

Relationships with other departments

Access from the ambulatory patient entrance, reception, and registration areas of the facility is most important.

GENERAL SPACE REQUIREMENTS, ENDOSCOPY			
Room	Suggested Area (net square feet)	Optimal Dimensions (feet)	Necessary Adjacent Support Spaces
Endoscopy procedure room (upper or lower)	225–280	15 x 15	Toilet (lower only) Scope cleanup room Clean scope storage
Bronchoscopy room	225–280	15 x 15	
ERCP room (R/F room)	320–350	16 x 22	Control area (radiographic)
Patient prep/recovery space	80–120	10 x 10	Dressing/prep area/toilets
Scope cleanup room	100–150	10 x 15	

Orientation and minimal travel distance for outpatients should dictate location.

The need for radiographic/fluoroscopic imaging associated with ERCP studies suggests that proximity to imaging services is important. In reality, these procedures are few in number and are often conducted in the imaging area as scheduled procedures. Alternatively, a procedure may be performed in the endoscopy area with the use of portable imaging equipment. Occasionally, a well-equipped endoscopy lab has fixed imaging equipment in one or more procedure rooms to facilitate all service from one location. However, the utilization rate of such dedicated equipment is typically too low to be cost-justified.

Easy vertical and horizontal access from the inpatient care units should be provided, without passage through public areas. Although endoscopy is occasionally needed for patients in the emergency department, physical proximity is not necessary.

In many new facilities, designers are consolidating space by using one centralized prep/recovery area for all patients undergoing invasive procedures. This configuration demonstrates the flexible use of space between prep and recovery. It also serves clinic needs to acccomodate to varying patient volumes during the week. In some instances, it also allows the reduction of staff, based on shared, overlapping resources. This concept suggests that the location of endoscopy be coordinated with other invasive procedure services (i.e., imaging—angiography or interventional radiology—surgery, and cardiac cath lab).

Key spaces

State and local building codes address the specific sizes of the various endoscopy rooms. These codes should, however, always be reviewed for minimum standards necessary for plan approval. Best practice standards within the healthcare industry, including some generations of the AIA *1996–1997 Guidelines for Design and Construction of Hospital and Health Care Facilities*, suggests guidelines for selected procedure spaces, as shown in the table above.

Key design considerations

The design of the endoscopy area should address the following considerations:

- Often both inpatients and outpatients are studied within the centralized area of this service. Combining inpatients and outpatients within the procedure areas is not of concern, but attention to the differences between these patients in the prep/recovery process is important. Privacy for each patient must be provided. Separate dress-changing areas are preferred over cubicles. Private prep/recovery spaces that include a changing area are preferable. This arrangement also allows a visitor to join the patient with greater privacy.

- Direct access between the procedure rooms and the patient prep/recovery area is fundamental to good design. Both patients and staff move frequently between these zones. The work core of support space for clean-up and administrative follow-up should be located close to the hub of activity.

- Centralized patient observation in a combined patient prep and recovery area is desirable. It affords optimal use of staff and facilities by allowing a flexible use of space. Consolidation of this area with the similar prep/recovery areas of other invasive procedure services should be considered when possible (surgery, cath lab, angiography, interventional radiology).

- The patient is alert through the entire course of prep and recovery—sedation usually occurs in the procedure room and wears off relatively quickly. A pleasant, relaxing environment that puts the patient at ease is highly preferable to the traditional clinical atmosphere.

Special equipment and furniture requirements.
Special design considerations for endoscopy are minimal, but should include the following:

- Fiber-optic light sources, video imaging, physiological monitoring, computerized patient information management and storage are utilized in all procedure rooms. These systems are portable and typically held on easily movable carts. Occasionally, the systems may be fixed on movable ceiling-mounted articulating arms. However, this solution is fairly expensive and not as flexible as the portable approach.

- If provided, a fixed C-arm for radiographic/fluoroscopic studies may be attached at the ceiling in the procedure room intended for ERCP studies.

- Endoscopy procedures typically use a stretcher for the patient. An articulating table capable of allowing sitting and lying positions is used for bronchoscopy. Both platforms are considered movable; the bronchoscopy table requires power.

- Each procedure room needs a 34-inch work counter space at least 6 to 8 feet in length for the layout of scopes. All other equipment in these rooms is considered movable.

- Medical gases are not required for the procedures. However, if inpatients are examined, wall outlets for gas should be provided in the procedure room and prep/recovery areas. Occasionally, drop outlets (from the ceiling) for medical gas may be utilized in the procedure room to reduce obstructions to movement within the room.

Supporting spaces

A number of supporting spaces for endoscopy are required:

- Preprocedure prep areas
- Space for medications, clean supply holding, clean and soiled linen holding, soiled utility room, nourishments, and equipment holding
- Diagnostic work areas
- Areas for support services for administration and staff:

  Reception/registration/scheduling work areas

  Waiting area with consult room

  Offices for the nurse manager

  Record storage areas

  Staff lounge with pantry, lockers, and toilets

Special planning and design considerations

Special design considerations for endoscopy include the following:

- Variable light control within all procedure rooms is needed for video monitoring.
- Isolation of the bronchoscopy room because of the potential presence of infectious disease agents is recommended, if not required by building code.
- Dispersion of unpleasant odors via airflow and air exchange in the prep/recovery areas. Building codes do not usually address this specific condition, but exhaust and vertiliations is a need patient recovery positions.
- Cleaning agents used manually or within special scope-washing

equipment typically require special exhaust measures to control noxious fumes and protect staff; 100 percent exhaust is typically required. Local building codes should be consulted for specific requirements. Continuous exhaust registers located behind and at the level of the work countertop are often employed. These registers include a transparent protective screen between the employee and work surface, effectively creating a built-in fume hood.

- Bacteria-resistant, cleanable building finishes should be used in all procedure and recovery areas.

Trends

The application of endoscopic procedures will continue to rise as new techniques and capabilities are created. The contribution of the endoscope toward lowering risk of radiation exposure (X-rays) and infections (surgery) is significant. Among the diagnostic and therapeutic technologies available today, endoscopy is one of the most promising and exciting.

It is likely also that the lines between surgery and endoscopy will blur in the future. This consolidation is already happening in many facilities. The only barrier is the level of sterile technique required in surgery that is not needed in endoscopy. It is possible, however, to resolve this issue with good design of patient flow. Physician practice patterns will change because of the capital cost considerations and the increasing acuity of patients undergoing endoscopic procedures. Improvement in the utilization of endoscopy space will result. This service, because of its growing number of applications, will be subject to the same demands for efficiency as surgery is today. As such, procedures will be scheduled regularly throughout the day. The net effect will be a reduction in space needed as a function of the number of procedures performed annually.

Obstetrics

Functional overview

The obstetrics department of a hospital is a major component of a comprehensive women's center. It is dedicated to the care of pregnant women prior to and through the delivery of the infant, as well as to the care of the newborn. Such a unit generally consists of a combination of labor, delivery, and recovery rooms, and nursery and support service areas, including areas for patients, families, and staff.

The layout of the department is dependent on the type of delivery and the number of projected deliveries. There are three main delivery models in obstetric care:

- *Traditional.* Consists of a separate group of rooms or areas through which the patient moves along various stages of the birthing process. The patient is admitted to a triage area and transferred to a labor room. The patient is then transferred to a delivery room for the birthing process. The patient is transferred again to recovery postdelivery. The postpartum unit is the final stop for the new mother. The infant is placed in a nursery adjacent to or within this unit. Of the three models, this one involves the most movement of the patient.
- *Labor/Delivery/Recovery (LDR).* Provides a room to accommodate all

three stages of the birthing process and is equipped for normal deliveries. The patient remains in the same room until recovery is complete. The patient is then transferred to the postpartum unit, the infant either moving to the nursery or accompanying the mother. Women who do not want to visit with family in the same room in which they have delivered prefer this model.

- *Labor/Delivery/Recovery/Postpartum (LDRP).* Provides a single room used for the entire stay of the patient. The infant may remain in the room or in the nursery for partial or full care. This model requires the least movement of the patient.

Service locations

Obstetrics is traditionally located in the acute care environment of a community, regional, or teaching hospital. Today, obstetrics departments are designed to provide lower-cost services in a family-oriented wellness environment. Facilities are increasingly reaching out, especially in large communities, to cluster birthing centers with other diagnostic and treatment functions. This reconfiguration will create ambulatory care centers with integrated physician office practices with both affiliated and non-affiliated physicians.

Operational considerations

Key activity factors and capacity determinants

In planning an obstetrics unit, the key activity factor or work load measure is the birth or delivery. Supportive activities provide a full spectrum of required obstetrics care services prior to and following delivery. In planning a comprehensive obstetrics unit, the hospital analyzes the present patterns of obstetrics care. The hospital focuses on the following determinants to arrive at the projected number of rooms and room types for labor, delivery, and recovery:

- The projected number of births to be served by the unit, given demographic trends and market share

- The occupancy rates, considering highs and lows in the hospital annual census

- The projected number of patients in the unit during peak periods and the length of the peaks

- The number of high-risk births utilizing the cesarean section room

- The average length of stay (ALOS) for women during labor, delivery, and recovery periods

- The number of high-risk women needing antenatal services.

The following information will allow appropriate planning of a unit adapted to the specific needs of a hospital, whether it selects the traditional, LDR, or LDRP delivery concept.

The American College of Obstetricians and Gynecologists recommends the following room ratios in the traditional delivery setting:

1 Labor room: 250 annual births

1 Delivery room: 400 to 600 annual births

1 Recovery room: for every 2 labor beds

In an LDR setting, the general planning guideline for determining the number of LDR rooms needed is

1 LDR room: 350 noncesarean annual births (based on an ALOS of 12 hours)

For the LDRP concept, the formula is LDRP rooms (total) =

$$\frac{\text{Number of annual births} \times \text{ALOS}}{365 \times \text{planned occupancy rate}}$$

Patient and work flow

Direct access for patients, beginning with clearly marked entrances and parking areas, is of high priority because of the critical timing of the labor and delivery process and the anxiety it may produce. Patients arrive at the obstetrics area from a number of sources, including the main women's center entrance, the emergency department (especially after hours), and the physician's office. Direct access to the emergency and surgery departments are handled by segregated horizontal access or dedicated vertical access that utilizes oversized, dedicated-keyed elevators.

Today most healthcare facilities direct patients through a central triage area. As this point, physicians decide whether to observe or advance a patient to an LDR/LDRP room or to a cesarean section room for immediate delivery. The area may be adjacent to or shared with a cesarean section recovery area for staffing efficiency and flexibility in assigning patients beds. Immediate proximity of this area to the cesarean section suite is essential for efficient transport time.

Patients in active labor are transferred to a labor room, an LDR room, or an LDRP room, where family members may join them. The LDR/LDRP design concept incorporates locating rooms around the perimeter of the facility for daylighting and should allow direct access from triage, the cesarean section area, resuscitation, and the neonatal intensive care unit (NICU). Adequate patient and family amenities ensure a

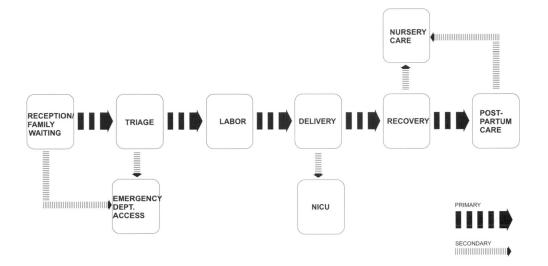

RECEPTION/ FAMILY WAITING → TRIAGE → LABOR → DELIVERY → RECOVERY → POST-PARTUM CARE

NURSERY CARE

EMERGENCY DEPT. ACCESS

NICU

PRIMARY

SECONDARY

▲ *Flow diagram identifies patient circulation within the obstetrics area.*

successful labor and delivery area. In today's changing world, adequate security measures should also limit general public access through the unit, thus protecting mother and infant.

In the LDRP model, staff flow begins with patient contact at the reception area, then continues to the triage area, labor and delivery/recovery areas, and postpartum or discharge area. In an LDR/LDRP concept, the patient will experience the same nursing staff throughout the labor/delivery process. Staff will move clean equipment into the room for delivery and remove postdelivery equipment for cleanup. After postdelivery assessment, the infant often remains with the mother during recovery before being transported to the nursery for further assessment, cleaning, and gowning. Infants in stress are transported directly to a transition nursery or an NICU if directed by the neonatologist. After a delivery occurs in the cesarean section room, the mother is transferred to the recovery area. At that

point, the baby is observed in a resuscitation area or a transition nursery adjacent to the delivery suite.

Physician and staff gowning facilities should provide a one-way flow into the cesarean section suite, as in the surgery department. Physician and nurse work areas should be decentralized and located closer to the patient areas to improve patient care and staff efficiency.

Relationships with other departments

The obstetrics area is the focal point of a comprehensive women's center. Particular departments or services have strong ties with the women's center. The neonatal intensive care unit (NICU) should be located nearby because of the frequency and priority of infants being transferred to the intensive setting.

The postpartum/obstetrical inpatient unit and nursery require easy accessibility, separated from public traffic and with horizontal or vertical access to obstetrics. Emergency and surgery departments

GENERAL SPACE REQUIREMENTS, OBSTETRICS

Room	Suggested Area (net square feet)	Optimal Dimensions (feet)	Necessary Adjacent Support Spaces
Cesarean/delivery suite	360–400	20 x 20	(Min. 16 ft dim.) Infant resuscitation
Infant resuscitation	150	10 x 15	May be located within cesarean section room at 40 net sq ft
Delivery room	300–350	18 x 18	
Labor rooms (traditional)	120–150	10 x 15	Toilet
Triage/recovery bay	80–100 per bed	10 x 10	Nurse work area, toilet, supplies
LDR/LDRP rooms	360–400	18 x 20	Includes toilet and equipment storage

require dedicated access for emergent cases, which can be accomplished with dedicated elevator access or restricted corridor access.

In recently designed facilities, the trend is to consolidate all services dedicated to comprehensive women's care, including perinatal services, pediatrics, breast health services, and education centers, in addition to labor, delivery, recovery, and postpartum accommodations.

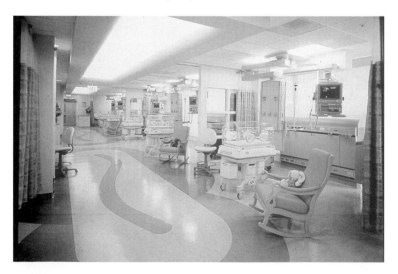

▼ A neonatal ICU at Utah Valley Medical Center in Provo, Utah.

Key spaces

National guidelines and state building codes address the required room types and, in many cases, the respective square footages. Best practice standards within the healthcare industry, including the AIA *1996-1997 Guidelines for Design and Construction of Hospital and Health Care Facilities*, suggest guidelines for key spaces within the obstetrics department, as shown in the table above.

Key design considerations

The design of the obstetrics area should address the following considerations:

- Determination of which delivery model (traditional, LDR, or LDRP) the hospital will provide. This will affect related areas, including inpatient units (obstetrics/postpartum) and nursery areas, as well as staffing models and overall patient care.

- Direct accessibility between triage/recovery and the cesarean section suite is fundamental for quick patient transport.

- Infant patient flow between delivery areas and resuscitation, transition nursery, and NICU (if applicable).

- Delivery equipment storage and flow for the LDR and LDRP concepts: shared vs. dedicated; centralized vs. decentralized.

Special equipment and furniture requirements

There are a number of special equipment and furniture requirements that should be considered, which focus mainly on LDR and LDRP rooms:

- Delivery lights are portable, recessed, or retractable. In recent years, the most popular kind has been recessed, adjustable delivery lighting controlled by a remote wand. If portable lights are utilized, adequate storage must be provided adjacent to or outside the room.

- The delivery process requires extensive movable equipment, including—but not limited to—a delivery cart, stool, mirror, anesthesia cart (in many cases), and a bassinet/isolette. This equipment is typically stored in an adjacent storage alcove or room and may be shared, especially in the LDRP model.

- The LDR/LDRP model requires a scrub sink, work counter, and supply storage within each room.

- Computer dictating and integrated heart/fetal monitoring systems require space adjacent to the mother and are built in or on a movable cart or other furniture.

- Patient and family furniture requirements include a rocker or patient chair for the mother, sleeping accommodations for family members, and patient storage, usually within a

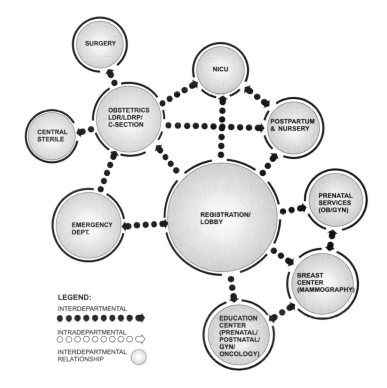

wardrobe that includes TV, VCR, and stereo equipment.

- Appropriate dedicated medical gas delivery systems for mother and baby are included, often in a concealed system.

- Cesarean section rooms are typically designed and equipped to replicate a typical operating room, with the addition of medical gases for infant resuscitation as required by code.

Supporting spaces

The following list includes supporting spaces in an obstetrics facility, based on national guidelines. Spaces may vary according to state health guidelines.

- Reception/waiting areas for patients and family members

▲ Interrelationship diagram illustrates key (or major) departmental relationships.

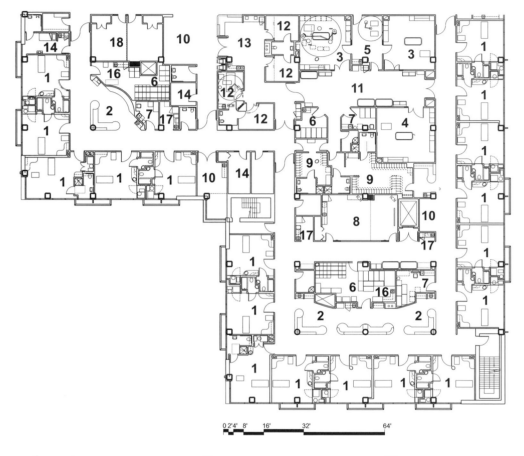

0 2'4' 8'   16'   32'   64'

1 LDR	**7** SOIL	**13** TRIAGE LAB
2 NURSE STATION	**8** LOUNGE/CONFERENCE	**14** OFFICE
3 C-SECTION	**9** LOCKERS	**15** ANESTHESIA STORAGE
4 HIGH RISK DELIVERY	**10** WAITING	**16** MEDICATION
5 INFANT RESUSCITATION	**11** SCRUB AREA	**17** NOURISHMENT ALCOVE
6 CLEANUP/EQUIPMENT	**12** TRIAGE	**18** TRAINING/CONFERENCE

▲ *Typical obstetrics floor plan illustrates the LDR model.*

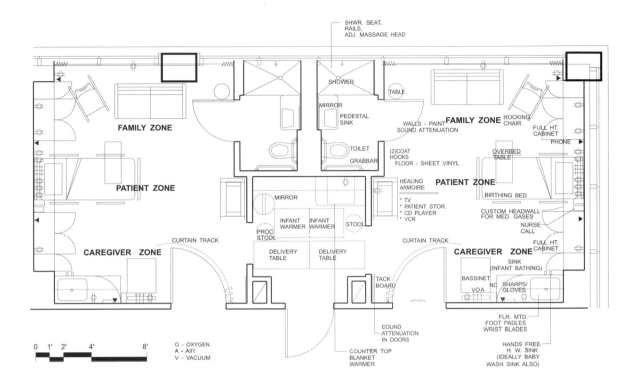

SHWR. SEAT,
RAILS,
ADJ. MASSAGE HEAD

SHOWER

TABLE

MIRROR

PEDESTAL
SINK

FAMILY ZONE

WALLS - PAINT
SOUND ATTENUATION

FAMILY ZONE

ROCKING
CHAIR

FULL HT.
CABINET

PHONE

TOILET

GRABBAR

(2)COAT
HOOKS

FLOOR - SHEET VINYL

OVERBED
TABLE

HEALING
ARMOIRE

PATIENT ZONE

PATIENT ZONE

* TV
* PATIENT STOR.
* CD PLAYER
* VCR

BIRTHING BED

CUSTOM HEADWALL
FOR MED. GASES

MIRROR

INFANT
WARMER

INFANT
WARMER

STOOL

NURSE
CALL

PROC.
STOOL

FULL HT.
CABINET

CAREGIVER ZONE

CURTAIN TRACK

DELIVERY
TABLE

DELIVERY
TABLE

CURTAIN TRACK

CAREGIVER ZONE

SINK
(INFANT BATHING)

BASSINET

NO

SHARPS/
GLOVES

TACK
BOARD

VOA

FLR. MTD.
FOOT PADLES
WRIST BLADES

SOUND
ATTENUATION
IN DOORS

HANDS FREE
H. W. SINK
(IDEALLY BABY
WASH SINK ALSO)

0 1' 2'   4'   8'

COUNTER TOP
BLANKET
WARMER

O - OXYGEN
A - AIR
V - VACUUM

A floor plan of typical LDR room.

- Nurses' work areas
- Support spaces for medications, nourishments, clean supplies, equipment, soiled supplies, and housekeeping
- Separate support spaces for the cesarean suite, including substerile, clean, soiled, and housekeeping supplies
- Administrative offices, lounge areas, lockers, toilets, and showers adequate to support the entire obstetrics area

Special planning and design considerations

There are a number of special planning and design considerations for obstetrics, as indicated in the following guidelines:

- Provide convenient access for visitors, but separate from patient and support traffic on and off the unit. Protect the patients' privacy and dignity.
- Create a family-centered, healing environment through the use of appropriate design vocabulary, materials, furnishings, and color. The use of artwork with full-spectrum color to complement the overall interior design can help create positive distractions and the peaceful imagery desired in this situation. In choosing the artwork, it is important to be sensitive to patients and their families, in care of both high-risk and normal deliveries.
- Reflect a focus on wellness and a sense of normalcy, and offer views of nature, landscape scenery, and water whenever possible.

77

• In the patient areas (LDR/LDRP), give patients and family members a sense of control over their environment through varied lighting and thermal controls, adequate storage space, and TV/VCR/music controlled at bedside.

Trends

Obstetrics is an area greatly affected by industry changes, legislation, patient choice, and competition. The decrease in length of stays from three days to 24 hours has leveled off to two days for normal deliveries and three days for cesarean sections. This change is aided by legislation resulting from a backlash against restrictive managed-care requirements. Obstetrics departments continue to be highly competitive in their efforts to capture market share and draw women to their facilities. Hospitals are redeveloping their obstetrics departments to align with a patient-centered focus and marketing their services accordingly.

The LDRP concept that was popular in the past decade has shifted to a more flexible LDR model, especially at facilities with birth rates greater than 3,000 births per year. The LDR and postpartum concept offers more flexibility in delivery of patient care in facilities with higher birth rates. This is achieved by allowing a higher turnover of delivery rooms and postpartum beds, which can also be utilized by gynocology and medical/surgery services. The mother/baby nursing care trend, which staffs one nurse to both mother and child while the infant rooms-in with the mother, also continues to gain popularity in the postpartum setting.

Hospitals continue to face pressures to consolidate or regionalize obstetrical services, which has resulted in a variety of affiliations and other agreements. Advances in prenatal care, neonatal care, and family-centered care will continue, all affecting the built environment. In addition, legislation, regulation, and market pressures will have a continuing impact on design.

Surgical Suite

Planning for the surgical suite, one of the most important areas of a hospital, involves many different disciplines. Consideration must be given to the

◢ A view of the LDRP room configured for delivery at HealthPark in Fort Myers, Florida

▼ A view of the LDRP room configured for pre- or postpartum at HealthPark in Fort Myers, Florida

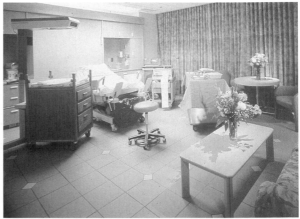

emotional needs of patients and their families. No other aspect of hospital care creates the level of fear and anxiety as surgery. Therefore, preplanning analysis must involve administrators, surgeons, anesthesiologists, surgical nurses, representatives of support areas (housekeeping, pharmacy, central sterile supply, and laboratory), and individuals who consider the needs of the patient and family.

Surgical procedures are performed on patients for a wide variety of reasons (i.e., to correct a potentially life-threatening situation or to provide an improved quality of life). Procedures may be performed in surgical suites that are designed specifically for treatment of outpatients, such as ambulatory procedure units, or in suites that are designed for treatment of both inpatients and outpatients.

The ambulatory procedure unit (APU) is discussed in detail in chapter 4 of this book. In brief, the APU is located off-campus or within the hospital, separate from the surgical suite or closely related to the surgery suite. It includes outpatient reception, surgery preparation, dedicated outpatient operating rooms, postanesthesia care unit (PACU), and an area for the final stage of recovery.

Normally, surgeons prefer to perform inpatient and outpatient surgery in the same operating suite during the same surgery schedule. Inpatients are those patients who have been admitted to the hospital prior to surgery. They are also those who, because of the severity of the surgery, are admitted to the hospital following surgery (e.g., same-day admits). In some cases, surgery is performed on an emergency basis as a result of trauma. Outpatients are admitted and prepared for surgery, undergo a surgical procedure, complete the recovery process, and are discharged on the same day.

General overview

The surgical process, although complicated, can be simplified into three distinct periods that relate to the patient's progress: "prior to surgery," "during surgery," and "after surgery." Each patient goes through these steps.

Prior to surgery (preoperative care). Prior to any surgery, the anesthesiologist (the physician in charge of administering the

▲ *An outpatient operating room at Methodist Care Center in Sugar Land, Texas.*

▼ *An outpatient recovery area at Mercy Regional Medical Center Ambulatory Care Center North in Laredo, Texas.*

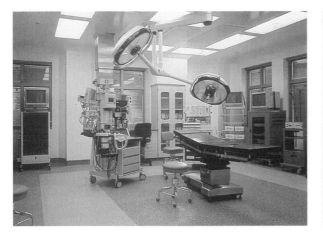

anesthesia) or the surgeon explains the different procedures of the surgery and its consequences, answering the patient's questions. At that point, the patient signs an authorization for the surgery procedure. For the inpatient, this takes place in the patient or preoperative holding room. For same-day surgery patients, the procedure occurs in the preoperative care area.

During surgery. In the operating room, the surgical procedure begins with the administration of anesthesia by the anesthesiologist. The anesthesiologist monitors and controls the patient's unconscious condition throughout the surgical procedure. The surgical team normally consists of a surgeon, an auxiliary surgeon, and a resident in surgery. Other staff include surgical nurses and a circulating nurse.

After surgery (postoperative care). Depending on the type of surgery and anesthesia, the patient will remain in the postanesthesia care unit (PACU) for as long as three hours. If the inpatient recovers without any problems, he or she is relocated to a patient room. The outpatient or same-day surgery patient will go to postoperative phase 2 recovery to complete the recovery process. In certain cases, such as in cardiovascular surgery, the patient is transported directly to an intensive care unit.

Services provided

A wide range of services are provided in the surgery suite. The primary services include anesthesia, preoperative holding, the operating rooms, the postanesthesia care unit (PACU), postoperative phase 2 recovery, and support from other departments, including pharmacy, laboratory, housekeeping, and central sterile supply.

Anesthesiology. This service provides general patient anesthesia, requiring support areas for the cleaning and storage of anesthesia equipment and supplies and offices for the anesthesiologists.

Outpatient prep/holding. Outpatients, normally treated in the inpatient surgical suite, are received and discharged from this area. After completing the required paperwork, a patient is taken to a holding room to change clothes and discuss the case with a physician. Following discussion and approval for surgery, the patient is transported to surgery for the procedure. The patient is transported back to the preoperative area for the recovery process in phase 2 recovery. A selected member of the patient's family is normally allowed to join the patient for this period, assisting the patient in recovery. This period lasts approximately one to three hours. Following full recovery the patient is discharged. It is important to design the traffic flow to allow separate entries and exits for arriving and discharged patients. The preoperative and phase 2 recovery areas can be designed as enclosed rooms or open areas separated by curtains. The preferences of medical and administrative staff can guide the design to the appropriate solution. Preoperative areas do not normally require medical gases, unless there is a desire to achieve flexibility between preoperative and postoperative areas. Postoperative areas do require medical gases. In addition, nurses' stations are positioned for direct visibility to patient cubicles.

Inpatient holding. Patients are received from the inpatient bed units and prepared for surgery in this area. The area requires medical gas and direct visibility from a nurses' station. A curtain separates each cubicle.

Operating rooms. Many different types of surgical procedures occur in operating rooms. This "inner zone" must meet the highest standard of cleanliness and aseptic conditions. There are specific requirements for each kind of operating room, according to the scheduled type of surgery. Some rooms are dedicated to specific surgeries, and others are used for many different types. Most rooms, however, require a variety and large quantity of medical gases, including oxygen and nitrous oxide, and a vacuum system. These gases are delivered via hose drops or medical gas columns. Nitrogen may be required to power certain instruments. Operating rooms require fluorescent fixtures, gas evacuation systems, ceiling-supply air systems and a low-return air system that meets code requirements for air changes per hour. In addition, building codes require a large volume of electrical power with a certain quantity assigned to emergency power. Certain specialty operating rooms may require microscope columns, laminar air flow systems, other specialty instrumentation, or adjacent workrooms.

Postanesthesia care unit. Described under "After surgery," page 80.

Surgery specialties

The specific procedures provided by hospitals vary according to population need, the hospital mission, and the available surgical specialists. All surgical specialties are grouped in the following categories:

Cardiothoracic surgery

Dental surgery

ENT (ear, nose, and throat)/otolaryngology surgery

General surgery

GYN (gynecology) surgery

Neurosurgery

Oncology surgery

Ophthalmology surgery

Orthopedic surgery

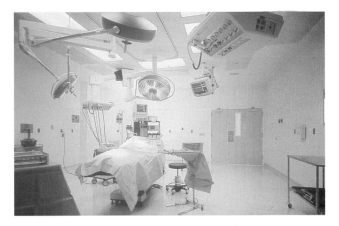

▲ A general operating room at HealthPark Medical Center in Fort Myers, Florida.

▲ A surgical suite family waiting area at All Saints Episcopal Hospital–Cityview in Fort Worth, Texas.

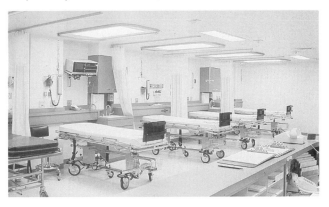

▲ A postanesthesia recovery room at Duncan Regional Hospital in Duncan, Oklahoma.

Pediatric surgery

Plastic surgery

Transplant surgery

Trauma/burn surgery

Urology surgery

Vascular surgery

Combination with other elements

The surgical suite is often combined with preadmittance testing and the ambulatory procedure unit, located conveniently for patient access. This area performs patient testing and administration functions prior to the day of surgery.

Key activity factors

The key element for determining the size of the surgical suite is the number of operating rooms. The basic criteria for determining the number of operating rooms are the total number of procedures and number of minutes expected annually for the target year. Calculations are made to determine the total volume of expected surgical operations.

Total number of procedures. The number of procedures performed in a given period of time is measured against operating room capacity, including procedure and cleanup time. Surgery generally takes place in a seven-to-eight-hour, five-day-a-week period beginning at 7:00 A.M. with emergency and some elective surgery occurring during the weekend. When a shortage of operating rooms occurs, it is not uncommon for surgery to take place in the evenings and on weekends.

Total number of procedure minutes. The number of procedure minutes is the period of time measured against operating room capacity, including procedure and cleanup time.

Key capacity determinants

The total volume of expected operations in conjunction with the anticipated work period is used to calculate the number of operating rooms needed. The number of operating rooms forms the basis for determining the number of preoperative holding areas, PACU recovery beds, and phase 2 recovery bays. Other square footage determinants include surgery support departments such as pharmacy, laboratory, and housekeeping. Current state and federal standards also have a bearing on the number and sizes of the required rooms.

Flow of various individuals

Work flow in the surgical suite must be considered in relation to several different groups: patients, visitors, medical staff, nursing staff, and logistical support.

Patients. Patients enter the suite from inpatient nursing units, the same-day surgery area, or emergency. Inpatients generally go to a holding area for surgery preparation, then to their assigned operating rooms. Outpatients are transported to their assigned operating rooms. After surgery, patients are transported to the PACU for recovery. Next, they go to their assigned patient rooms or phase 2 recovery.

Visitors. Visitors wait during surgery in the family waiting area. In some facilities, inpatient family members or visitors wait in the patient's private room. Outpatient and same-day surgery visitors wait in the preoperative waiting area until after the surgery, when a limited number of visitors may be allowed to attend to the patient while he or she is in the phase 2 recovery area.

Medical staff. All surgical staff members change into sterile clothing in dressing

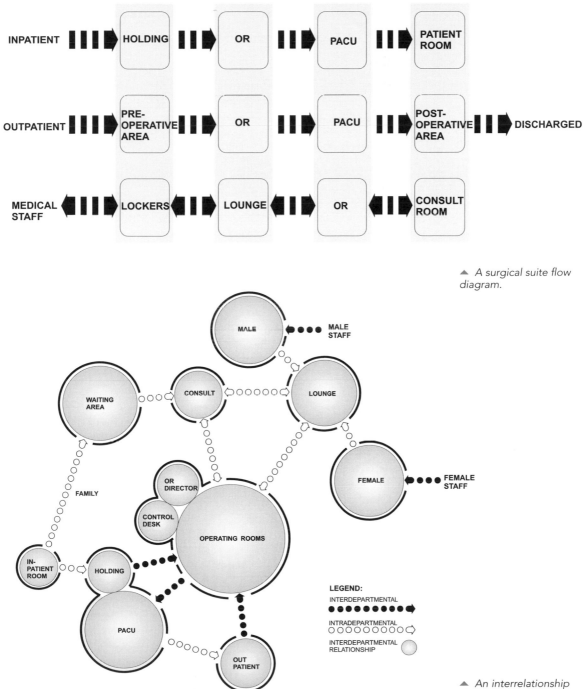

▲ A surgical suite flow diagram.

▲ An interrelationship diagram of a surgical suite.

▶ *A general operating room plan.*

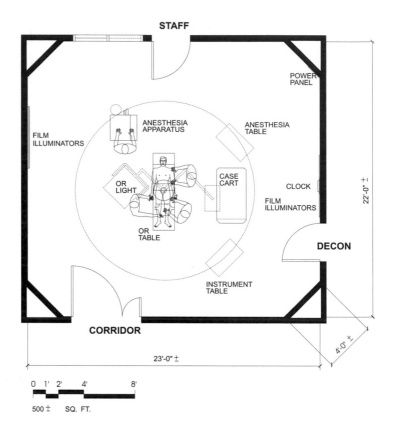

STAFF

POWER PANEL

FILM ILLUMINATORS

ANESTHESIA APPARATUS

ANESTHESIA TABLE

CASE CART

CLOCK

OR LIGHT

FILM ILLUMINATORS

OR TABLE

INSTRUMENT TABLE

DECON

22'-0" ±

CORRIDOR

23'-0" ±

4'-0" ±

0 1' 2'   4'   8'

500 ±   SQ. FT.

areas and enter the surgical suite through a lounge. They can consult the surgery schedule for room assignments. Everyone participating in the surgery scrubs before entering the operating room from the perimeter corridor. After each surgery, the surgeon speaks with the patient's family in a consultation room. Between surgical cases, physicians can take a break in the surgery lounge. There they can utilize the physician dictation areas to record the proceedings/outcome of the surgery.

Relationships with other departments
Patient areas, such as the emergency department, the cardiovascular intensive care unit, the intensive care unit, and patient rooms, require direct horizontal or vertical access to surgery. This layout accommodates the safe and rapid transport of patients. Support areas, such as pharmacy, laboratory, respiratory therapy, and central sterile processing and housekeeping services, should have access to surgery through nonpublic and nonsterile corridors. In addition, the laboratory requires a satellite location in surgery for processing and interpreting frozen pathological sections. Central sterile processing requires either horizontal or vertical adjacency to surgery to transport sterile supplies and instruments rapidly and directly. Pharmacy requires access via pneumatic tube to surgery or the placement of a satellite pharmacy in surgery.

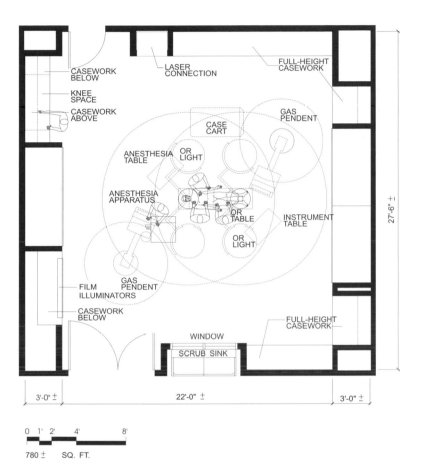

CASEWORK
BELOW

KNEE
SPACE

CASEWORK
ABOVE

LASER
CONNECTION

FULL-HEIGHT
CASEWORK

CASE
CART

GAS
PENDENT

ANESTHESIA
TABLE

OR
LIGHT

ANESTHESIA
APPARATUS

OR
TABLE

INSTRUMENT
TABLE

OR
LIGHT

FILM
ILLUMINATORS

GAS
PENDENT

CASEWORK
BELOW

FULL-HEIGHT
CASEWORK

WINDOW

SCRUB SINK

27'-6" ±

3'-0" ±

22'-0" ±

3'-0" ±

0 1' 2'   4'   8'

780 ± SQ. FT.

◀ *An orthopedic operating room plan.*

Space summary

Key design elements must be considered in planning a surgery suite. General operating rooms should be of standardized size and configuration (a square shape is best). The sizes of specialized operating rooms are important to proper room functioning. The specialized operating rooms listed here are key spaces within the surgery suite and have specific area and dimensional requirements. The designer should consult national and state standards for those requirements. The following net square footages (NSF), exclusive of any built-in cabinets, can serve as a basis for early planning:

General operating room
400 NSF, 20-minimum dimension

Cardiovascular surgery
600 NSF, 20-minimum dimension
(requires an adjacent pump room)

Cystoscopy rooms
350 NSF, 15-minimum dimension

Orthopedic surgery
600 NSF, 20-minimum dimension
(requires an adjacent storage room)

Neurosurgery
600 NSF: 20-minimum dimension
(requires an adjacent storage room)

▶ *A cardiovascular operating room plan.*

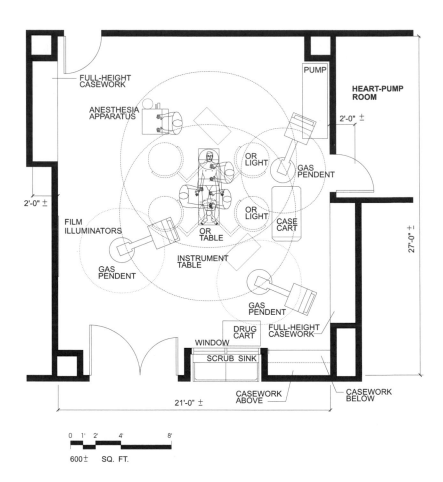

FULL-HEIGHT CASEWORK

PUMP

HEART-PUMP ROOM

2'-0" ±

ANESTHESIA APPARATUS

OR LIGHT

GAS PENDENT

OR LIGHT

CASE CART

FILM ILLUMINATORS

OR TABLE

INSTRUMENT TABLE

GAS PENDENT

GAS PENDENT

27'-0" ±

2'-0" ±

DRUG CART

FULL-HEIGHT CASEWORK

WINDOW

SCRUB SINK

CASEWORK ABOVE

CASEWORK BELOW

21'-0" ±

0 1' 2' 4' 8'

600± SQ. FT.

Operational relationship

There are several operational issues that affect surgical suite design—for example, integrated versus independent outpatient facilities, perimeter work corridor versus interior work core, and integrated versus separate central sterile supply.

Integrated versus independent outpatient facilities. This important consideration addresses the question of the outpatient service location. Outpatient surgery can be an integrated part of the inpatient surgery suite or separated in an independent outpatient suite that includes both preoperative areas and operating rooms. These areas may be located on or off campus. The appropriate location of this service will involve the medical staff and hospital administration.

Perimeter work corridor versus interior work core. A perimeter work corridor layout circles the operating rooms. The layout provides a single corridor system that is used to transport patients, physicians, nursing staff, and clean and soiled supplies. Closed clean and soiled case carts and double bagging of waste products are used to maintain sterile conditions. An interior work core

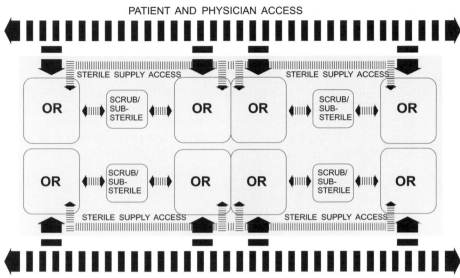

PATIENT AND PHYSICIAN ACCESS

STERILE SUPPLY ACCESS   STERILE SUPPLY ACCESS

OR   SCRUB/SUB-STERILE   OR   OR   SCRUB/SUB-STERILE   OR

OR   SCRUB/SUB-STERILE   OR   OR   SCRUB/SUB-STERILE   OR

STERILE SUPPLY ACCESS   STERILE SUPPLY ACCESS

PATIENT AND PHYSICIAN ACCESS

◀ A diagram of a surgical suite's perimeter corridor concept.

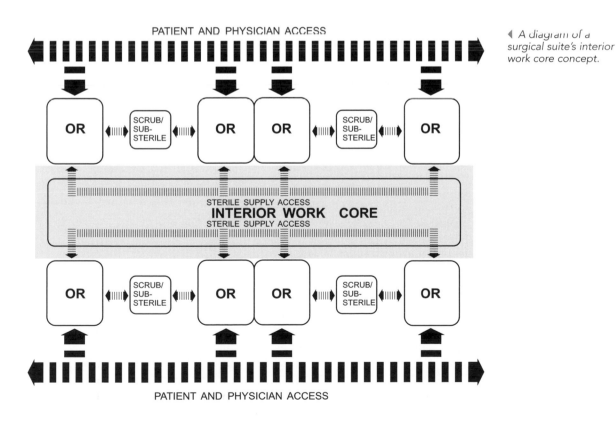

PATIENT AND PHYSICIAN ACCESS

OR   SCRUB/SUB-STERILE   OR   OR   SCRUB/SUB-STERILE   OR

STERILE SUPPLY ACCESS
INTERIOR WORK CORE
STERILE SUPPLY ACCESS

OR   SCRUB/SUB-STERILE   OR   OR   SCRUB/SUB-STERILE   OR

PATIENT AND PHYSICIAN ACCESS

◀ A diagram of a surgical suite's interior work core concept.

▲ A surgery interior work core at McAllen Regional Medical Center in McAllen, Texas.

Medical gas evacuation system

Nurse call system

Scrub sinks

Surgery lights

Movable medical equipment. The surgery suite uses a large amount of movable equipment. The following list is representative of equipment items used in an operating room:

Powered surgery tables

Portable lasers

C-arm radiographic machines

Anesthesia machines

Heart pump machines

Tabletop sterilizers (autoclaves)

Flash sterilizers

Blanket warmers

Diagnostic ultrasound units

separates clean distribution from the soiled distribution system. Placed between two rows of operating rooms, the interior work core is used for sterile supplies and instruments.

Integrated versus separate central sterile supply (CSS). Central sterile supply is placed adjacent to surgery or on another floor; if it is placed directly above or below the surgical suite, it is linked by elevator or dumbwaiter. Although the surgical and CSS staff normally prefer an adjacent relationship, physical building constraints often have a bearing on the location of central sterile supply.

Fixed medical equipment. Surgery uses expensive and delicate equipment. The type and quantity of equipment vary widely according to specific requirements of the surgery staff. The following list is representative of major items of fixed equipment:

Cystoscopy table (can be mobile)

Film illuminators

Laminar flow (optional)

Medical gas

A department as complex as surgery requires many work areas with specific functions. Although a complete description is not possible within the constraints of this chapter, the following list includes those spaces required for most surgical suites. This list will vary in detail according to the needs of the particular facility. For example, the outpatient prep/phase 2 recovery area may not be needed in some facilities.

Public Areas

Family waiting (inpatient and outpatient)

Consultation/bereavement

Reception/file storage

Admitting/cashier stations

Public toilets (shared)

Outpatient Prep/Phase 2 Recovery

Changing areas

Prep/recovery positions

Patient toilets

Patient lockers

Nurses' station

Nourishment

Wheelchair/stretcher alcove

Housekeeping/trash/recycling Room

Clean utility

Soiled utility

Surgery

General operating room(s) (ORs)

Major operating room(s)

Heart (cardiovascular) operating room(s)

Pump room (adjacent to the heart room)

Orthopedic operating room(s)

Orthopedic storage room

Neurosurgery room(s)

Neurosurgery equipment room

Substerile rooms (one between each two ORs)

Scrub alcoves (one between each two ORs)

Alternate OR/cystoscopy

Sterile instruments area

Support Areas

C-arm alcove

Clean utility/case cart staging

Medication room (sink, refrigerator, narcotics locker)

Nurses' station/control station/electronic status board

Soiled utility

Frozen section laboratory

Medical gas storage (inside or outside the facility)

Equipment/storage room

Housekeeping

Blood bank storage

Wheelchair/stretcher alcove

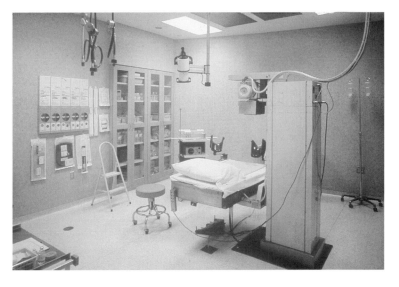

Postanesthesia Care Unit (PACU)— Phase 1 Recovery

Holding/anesthesia, prep positions

Patient recovery positions

Isolation/anteroom (desirable)

Nurses' station

Clean utility/equipment

Soiled utility

Trash room

Medication room

Supervisor's office

Staff toilet

Hand washing sinks (one for every four beds)

Stretcher alcove

Physician/Staff Areas

Physician area

Physicians' lounge (may be combined with nurses' lounge)

Male lockers/dressing area

Male toilet/shower

Female lockers/dressing area

Female toilet/shower

Physicians' sleeping rooms

▲ A cystoscopy room at Hanover Medical Park in Hanover County, Virginia.

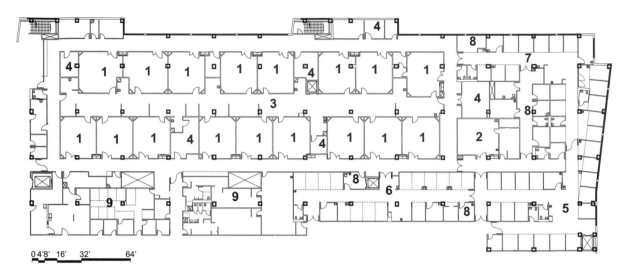

1 OR
2 SPECIAL PROCEDURE
3 STERILE CORRIDOR
4 OR STORAGE
5 PRE-OP

6 POST ANESTHESIA RECOVERY UNIT
7 PHASE 2 RECOVERY
8 SUPPORT
9 STAFF

▲ *A surgical suite floor plan at McKay-Dee Hospital Center in Ogden, Utah*

Staff area
    Staff lounge (may be combined with physicians' lounge)
    Female lockers/dressing area
    Female toilet/shower
    Male lockers/dressing area
    Male toilet/shower

Offices
    Office, medical director
    Office, surgery manager
    Secretary

Anesthesiology
    Office, department chairman
    Secretary
    Office, manager
    Office, anesthetist, shared
    Conference/library/lounge

Technical work area/storage
On-call room(s)
On-call toilet(s)

Trends

Surgical facilities will continue to separate outpatient cases from inpatient cases. The trend is, however, toward integrating outpatient with inpatient surgery for greater efficiency in the use of staff and instruments and cost reduction. This trend puts additional pressure on the surgery staff to maintain outpatient standards of care within the inpatient hospital setting. Outpatients will continue to require direct and convenient means of entering the outpatient area.

Pain management services will expand as new and better means of reducing pain are developed. The preoperative patient areas will continue to be key locations for pain management services. The integration of invasive imaging (cath lab) within the surgical suite will increase as a means of delivering invasive imaging in a surgical environment. A developing trend is to combine surgery with magnetic resonance imaging. Each of these trends carries with it the promise of improved surgical services and better care for the patient.

THERAPY DEPARTMENTS

Oncology

Oncology therapy is treatment for cancer patients. Two common forms of cancer treatment are chemotherapy and radiation therapy. Chemotherapy is the intravenous admission of chemicals that attack cancer cells. Radiation therapy is the exposure of cancer cells to radiation. This radiation can be introduced to the body either through direct implantation—called brachytherapy—or by means of a beam of radiation from a linear accelerator or a screened radioactive source. Because radiation is not selective regarding the type of cells it kills, treatment planning for radiation therapy is quite complex. Both chemotherapy and radiation therapy require patient preparation and recovery. Most chemotherapy and radiation therapies are provided in an ambulatory care setting. Because of the difference in treatment modalities, the two therapies can be separated from each other. However, 30 percent of cancer treatment regimens involve both chemotherapy and radiation therapy.

Patient examination and treatment, as well as treatment planning, are key activity factors. The number of patients being treated and the type of healing environment needed determine space requirements. In radiation therapy, equipment requirements are extensive, as are requirements for shielding. In both chemotherapy and radiation therapy, proper staff supervision is critical to the efficient utilization of space.

Chemotherapy is administered in a nontechnical area designed as patient-friendly space. The process is traumatic, stressful, and lengthy. The amount of space required depends on the total patient volume and type of desired treatment. Separate patient rooms and individual cubicles provide privacy, while open treatment bays encourage interaction with other patients. Creating a healing environment is the design goal for the chemotherapy facility.

Radiation therapy is performed in an area housing highly technical equipment, operated by highly specialized staff. The therapy is usually administered by linear accelerators. A shield must confine the dangerous beam of radiation created by the linear accelerators.

▼ A linear accelerator room at Wellington Regional Cancer Center in Wellington, Florida.

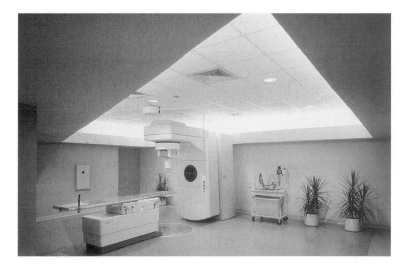

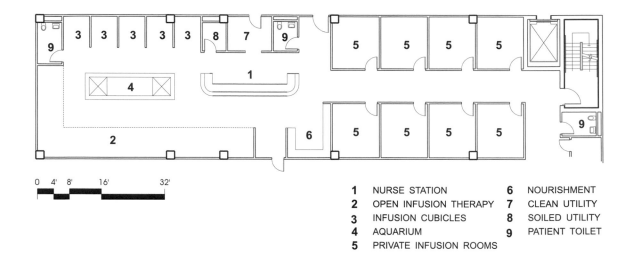

1	NURSE STATION	6	NOURISHMENT
2	OPEN INFUSION THERAPY	7	CLEAN UTILITY
3	INFUSION CUBICLES	8	SOILED UTILITY
4	AQUARIUM	9	PATIENT TOILET
5	PRIVATE INFUSION ROOMS		

▲ A chemotherapy/infusion therapy department plan at Schumpert Cancer Center in Shreveport, Louisiana

Flow of patients

The flow of oncology patients is very predictable, because patients undergoing either chemotherapy or radiation therapy are usually ambulatory and regularly scheduled. Facilities are needed for those patients who are weak and nauseous following treatments. Radiation therapy involves initial examination and consultation with the patient, treatment planning by the staff, treatment simulation using diagnostic x-rays to confirm the treatment and then the radiation treatment. Both therapies usually consist of more than one treatment.

Oncology therapy has few relationships with other departments because most cancer patients are ambulatory. A key factor is direct exterior access to chemotherapy and radiation therapy, respecting patient privacy. Oncology does need access to emergency facilities, but not directly to the emergency department. Chemotherapy requires a connection to the pharmacy for preparations of administered chemicals.

Key spaces

The equipment and shielding requirements for radiation therapy are the most significant for any area in oncology. Linear accelerators aim and focus a beam of high-level radiation. To confine the effects of the beam to the treatment vault itself, substantial radiation shielding is required. Although lead and steel are highly effective shields, concrete is more commonly used because of its lower cost. Eighteen to 20 megavolt linear accelerators produce a beam that can be shielded by approximately 8 ft solid concrete.

To aim the beam, the linear accelerator must be capable of 360 degree rotation. In turn, a room with a 10 ft overhead clearance and a 360 degree shield along the sides requires a significant amount of floor area and building height. Because of the permanency of this kind of construction, careful planning for placement is imperative.

Typical room sizes for radiation therapy are as follows:

Therapy vaults—high energy	600 sq ft
Therapy vaults—low energy	500 sq ft
Control areas	130 sq ft
Equipment	100 sq ft
Entry maze	140 sq ft
Simulator	300 sq ft
Treatment planning	200 sq ft
Dosimetrist's office	120 sq ft
Mold room	250 sq ft
Patient toilets	60 sq ft
Sub-waiting areas	20 sq ft each
Family waiting areas	18 sq ft each

Brachytherapy is the implantation of a radioactive source in or near the site of a cancerous mass. Implantation can be implemented surgically or by catheter. A patient must be monitored during therapy, usually in a patient room that is specifically shielded to prevent exposure to other patients.

Typical room areas for chemotherapy are as follows:

Open treatment bays	60 sq ft
Treatment cubicles	60–80 sq ft
Treatment groups	100–150 sq ft
Nurses' station	150+ sq ft
Patient toilets	50–60 sq ft (ADA compliant)
Family waiting areas	15 sq ft per person
Examination rooms	120 sq ft

Key design considerations

The stress and anxiety felt by many cancer patients can be eased somewhat if there is an opportunity for camaraderie with other patients in mutual support.

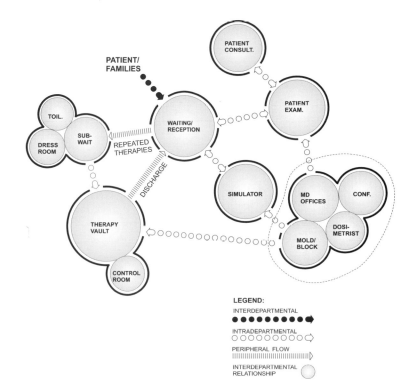

An interrelationship diagram of the oncology department.

The design of the facilities for oncology therapy should provide opportunities for such interaction. Because of the effects of therapy on the physical appearance of patients, privacy and discretion are key design considerations.

The need for staff to supervise patients during and after their treatment influences all design solutions. Treatment planning is a staff function that is screened from patients physically and audibly. A hot lab houses radioactive substances that are prepared for brachytherapy implantation. The room must be shielded and located adjacent to the room where implantation takes place. Preparation in the pharmacy for chemotherapy requires laminar flow mixing hoods to ensure the sterility of the administered agents.

ANCILLARY DEPARTMENTS

▶ *A plan and section of a
linear accelerator vault.*

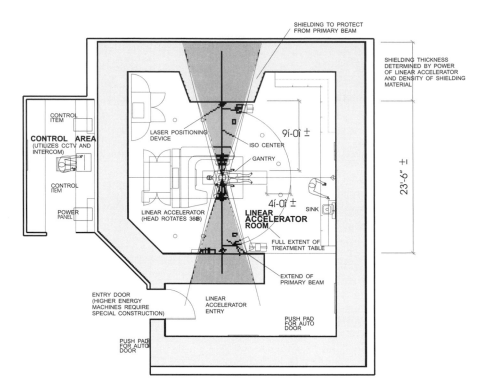

SHIELDING TO PROTECT
FROM PRIMARY BEAM

SHIELDING THICKNESS
DETERMINED BY POWER
OF LINEAR ACCELERATOR
AND DENSITY OF SHIELDING
MATERIAL

23'-6" ±

9'-0" ±

CONTROL
ITEM

CONTROL AREA
(UTILIZES CCTV AND
INTERCOM)

LASER POSITIONING
DEVICE

ISO CENTER

GANTRY

CONTROL
ITEM

4'-0" ±

POWER
PANEL

LINEAR ACCELERATOR
(HEAD ROTATES 360°)

**LINEAR
ACCELERATOR
ROOM**

SINK

FULL EXTENT OF
TREATMENT TABLE

EXTEND OF
PRIMARY BEAM

ENTRY DOOR
(HIGHER ENERGY
MACHINES REQUIRE
SPECIAL CONSTRUCTION)

LINEAR
ACCELERATOR
ENTRY

PUSH PAD
FOR AUTO
DOOR

PUSH PAD
FOR AUTO
DOOR

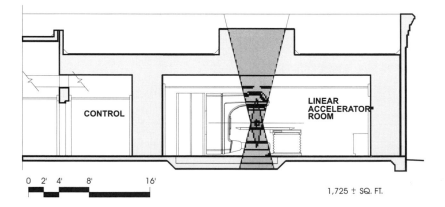

CONTROL

**LINEAR
ACCELERATOR
ROOM**

0 2' 4'   8'   16'

1,725 ± SQ. FT.

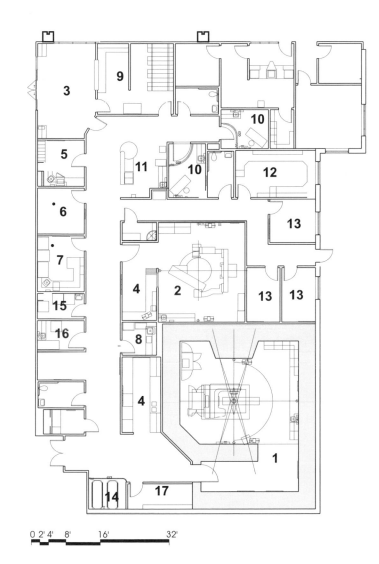

◀ A typical oncology department layout at Louise Obici Memorial Hospital in Suffolk, Virginia.

1	LINEAR ACCELERATOR	7	BLOCK ROOM	13	OFFICE
2	SIMULATOR/CT ROOM	8	DARK ROOM	14	STRETCHER HOLDING
3	WAITING	9	RECEPT/RECORDS	15	SOILED ROOM
4	CONTROL	10	EXAM ROOM	16	CLEAN ROOM
5	WORK/STAFF	11	NURSE STATION	17	STORAGE
6	CONSULT/CONF.	12	DOSIMETRY		

▶ A chemotherapy/infusion therapy area at Schumpert Cancer Center in Shreveport, Louisiana.

Patients' dressing areas, lockers, and toilets, as well as staff lounges, lockers, and offices, are needed to support treatment areas.

Physical Medicine and Rehabilitation

Physical medicine and rehabilitation (PM&R) offers services to individuals who are physically disadvantaged, with the purpose of returning them to their maximum physical capabilities. These services may include physical therapy, occupational therapy, speech pathology, audiology, and specialized programs; they may be supported with the development of orthotics and prosthetics to assist in their functioning. Physical medicine and rehabilitation are provided on an inpatient, outpatient, or in-home basis.

Physical therapy

Physical therapy concentrates on gross neuromuscular and skeletal activity, with emphasis on regaining movement, circulation, and coordination of body and limbs. Typical components of the physical therapy service are treatment areas, a gymnasium, and a hydrotherapy area. Treatment areas may be individual cubicles or rooms. A number of therapies can be administered in these areas, including thermal therapy, electrical stimulation, massage, and manipulation. A gymnasium is generally configured with equipment for several functions located in a common space, such as mats, platforms, gait training stairs, parallel bars, and weights, as well as other resistive equipment and orthotic and prosthetic training services. The gym can also serve as a multipurpose space, supporting other uses such as sports events (e.g., wheelchair basketball) and community activities. In long-term rehabilitation facilities, the physical therapy program may be expanded into recreational therapy for patients.

Hydrotherapy is a treatment with warm to hot circulating water in tanks. The tanks are used either for the extremities, such as the legs and arms, or for full-body submersion. Hubbard tanks, which are configured to allow each limb to be fully extended, are also used. The warm to hot water circulating around the body or parts of the body stimulates blood circulation, promoting healing and reduction of pain. Larger therapy pools allow patients to exercise while suspended in water, thus reducing the impact of body weight during therapy. The humidity of these areas should be carefully controlled through the mechanical ventilation system.

Occupational therapy

Occupational therapy focuses on optimizing a patient's independence while concentrating on finer physical movements. Activities of daily living (ADL), vocational training, and, in some cases, a work-hardening program are used to rehabilitate the patient.

The activities of daily living are routine tasks that individuals are required to perform. The area provided for this therapy includes a mock bedroom, kitchen, and bathroom. These areas provide the patient with an opportunity to learn the basic essentials of cooking, hygiene, and dressing with the benefit of an attending therapist.

The vocational training area houses a variety of equipment, including word processors, computers, cash registers, and telephone switchboards, simulating a work environment. The area may also include wood and metal workshops. Some occupational therapy services include work-hardening programs, which simulate an industrial environment, providing both education and therapy for a more rigorous work setting. Patients learn to perform work tasks and to protect themselves from further injury. Because of the noise made by equipment, it is important to address acoustics in the vocational training area.

Speech pathology and audiology

A patient's injuries or disease may result in communication disabilities. These are most commonly related to cerebrovascular (stroke) and head trauma. The purpose of therapy is to assist a patient in regaining control or adapting to a specific communication disability, which may include cognitive retraining. Communication disabilities include problems with speech and/or hearing. Audiology is most effectively supported diagnostically by two-compartment sound-isolated booths. In the booths patients are accurately tested for hearing loss, as well as the effectiveness of prescribed hearing devices.

Specialized programs

Many providers have specialized programs in physical medicine and rehabilitation. These may include a pain clinic, cardiac rehabilitation, sports

A general gymnasium at the Dallas Rehabilitation Institute in Dallas, Texas.

A hydrotherapy area including a therapy pool, full body tank, and extremity tanks at the Warm Springs Rehabilitation Facility in Dallas, Texas.

medicine, and hand therapy. Specialized areas may be required for these programs. However, many are similar in configuration to the areas for the services already described.

Settings

Physical medicine and rehabilitation services may be housed in a variety of settings, including hospitals, ambulatory care centers, and comprehensive specialty rehabilitation facilities. Care is provided under several physician specialities such as physiatry, orthopedics, neurology, cardiology, and others. The specialty centers may include rehabilitation treatment for cerebrovascular/stroke, spinal cord injury, head trauma, amputation, developmental disabilities, neurological degeneration, complicated fractures, cardiac conditions, or genetic disorders.

▼ An interrelationship diagram of the physical medicine and rehabilitation departments.

Operational considerations

The size, internal relationships, configuration, and location of physical medicine and rehabilitation services are dependent on their work loads. Work load is determined by the number of inpatient or outpatient visits and treatments received within the operating hours of the services. Capacity is determined by such factors as the number of treatment cubicles, mats, therapy positions or stations, cognitive retaining rooms, and hydrotherapy tanks.

Patient and work flows shape the design of the PM&R area. Because of their various disabilities, patients require convenient access to the services. In hospitals, the PM&R services are often located near the elevators at grade. This location is easily reached by inpatients and outpatients. Patients must be visible and accessible to staff. Satellite therapy areas may be located on nursing units for the convenience of less mobile patients. Many initial therapies occur in the patient's room.

PM&R services are related to other departments and services within a hospital. The most common relationships are with nursing units, such as orthopedic, cardiac, neurological, and other units. These services should also be accessible to outpatient entrances, with a dedicated entrance near convenient parking.

Support areas

The following are suggested support areas for PM&R:

- Lounge, personal lockers, toilet, and, possibly, a place to shower
- Meeting space for continued education and training
- Clean workroom, soiled utility, housekeeping, equipment storage, wheelchair and stretcher storage

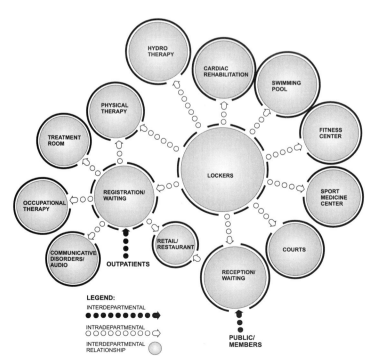

LEGEND:
INTERDEPARTMENTAL
●●●●●●●●➤
INTRADEPARTMENTAL
○○○○○○○○○⇨
INTERDEPARTMENTAL
RELATIONSHIP ●

Larger facilities may also have an orthotics and prosthetics department. The department supplies, manufactures, and fits devices to assist patients' mobility and dexterity. These devices may include artificial limbs, assistive appliances, braces, crutches, and wheelchairs.

Space needs

According to the AIA *1996–1997 Guidelines for Design and Construction of Hospital and Health Care Facilities*, typical physical medicine and rehabilitation services include five major areas:

- Administrative/work
- Physical therapy
- Occupational therapy
- Speech pathology/audiology
- Support/staff

The following are areas typically required in the department:

- Reception and waiting (outpatient or staging of inpatients)
- Administrative office and clerical space
- Patient toilet
- Wheelchair and stretcher storage
- Housekeeping closet
- Access to conference room
- Physical therapy
  - Individual therapy treatment areas with a minimum of 70 sq ft
  - Hand washing area
  - Exercise area (gym)
  - Clean linen storage
  - Equipment and supply storage
  - Soiled utility
  - Patient dressing areas, showers, and lockers (if required)
  - Hydrotherapy (when required)

- Occupational therapy
  - Patient work areas
  - Hand washing area
  - Equipment and supply storage
  - Activities of daily living areas
- Speech pathology and audiology
  - Evaluation and treatment area
  - Space for equipment and storage
- Orthotics and prosthetics
  - Work space
  - Space for fitting and evaluating
  - Space for equipment, supplies, and storage

These areas should be planned in a manner that encourages quality patient care, appropriate space for the proposed work load, and staff efficiency.

Special planning and design considerations

An overriding issue in PM&R is accessibility for patients with restricted mobility. In treatment areas, space must accommodate not only the patient and therapist but also the transportation modalities used to get the patient to therapy—such as a stretcher, wheelchair, or walker. Slip-resistant floor surfaces should have no tripping hazards and must accept wheelchairs and walking accessories.

Heating, ventilation, and air-conditioning systems should address several demands in the PM&R department. Humidity control is required in hydrotherapy and therapy pool areas. Orthotics and prosthetic manufacturing areas require special consideration of acoustical needs and control of fumes and dust.

Trends

Physical medicine and rehabilitation services will be performed more often in

1	WAITING/RECEPTION	**7**	OCCUPATIONAL THERAPY/ACTIVITIES OF DAILY LIVING
2	SPEECH THERAPY	**8**	STAFF WORK AREA
3	TREATMENT PLINTHS	**9**	FITNESS CENTER
4	GYMNASIUM	**10**	DIRECTOR'S OFFICE
5	HYDROTHERAPY	**11**	DICTATION LOCKERS/SHOWERS/TOILET
6	CARDIOPULMONARY	**12**	OFFICE

▲ *A floor plan for a physical medicine and rehabilitation area at Louise Obici Memorial Hospital in Suffolk, Virginia.*

outpatient and home care settings. These services will also be more and more decentralized within the community for convenience and ease of access. There is a trend toward the development of specialty centers of excellence for certain rehabilitation services such as those provided for spinal cord injuries, head trauma, stroke, and development rehabilitation. However, physical medicine and rehabilitation will continue to play an important role in the continuity of care—from inpatient to home care—in both medical and surgical specialties.

Renal Dialysis

Renal dialysis is the simulation of kidney functions for patients in chronic end-stage renal failure or temporary acute kidney failure. The simulation may be performed by two primary methods—hemodialysis or peritoneal dialysis.

Hemodialysis is the filtering of an individual's blood to remove the uremic toxins and water typically removed by the kidneys. The process is implemented by a machine connected to the body's veins through large-bore needles and plastic tubes. These needles may be placed in surgically created fistulas or artificial implants. These are more commonly located in the arm, but the needles may also be placed in the neck or leg regions. The blood is circulated through a membrane filter whereby toxins and water are removed. Alarms on the machine monitor biophysical parameters such as the patient's body temperature, relative blood volume, and hematocrit and electrolyte balances. This procedure may be required three days a week and varies in duration from two to four hours. Home dialysis with this method is possible, but limited by cost and caregiver availability.

Peritoneal dialysis is the removal of uremic toxins and water from the body through the peritoneal cavity around the abdominal organs. This is performed by

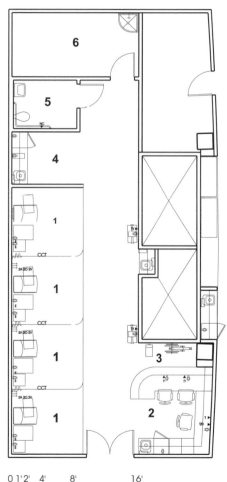

◀ An inpatient renal dialysis unit at Louise Obici Hospital in Suffolk, Virginia.

0 1' 2'   4'   8'   16'

1 DIALYSIS STATION
2 NURSE WORK AREA
3 WEIGH-IN
4 NOURISHMENT
5 TOILET
6 STORAGE

perfusing specific warm, sterile chemical solutions through the cavity. An artificial opening is surgically created in the abdominal wall for this procedure. Dialysis by this method is typically performed several times daily, depending on the size and weight of the patient—which may also limit its practicality. Peritoneal dialysis is considered a less efficient method than hemodialysis; however, it is the most common home dialysis treatment.

Settings

Renal dialysis may occur in a variety of settings, including hospitals, physician's offices, and freestanding dialysis centers, as well as in the home. These settings vary in size and configuration, depending on types of inpatients and outpatients served.

Operational considerations

A renal dialysis unit or center is designed around several operational considerations. The number of patients treated, the hours and frequency of treatment required for patients, and the hours of operation are all items for discussion. Capacity is determined by the number of dialysis positions.

Patient and work flow through a dialysis unit includes several components. The patient is weighed upon arrival. Following this evaluation, the hemodialysis patient is connected to the dialysis machine. The machine is set to operate for a set amount of time. The patient is disconnected from the machine and reweighed, and fluid loss is recorded. An inpatient may return to his or her room and an outpatient may return home. Portable machines are becoming more popular in hospitals, allowing patients to remain in their rooms for treatment.

The treatment area can be open or partially enclosed, yet permitting visibility for nursing and technical staff. The nurses' station is centrally located, allowing visual observation of all patient treatment stations. Treatment positions are at least 80 sq ft (7.43 sq m) and at least 4 ft from other positions. Privacy should be addressed in the layout and design of the treatment position. Isolation positions may also be required for infectious cases. Tables may be placed beside recliners and stretchers as a convenience for the patients.

When a facility for renal dialysis is combined with the physician's office, the nephrologist may schedule an office visit at the same time a renal dialysis procedure is scheduled. The appointment may include not only a visit with the physician, but also a visit with a dietitian or social worker to address specific issues regarding nutrition or personal resources.

Inpatient renal dialysis services should be closely related to inpatient units for convenience and ease of access. After undergoing a renal dialysis procedure, a patient may be weak and faint. Therefore, outpatient services should have immediate access to the parking lot.

Support areas

A number of support areas are provided for the dialysis patient during treatment:

- Nurses' station

- Medication preparation and dispensing station

- Examination room of at least 100 sq ft (9.29 sq m) If home training is provided, a separate room of 120 sq ft (11.15 sq m) should be available.

- Clean workroom

- Soiled workroom
- Separate reprocessing area
- Nourishment stations
- Housekeeping closet
- General storage and storage alcoves
- Water treatment and dialysis preparation
- Patient toilet and personal storage
- Appropriate staff facilities
- In an outpatient setting, a waiting area and supporting offices

Space needs
According to the AIA *1996–1997 Guidelines for Design and Construction of Hospital and Health Care Facilities,* a typical renal dialysis service should include the following:

Waiting and reception (in outpatient facilities)

Treatment positions

Isolation treatment position (if required by the program)

Nurses' station

Medication station (if required)

Home training room (if required)

Examination room

Clean workroom and linen storage

Soiled workroom

Reprocessing room (if required)

Nourishment station

Housekeeping closet

Equipment repair (if required)

Storage

Central batch delivery system and water treatment

Patient toilet

Patients' personal storage space

Supporting offices and staff facilities (if required)

Special planning and design considerations
It is important for the designer of a renal dialysis service to be sensitive to the patient's situation during treatment. Typically, a patient is in a recliner or on a stretcher, which makes lighting and ceiling treatments important. During the actual connection to the machine, adequate lighting is required. After the connection, a more indirect light is desirable. Many centers provide shared television sets for patients' entertainment. However, it is difficult to find television programs that interest everyone. Thus, individual television sets are preferable. Acoustical considerations are also important, especially for patients who prefer to sleep during treatment.

Trends
End-stage renal failure is affecting a larger percentage of patients because of the continued aging of our population. As a result, the growth of renal dialysis centers will continue. Outpatient centers are being developed by major providers nationally. The trend toward consolidation of major national and international dialysis providers is expected to continue. Currently, close to 50 percent of patients in the United States receive treatments from ten major national providers. Home dialysis is also expected to grow as the procedures continue to be simplified by new machines.

Respiratory Care
Respiratory care is the care of the respiratory system—primarily the lungs. There are two distinct areas of activity. The first is inhalation therapy, involving a variety of techniques ranging from simple oxygen supplementation to assisted

breathing with the use of respirators or ventilators. Diagnosis, by calculating the respiratory system's effectiveness through pulmonary function studies and arterial blood gas analyses, is the second activity.

Context

Although the two activities have traditionally been grouped together, they are very different. Inhalation therapy is typically rendered at the patient's location—on nursing units, in outpatient treatment areas and physicians' offices, and even in the home. Increasingly, inhalation therapy is being decentralized to the hospital nursing areas such as critical care, pulmonary units, and neonatal units, which require its support. In many cases, inhalation therapists are integrated into nursing teams or nurses are cross-trained as inhalation therapists. The study of pulmonary function has remained a discrete activity, requiring specific equipment for diagnosis of pulmonary capacity and status. It may constitute a single department or be combined with other diagnostic activities in a multifunction diagnostic center within a hospital or ambulatory care facility.

Operational considerations

Activities and capacities

The key activity factor or work load measure for inhalation therapy is number of procedures or hours of therapy. However, because these procedures occur outside the department—rather than in a procedure room—the key capacity determinants are the number of therapists and pieces of equipment. The key activity factor or work load measure for pulmonary function is the procedure. The key capacity factor is the number of procedure rooms.

Patient and work flow

For pulmonary function testing, patient and work flow is similar to that of other diagnostic departments. The patient arrives, checks in, waits briefly, undergoes the procedure, and departs. The results of the testing are recorded, interpreted, and filed.

For inhalation therapy, the process is more complicated. As noted earlier, the therapy is typically rendered at the patient's location, with staff and equipment coming to the patient. However, following the procedure or treatment, the therapist must record observations on the patient. Traditionally, this was done within the department at charting positions. With the development of computerized records and specialized hand-held devices for recording inhalation therapy activity, this occurs on the nursing unit or at the point of care.

Another necessary process is the returning of equipment to a ready-to-use

▼ *A pulmonary function interrelationship diagram.*

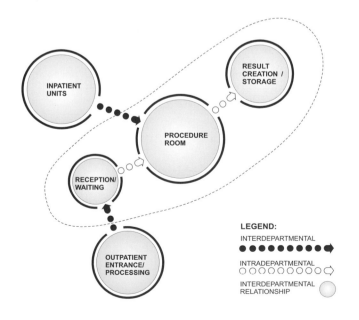

INPATIENT UNITS

RESULT CREATION / STORAGE

PROCEDURE ROOM

RECEPTION/ WAITING

OUTPATIENT ENTRANCE/ PROCESSING

LEGEND:
INTERDEPARTMENTAL
●●●●●●●●●➤

INTRADEPARTMENTAL
○○○○○○○○○▷

INTERDEPARTMENTAL RELATIONSHIP ○

state. Following treatment, equipment must be cleaned and disinfected before being used with the next patient. Today, many of the pieces that contact the patient directly are disposable. The rest of the equipment must undergo a process of decontamination and cleanup. This may occur at a centralized location in the department or in satellite equipment storage areas near the nursing units.

Relationships with other departments

Inhalation therapy primarily occurs on critical and acute care nursing units. It may also be provided in emergency, observation, and day hospital settings.

The pulmonary function service, used by inpatients and outpatients, should be accessible from outpatient intake and registration areas. It is often combined with cardiology diagnostic services to create a cardiopulmonary department.

Space summary

Pulmonary function testing room
Pulmonary function testing is the process of determining the lungs' functional capacity through spirometry (i.e., measuring the volume of the lungs in the states of both inhalation and exhalation). The spirometer is not a large piece of equipment. However, it may be utilized in conjunction with a treadmill for testing the patient under stress.

Recommended dimensions: 10 ft × 12 ft for simple spirometry; 18 ft × 12 ft with a treadmill or for a chamber-style unit (one that the patient actually enters for the procedure).

Ceiling height: 8 ft is adequate

Key design considerations:
- Casework should be provided for general work. An arterial blood gas machine is often included in this space.

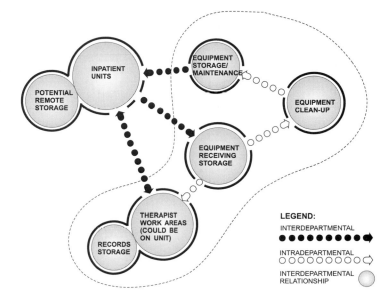

- Size and configuration should permit easy maneuvering with emergency equipment if a treadmill is provided.

Special equipment: Spirometer, with or without treadmill

Individual supporting spaces: None

Supporting spaces
- Equipment receiving/decontamination
- Equipment processing
- Equipment storage and maintenance
- Therapist charting/work
- Supply storage
- Staff conference
- Records storage

Special planning and design considerations

Decentralization
Inhalation therapy continues to be decentralized. With the use of multi-tasking and the creation of care teams,

▲ An inhalation therapy interrelationship diagram.

▶ *A typical pulmonary function room plan.*

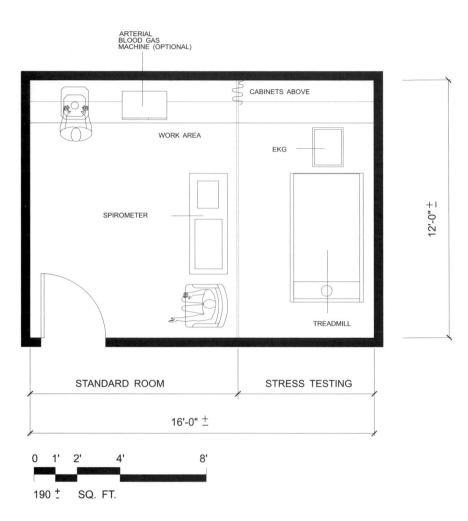

ARTERIAL BLOOD GAS MACHINE (OPTIONAL)

CABINETS ABOVE

WORK AREA

EKG

SPIROMETER

TREADMILL

12'-0" ±

STANDARD ROOM

STRESS TESTING

16'-0" ±

0 1' 2' 4' 8'

190 ± SQ. FT.

this trend can be expected to continue, separating this activity from pulmonary function testing.

Biohazard waste disposal
Because inhalation therapy equipment may acquire infectious materials during the treatment process, care must be taken in disposing of these components. Containment and disposal of such waste is coordinated with the institution's overall biohazard waste disposal system.

Trends
With continuing pressure for cost containment, inhalation therapy services will more often be rendered in the home, where they are least costly. This trend is due to the development of smaller, simpler, and less expensive equipment.

LOGISTICAL SUPPORT DEPARTMENTS

Central Sterile Processing

Functional overview

Central sterile processing (CSP) is a service whereby medical/surgical supplies and equipment—both sterile and nonsterile—are cleaned, prepared, processed, stored, and issued for patient care. Its primary function is the sterilization of instruments for surgery, labor and delivery, and other departments. It also is responsible for the distribution of sterile and clean disposable (purchased goods that are used once and then discarded) items. This department is under considerable pressure to reprocess surgical instruments more quickly, efficiently, and safely. Careful attention to the requirements for sterile separation and instrumentation are required to design tomorrow's central sterile processing department.

Combined with other elements

Central sterile processing is often next to surgery. It can be located either below or above surgery. This requires elevators or dumbwaiters to provide direct access for both clean and soiled materials to and from surgery. In some facilities, central sterile processing is collocated with materials management.

Operational considerations

The size of the central sterile processing area depends on the number of surgical and obstetrics cases treated in a given period and the amount (cu ft) of sterile storage required. In addition, the number of open heart and/or orthopedic cases treated in a given period must be considered. Key capacity determinants include the number and type of sterilization instruments, the exchange case cart distribution system, and instrument holding and equipment cleaning in the CPS department.

Work flow

The department is divided into three zones to accomplish the functions of decontamination, assembly and sterile processing, and sterile storage and distribution. These zones include the following:

1. Decontamination zone

2. Assembly/sterilization zone

3. Storage and distribution zone

The work flow for central sterile processing is centered on the processing of soiled instruments through the four zones. A distinct separation must be maintained between the soiled and sterile areas. The technical staff works on either the soiled side or the sterile side and cannot cross from one side to the other.

Decontamination zone. Reusable equipment and soiled instruments and supplies are received from surgery, labor/delivery, and other departmental areas for initial or gross cleaning. These items are cleaned and decontaminated by means of manual or mechanical processes and chemical disinfection. The exchange cart is cleaned in a pass-through cart washer and readied in the assembly zone to carry items back to the departments. Items of equipment used in this area include the following:

Biohazardous waste management systems

Washer/decontaminator—used to clean heat-tolerant items

Ultrasonic washer—used to remove fine soil from surgical instruments after

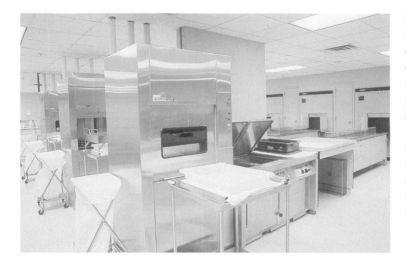

manual cleaning and before sterilization

Healthcare decontamination systems (pass-through washer sterilizers or tunnel washers)—used to sterilize instruments in perforated or mesh-bottom trays

Cart washers—used to clean carts and other transport vehicles

Assembly/sterilization zone. After the instruments have been cleaned and inspected, they are typically assembled into sets or trays, according to detailed instructions. Each set or tray is wrapped or packaged in a nonwoven textile pouch or a rigid package/container system for terminal, or final, sterilization. At that point, the sets are prepared for issue, storage, or further processing.

After assembly, the instruments receive final sterilization. The cleaned instruments are transferred to the sterile storage area until issued. Equipment used most commonly in this zone includes the following:

High-pressure sterile processing systems (steam or electric)

Low-pressure sterile processing systems

ETO (ethylene oxide) gas sterilizer and aerators

ETO gas aerators

Chemical sterilization systems

Microwave sterilization systems

Storage and distribution zone. Following the sterilization process, instruments are stored in sterile storage or sent to the appropriate department. Other functions of this zone include case cart preparation and delivery; exchange cart inventory, replenishment, and delivery; telephone and requisition order filling, and delivery of patient care equipment.

Relationships with other departments

Central sterile processing's most important relationship is with surgery. For this reason, the department must be located directly adjacent to or immediately above or below surgery. Obstetrics receives sterile items from CSP, but is secondary to surgery. Materials management receives disposable items and other goods for CSP. Linen is normally provided by an outside service and is sometimes distributed to CSP if used for sterile wraps.

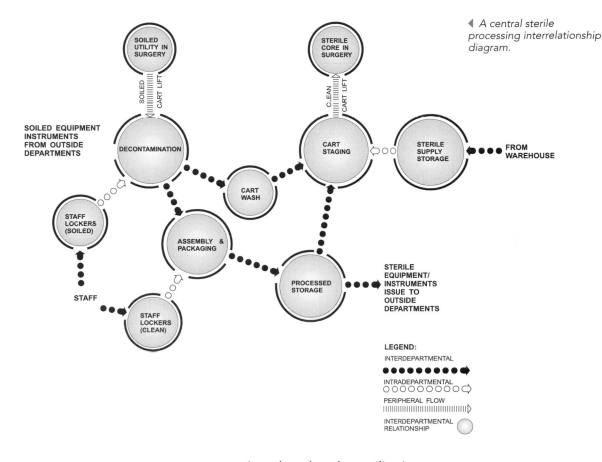

A central sterile processing interrelationship diagram.

Diagram labels:
SOILED UTILITY IN SURGERY · STERILE CORE IN SURGERY · DECONTAMINATION · CART STAGING · STERILE SUPPLY STORAGE · CART WASH · STAFF LOCKERS (SOILED) · ASSEMBLY & PACKAGING · PROCESSED STORAGE · STAFF LOCKERS (CLEAN)

SOILED EQUIPMENT INSTRUMENTS FROM OUTSIDE DEPARTMENTS

FROM WAREHOUSE

STERILE EQUIPMENT/ INSTRUMENTS ISSUE TO OUTSIDE DEPARTMENTS

STAFF

SOILED CART LIFT · CLEAN CART LIFT

LEGEND:
INTERDEPARTMENTAL
INTRADEPARTMENTAL
PERIPHERAL FLOW
INTERDEPARTMENTAL RELATIONSHIP

Space summary
Although the instrumentation of central sterile processing can be complex, its spaces are relative simple. National and state codes should be consulted for compliance. As mentioned earlier, the department is divided into three zones with specific work areas within each zone.

Decontamination areas
  Soiled cart staging
  Decontamination work area
  Biohazardous waste management systems
  Ultrasonic cleaners
  Healthcare decontamination systems

(pass-through washer sterilizers)
Cart washers
Trash holding
Soiled toilet/locker/vestibule
Soiled housekeeping closet
Instrument room

Assembly/sterilization
  Clean work area / prep packaging
  Sterilizer area
  High-pressure sterile processing systems (steam or electric)
  Low-pressure sterile processing systems
  ETO gas sterilizer and aerators
  ETO gas aerators

A central sterile processing floor plan at McKay-Dee Hospital Center in Ogden, Utah.

1	DECONTAMINATION	6	OFFICE	10	TERMINAL STERILIZER
2	WRAP/PACK	7	PASS-THROUGH	11	ETHYLENE OXIDE STERILIZER
3	STERILE STORAGE		WASHER/STERILIZER		
4	STAFF	8	CART WASH		
5	SUPPORT	9	CART STORAGE		

Chemical sterilization

Clean lockers

Linen room

Clean housekeeping closet

Storage/distribution

Office, supervisor

Processed instrument storage/equipment

Equipment storage

Cart staging

Trends
Central sterile processing will move toward total integration with surgery. This move is in response to physicians' continued concern regarding the handling of surgical instruments and the need for nurses to prepare the case trays for sterilization.

Food Services
The food service department is responsible for all activities involving food, nutrition, and beverages in the healthcare facility. The department's primary function is to provide nutrition and dietetic care to both inpatients and outpatients. Ancillary services include the operation of dining facilities for employees, visitors, and physicians,

catering and vending services, meal service for child care centers and satellite facilities, and providing education in nutrition for all campus facilities, clinics, and long-term care units.

Setting
Economics and convenience dictate the setting for the food service department. Ambulatory care centers, long- and short-term facilities, hospitals, and surgical day clinics may all include an in-house food service department. The size and complexity of the operations are contingent on cost. A food service may also be operated as a satellite from a remote or centralized facility, although such operations have unique equipment and procedural requirements.

Operational considerations
The department's work load hinges upon the number of meals served; operational factors such as food production methods, menu selection, staffing, and hours of operation play a key role. Capacity determinants may include food production methods, the size of production equipment, dry/refrigerated storage space, and the number of dining rooms, floor pantries, and warming kitchens.

Work flow also affects an operation's work load and capacity. Cross-traffic, double handling of goods, and poor controls impact costs, efficiency, and food quality. Generally, products should flow as follows:

1. Receiving area
2. Prep area
3. Cooking line
4. Finished product assembly
5. Tray assembly
6. Dish washing

▲ A food court at Valley Children's Hospital in Madera, California.

To ensure an optimal work flow and efficient service, the food service department and its supporting spaces must adhere to particular adjacency requirements:

Receiving area. Locate near the loading and unloading dock for quick, safe food receiving.

Kitchen. Locate near the servery, conference/meeting rooms, service elevators to patients' rooms, and auxiliary services, such as vending and catering.

Floor pantries. Locate near the service elevator core.

Vending. Locate next to the employee/visitor's dining facility, to accommodate late service, and at other strategic points throughout the facility.

Physicians' dining. Locate next to the servery and the dining room.

Employee/visitor's dining. Locate adjacent to the kitchen and food production area. The seating area should be placed next to the servery, providing easy access for foot traffic. Guests need quick access to the visitors' parking lot.

▶ *An interrelationship diagram of the dietary flow process.*

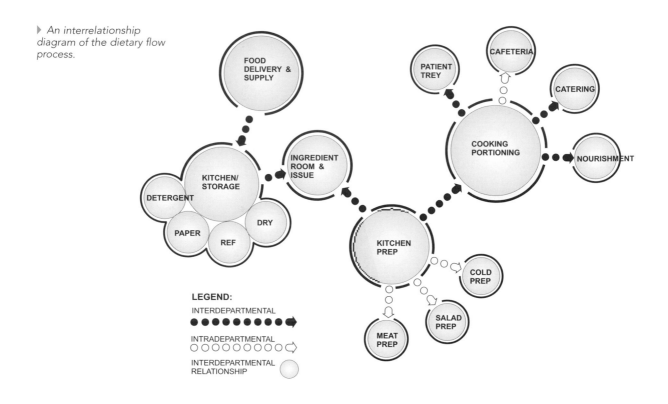

FOOD DELIVERY & SUPPLY

KITCHEN/ STORAGE

DETERGENT

PAPER

REF

DRY

INGREDIENT ROOM & ISSUE

KITCHEN PREP

COLD PREP

SALAD PREP

MEAT PREP

PATIENT TREY

CAFETERIA

CATERING

COOKING PORTIONING

NOURISHMENT

LEGEND:

INTERDEPARTMENTAL
●●●●●●●●●➤

INTRADEPARTMENTAL
○○○○○○○○○⇨

INTERDEPARTMENTAL
RELATIONSHIP ⬤

▼ *An indoor dining area at Roseville Hospital in Roseville, California.*

▼ *The kitchen/bakery area at Texas Scottish Rite Hospital for Children in Dallas, Texas.*

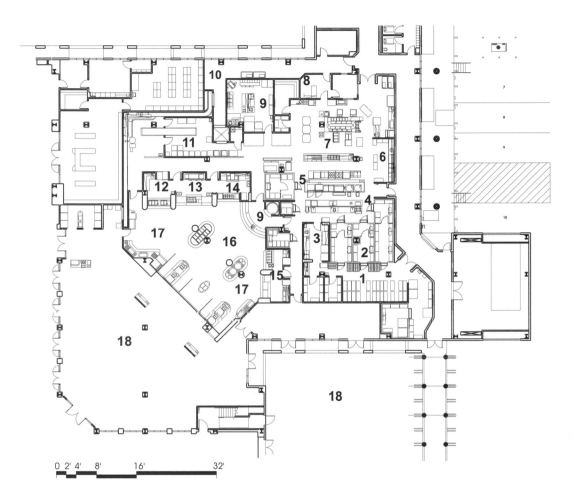

1	DRY STORAGE	**7**	TRAY ASSEMBLY AREA	**13**	SHORT ORDER
2	REFRIGERATED STORAGE	**8**	OFFICES	**14**	PIZZA STATION
3	INGREDIENT ROOM	**9**	BAKERY	**15**	ENTREE
4	PREPARATION AREA	**10**	SOILED DISH AREA	**16**	DESSERTS
5	COOKING AREA	**11**	CLEAN DISH AREA	**17**	BEVERAGE
6	POT WASH AREA	**12**	SPECIALITIES	**18**	DINING

▲ *A dietary floor plan at Mercy Health Center in Laredo, Texas.*

▶ *Simulated outdoor dining area at Texas Scottish Rite Hospital for Children in Dallas, Texas.*

Offices. Locate offices for management and supervisors near the appropriate production areas to foster communication with line workers.

Food production methods

Four major production systems are available to the food service department. They may be combined to address the specific needs of a facility.

Cook-serve

The system of choice for generations has been cook-serve. It still produces the highest-quality products. However, changes in healthcare delivery methods, cost cutting, departmental reengineering, and a shortage of qualified management and kitchen labor are diminishing food quality and increasing production costs. Moreover, the introduction of the HACCP (Hazard Analysis Critical Control Points) system and other regulations have forced many hospitals to consider using advanced food preparation systems.

In a cook-serve system, food is prepared a few hours before serving time. Bulk foods are prepared from scratch (raw materials), finished, and served immediately. Convenience products have supplemented this traditional preparation method. For example, kitchen personnel no longer peel potatoes or butcher meat. In most cases, the products arrive preportioned and ready for processing; frozen prepared items need only be rethermalized and served.

The cook-serve system is not the most economical or the most beneficial production method for accommodating patient population growth. It is unable to safely provide a large quantity of high-quality food at a reasonable cost. In addition, the finished products can be transported only a short distance and yet remain safe for consumption, pursuant to health department regulations.

Cook-chill

Cook-chill food production is a processing system that functions on the principle of cooking food to a just-done state, followed by rapid chilling and storage under tightly controlled temperatures. Cook-chill production is inventory-based, whereas cook-serve is consumption-based.

In a cook-serve system, a specific menu and service time drive production, which requires precise scheduling. A cook-chill system, on the other hand, is far more flexible. Virtually all meals are prepared weeks in advance and stored in the food bank. Production is based on replenishing the inventory, which affords much greater scheduling flexibility. Employee overtime is not needed, nor is cooking on weekends or holidays required. The system can also accommodate most menus, regardless of menu cycle.

Two methods are currently employed for rapid temperature reduction. The first is blast chilling, which uses high-velocity convected cold air and water-bath chilling. Conventionally prepared foods, placed in a pan and chilled by convected air, have a safe shelf life of up to five days. Cooked foods placed in a casing, vacuumed, and chilled by the water-bath method, have a safe storage life of up to 45 days. The extended shelf life is largely due to the protective casing, which prevents spoilage attributed to the presence of oxygen and microbes.

Water-bath chilling is a U.S. Department of Agriculture (USDA) approved system of batch food processing. Food is cooked to the peak of readiness (90 percent), packaged in a tough casing, impervious to oxygen, at the pasteurization temperature of 165 degrees, then rapidly chilled to 40 degrees F or below for no longer than an hour. This enables the fresh product, which has not undergone the structural disruption of freezing or the high-retort temperature of canning, to be refrigerated at 28 to 32 degrees F for four to six weeks. This temperature range is vital in maintaining the quality and safety of the food.

An on-site cook-chill system is economical when the number of beds served is at least 300. A cook-chill system is limited in the number of products it can provide. It cannot be used for all menu items, but must be complemented by cook-serve items.

Quick-chill/rethermalization

Quick-chill rethermalization systems are increasingly replacing cook-serve operations. Although the quick-chill process is based on the cook-serve system, the final steps are different. Foods are chilled at the end of the cooking process. This allows the operation to use a cold tray assembly system, with the food rethermalized either in the kitchen or on the patient floors.

A hot tray assembly line is a complex and labor-intensive system to operate. Food must be held at 140 degrees F until served to patients. Leftover food is often wasted, which increases the food cost per patient day. Furthermore, approximately 10 percent more food must be prepared to allow for patients' changing the menu.

In a cold tray line, food must be held below 40 degrees F until rethermalization time prior to serving the patient. The time between dish-out and serving must be minimized. However, the food can be saved as long as it is kept cold throughout the process. With quick-chilling, products can be stored in inventory up to five or six days, eliminating the need for weekend cooks and kitchen staff. Only tray assembly staff are needed, thus reducing labor costs between 8 and 10 percent, according to national studies.

This system can also be supplemented with convenience foods. Many vendors provide bulk convenience foods in personal-size servings or half-sized pans. Convenience foods work well in centralized food delivery systems.

Floor pantry/kitchenless system

The kitchenless concept was developed to address the safety and quality of food delivery in an urban healthcare setting. This system does not replace the main

115

dietary operation. It converts the production kitchen from a cook-serve facility to an on-demand assembly kitchen. The concept is based on individually prepackaged, preportioned convenience meals held in a refrigerator or freezer in each pantry. Meals are assembled cold and heated in a convection oven on the patient floor. Once meals are heated, they are delivered as soon as possible to the patients. The system can also operate from a centralized location.

The kitchenless system is limited, however, when used for breakfast, freshly made entreés, toast, and similar items. These items must be individually produced for each patient, which requires short-order cooking.

Space requirements

Generally, a food service department consists of seven key areas: public serving, receiving and storage, food prep, food production/cooking/portioning, assembly, dish washing, and support. Although each food production method has specific requirements, a typical space program for a full-service in-house operation would be similar to the following:

Public serving area

- Cafeteria seating
- Food court/scramble serving area
- Private/physician/visitors dining
- Vending area
- Janitor's closet
- Table and chair storage
- Public toilets

Receiving and storage area

- Receiving area/scale
- Recycling/returns

- Breakdown
- Cart and can wash
- Dry storage
- Paper storage
- Detergent/cleaning supplies
- Refrigerated/frozen storage
    Meat cooler
    Meat freezer
    Produce cooler
    General freezer
    Dairy cooler
- Vending supply storage
- Supplies (other)
- Ingredient control room (cook-chill)
    Ingredient room
    Issue cooler

Food prep area

- Salad prep
- Salad cooler
- Vegetable prep
- Cook's cooler
- Meat prep
- Meat cooler
- Catering prep
- Catering storage
- Cafeteria prep
- Catering/cafeteria cooler
- Beverage dispensing room
- Food production area
- Cook line
- Tray assembly
- Bulk production (cook-chill)
- Portioning (cook-chill)
- Blast chiller (cook-chill)

- Food bank cooler (cook-chill)
- Holding freezer (cook-chill)
- Remote facilities cooler (cook-chill)

Assembly area

- Patient tray assembly
- Catering assembly/setup
- Cafeteria assembly
- Nourishment area
- Cart holding area
- Tray support storage
- Dietitian's office

Dishwashing area

- Chemicals and detergent storage
- Dish washing/pot washing
- Soiled cart holding
- Cart wash
- Trash holding
- Janitor's closet
- Clean cart holding

Support area

- Director, food and nutrition
- Dietitian administrator
- Cafeteria manager
- Kitchen production manager
- Service coordinator (catering/vending)
- Dietary technician
- Workstation/purchasing/secretary
- File/fax/copier/supplies
- Toilets

Design considerations

Delivering safe, high-quality food is paramount to the dietary services department. Increasingly, food establishments are operating under HACCP guidelines. One of the basic tenets of this system is that hot food must be maintained at 140 degrees F and cold food at 40 degrees F. Therefore, finished products can be transported only a short distance if they are to remain safe for consumption.

Efficient, cost-effective, and safe food production is based on a continuous system, with specific methods for raw product flow, preparation, cooking, assembly and dispensing. To prevent cross-contamination, clean and soiled areas and products must be segregated. These functions require adequate space and a designated flow pattern.

Cross-contamination must also be addressed in the receiving area. Boxes and containers may contain living organisms and so must not be loaded directly into the production kitchen holding coolers. Sufficient space is needed for receiving, weighing, and storing products to ensure product safety, strict inventory controls, and the proper rotation of goods.

Trends

For decades, a simple concept dominated cafeteria service: Recreate an army mess hall, with a long line of serving stations supported by an oversized kitchen or commissary. The demands of younger patients, staff, and visitors accustomed to a variety of dining options and the increasing need to find new revenue streams have spurred more flexible, innovative designs.

One of the latest developments is the food court and market designs, similar to those found in high-end food outlets and shopping malls. Employees, visitors, and outpatients are able to move freely through food displays or boutiques, which are either self-service or staffed. The atmosphere promotes social activity and helps relieve stress. The variety of food offerings also satisfies more discriminating customers.

On the production side, new technologies and equipment have allowed kitchens to consolidate functions. These advances have enabled healthcare facilities to prepare products for inventory, rather than immediate consumption, capitalizing on economies of scale.

SUPPORT SERVICES

Environmental and Linen Services

The environmental services department is responsible for maintaining a clean and sanitary environment in the hospital, including floors, carpeting, tile, drapery, windows, lights, vents, and upholstered items. This department is also responsible for furniture moves, conference and classroom setups, replacement of patient room furniture, and trash collection. Environmental services typically contracts with outside vendors or arranges with the maintenance department for pest control, waste removal, exterior window washing, furniture repairs, window coverings, and the purchasing of trash receptacles and mattresses.

The number of housekeeping rooms or closets is determined by the needs of the facility. A service sink or floor well with a drain is provided for mops and other cleaning equipment. Shelves or carts for the storage of cleaning chemicals and supplies are also required.

Linen services are typically included within environmental services for the collection and distribution of linens and scrubs throughout the hospital. Linen services are typically contracted with vendors. However, some hospitals still operate full laundry services. Linen is stored on shelves or carts. Clean linen storage may be located in clean workrooms or linen storage alcoves. Soiled linen can be collected in carts in corridor alcoves or transferred to soiled utility rooms for pickup.

Settings

Hospital environmental and linen services serve the hospital and satellite facilities, including medical office buildings, ambulatory care facilities, and other related campuses.

Operational considerations

The environmental and linen services department is staff-intensive and should be near loading dock, materials management, and engineering/maintenance services, as well as close to elevators. Larger carts may be circulated throughout the hospital for restocking housekeeping carts located throughout the facility. Carts can also be delivered to the central department for restocking. Housekeeping carts are usually kept in the various housekeeping closets throughout the hospital. Linen carts are located in appropriate areas and are restocked on a "par" level or exchanged for a newly stocked cart.

Space needs

According to the AIA *1996–1997 Guidelines for Design and Construction of Hospital and Health Care Facilities*, the following areas are generally accepted as appropriate for environmental and linen services:

Environmental services
  Housekeeping closets
  Housekeeping storage and supplies
  Bed and equipment storage

Administrative offices

Vendor meeting room

Linen services

Linen storage

Receiving, sorting, and holding area for soiled linen

Centralized clean linen storage

Soiled and clean linen cart storage

Hand washing in soiled linen storage areas

Service entrance protected from inclement weather

Laundry or minimum laundry processing room for emergencies

Storage for laundry supplies

Staff facilities

Special planning and design considerations

Hospital finishes, furniture, and accessories are designed to withstand the rigors of constant cleaning and sanitizing. Such measures help to maintain standards of cleanliness that support a healing environment.

Trends

Outsourcing environmental and linen services is a growing trend in hospitals.

Engineering and Maintenance

The engineering and maintenance department is typically responsible for the entire physical plant and grounds of the hospital. Services include preventive maintenance, corrective maintenance, casualty prevention, minor construction, and construction administration. Work load and departmental needs are directly related to the scope of the facilities and the campus for which the department is responsible.

▲ A security safety command station at Texas Scottish Rite Hospital for Children in Dallas, Texas.

Settings

These services should be convenient and accessible to all areas of the facilities and the campus. Access to the dock area is necessary for building materials, supplies, and equipment. Enclosed access to all hospital departments and areas is also desirable. The department may be responsible for off-site facilities, such as ambulatory care centers and medical office buildings, as well as for the hospital and grounds.

Operational considerations

Engineering and maintenance services are integral to the day-to-day operation of the hospital. These services are responsible for keeping the facilities in proper working condition and helping them function effectively. Engineering is responsible for monitoring the mechanical, plumbing, heat, ventilation, air-conditioning (HVAC), and electrical systems, as well as preventive maintenance and repair. Supporting shop work areas, such as carpentry, electrical, plumbing, paint, welding, and HVAC, may be provided in appropriate areas of the hospital. They may also be located in a separate outbuilding for better acoustical and dust control. If such shops are located in an outbuilding, covered access or transportation to the dock area should be provided.

Space needs

According to the AIA *1996–1997 Guidelines for Design and Construction of Hospital and Health Care Facilities,*

components of engineering and maintenance services include the following:

Central energy plant

Medical gas park

Dock area

Compactors at dock area

Administrative offices (plan room, computer-aided drafting and design [CADD] room, environmental controls room, etc.)

▶ *A engineering and maintenance floor plan at Mary Washington Hospital in Fredericksburg, Virginia.*

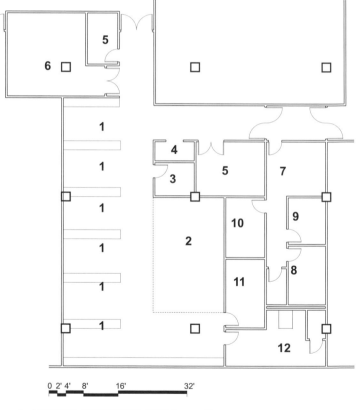

	1	VARIOUS SHOP WORK AREAS	7	SECRETARY & WAITING
	2	STORAGE	8	DIRECTOR'S OFFICE
	3	SUPERVISOR'S OFFICE	9	OFFICE
	4	JANITOR'S CLOSET	10	CADD ROOM
	5	LOCKED STORAGE	11	PAINT ROOM
	6	CARPENTER'S SHOP	12	LOCKERS/ SHOWER/ TOILET

Appropriate shops (carpentry, electrical, plumbing, paint, welding, HVAC, etc.)

Supply storage

Flammable storage

TV storage

Biomedical workshop

External grounds maintenance equipment storage

Staff facilities

Special planning and design considerations

Engineering and maintenance services require appropriate electrical and mechanical systems for shop operations meeting all requirements of the Occupational Safety and Health Administration (OSHA). Specifically, dust control and the storage of flammable fluids must be addressed.

Safety and Security

Safety and security services within a hospital setting provide general security, guard patrols, preliminary investigations, fire prevention, control policies and training, disaster planning and training, and other measures for the general safety of staff, patients, and visitors. Other services include lost-and-found and patient assistance, and transportation by vehicle. The department operates 24 hours per day, seven days a week.

Settings

Safety and security has high visibility near entrances and parking areas. It is common to place this function close to the emergency entrance, inasmuch as this is a 24-hour entrance to the hospital. The service has relationships to employee health, infection control, engineering, and risk management.

Operational considerations

This service typically includes a suite arrangement, one component of which is a command post. At the post, security guards monitor closed-circuit television cameras. A director's office is usually adjacent to the command post. Storage is required for lost-and-found and disaster planning equipment. More healthcare facilities are establishing car patrols on their campuses.

Space needs

Typical safety and security services include the following:

Command post

Director's office

Security supervisor's cubicle

Storage (lost-and-found, disaster planning equipment)

Trends

Greater emphasis is being placed on safety and security at healthcare campuses because of a rising perception of more violence and criminal activity. This activity, experts say, is attracted by the 24-hour operation of a hospital.

Materials Management

Functional overview

Materials management is responsible for the acquisition, general storage, daily inventory, and restocking of most, if not all, of the consumable materials used within a facility. This service may be provided for several facilities within a healthcare system to increase efficiency of operations, reduce total space require-ments, and maximize purchasing power. The following services are provided:

ANCILLARY DEPARTMENTS

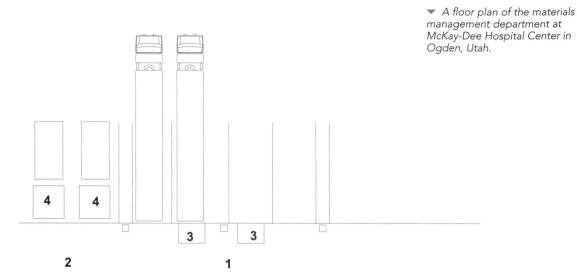

▼ *A floor plan of the materials management department at McKay-Dee Hospital Center in Ogden, Utah.*

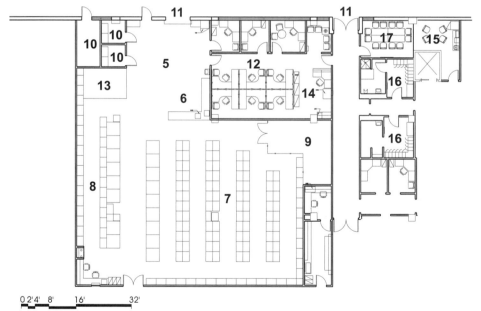

1 DOCK - CLEAN AREA	**7** BULK STORAGE	**12** OFFICES/ WORKSTATIONS
2 DOCK - SOILED AREA	**8** MEDICAL-SURGICAL SUPPLY	**13** SCALES/PALLET HOLDING
3 DOCK LEVELER/TRUCK BAY	STORAGE	**14** WAITING AREA
4 TRASH COMPACTOR	**9** NEW EQUIPMENT STORAGE	**15** LOUNGE
5 RECEIVING/STAGING AREA	**10** MEDICAL GAS CYLINDER STORAGE	**16** LOCKERS
6 CLERICAL WORKSTATION	**11** CLEAN ENTRANCE	**17** CONFERENCE ROOM

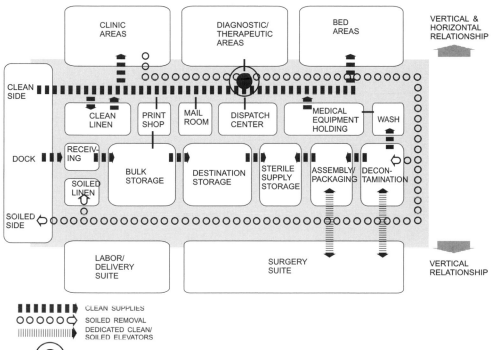

▲ *A materials management flow diagram.*

- Management of consumable goods such as medical-surgical supplies and administrative paper goods

- Receiving, breakdown, and stowage of supplies, in bulk cases and in units of issue

- Storage of special supplies (chemical reagents, X-ray film; stock intravenous [IV] solutions, flammable or other hazardous materials)

- Receiving and temporary holding of new equipment or furnishings

- Distribution and restocking of supplies to consumer units on a scheduled and on-call basis using preestablished (PAR) levels

- Inventory management to maintain supply and to secure optimal purchas-

ing agreements for operational economy

- Administration and management of the facility's supply system in cooperation with the managers of consumer units

Responsibilities of the materials management director may include managing the central sterile processing service (reprocessing/sterilizing reusable items) and overseeing the linen service. Materials management service excludes food products, which are managed by the food service department. Also, this department usually relies on the clinical lab for storage of radioactive materials or special products, such as reagents, which require refrigerated storage.

Service locations

A general storage area is required in facilities of all types. If serving a network of facilities, material management is often centralized at a "hub" facility, with management and distribution services provided to satellites. Demand for storage space and staff will be driven by the mix of services and volume of activity at each site. Each consuming unit in smaller facilities may itself manage material acquisition and storage. However, this service is typically centralized to achieve economies of scale and to minimize staffing requirements.

Key activity factors

Planning for this service is driven by the array of clinical services to be supported and the operational concept for the materials management program. The projected volumes of patient care services, types of general and specialty supplies required, relative proportion of inpatient versus outpatient care, and the administrative needs of the clinical services are components to be addressed in determining demand for materials management services. More important to space planning, however, is the frequency of deliveries and the type of supply system—external and internal—as well as the functional work flow intended for the service. These components make up the operational concept.

Key capacity determinants

The extent of centralized versus decentralized storage affects capacity. Inherently, decentralized storage requires more space. Some decentralization is necessary in all healthcare facilities for enhanced productivity. Capacity is determined by the on-site supply reserve and delivery frequency to bulk stores and local storage rooms. Capacity is driven by the storage system: fixed shelving or high-density movable shelving, the storage system volume—height in particular—and the extent of compartmentalization (separate areas for specialty storage, or bulk carton storage versus broken lot "unit of issue" storage).

Work flow

In materials management, work flow begins at the receiving service dock. Bills of lading and product condition are checked in the receiving area. This area must contain space for weather-protected products and temporary holding. Weighing scales are located in this area, as is a clerical work space. The dock area must be raised, often with dock levelers for receiving materials from tractor-trailer and bobtail trucks, and must have an apron at grade for smaller delivery vehicles.

Cartons of received supplies are moved directly into bulk storage areas on pallets or placed on heavy-duty shelving. Equipment and furniture are moved to a temporary holding space until they can be installed by engineering or environmental service staff. Hazardous or flammable supplies are stored in dedicated rooms. These rooms are often accessible directly from the dock to facilitate exterior access for vendors and to provide ventilated, safe storage outside the building.

From the cartons, daily-replenished supplies are moved onto more accessible shelves for ease of restocking by unit of issue. The "distribution room" or "clean/sterile supply area" is the principal storage room from which carts are loaded to restock each consumer department in the facility. Depending on the inventory management system, before distribution each item is usually marked with a bar code label to facilitate tracking and billing.

Bulk stores also hold cartons of prepackaged consumable sterile goods used in surgery, labor/delivery, or other special procedures areas. These items are distributed daily to the central sterile processing (CSP) area. The supplies delivered to the clinical areas may include both consumable and reprocessed goods. For this reason, CSP is often adjacent to the distribution room of materials management to optimize material flow over minimum distances. A "break-out" room between the distribution room and CSP typically serves as a vestibule, where supplies are removed from cartons to shelves.

The replenishment system for consuming units is an important determinant of necessary space. There are two basic approaches—replenishment or use of exchange carts. A hybrid of the two is often employed. Pure replenishment requires a periodic inventory, by the materials management staff, of items consumed in each consumer area; the collection of those items from the centralized supply distribution room onto a cart; and the delivery and restocking of those items in the cabinets or on carts in the consumer unit. These storage areas are typically identified as the clean supply or clean utility rooms of the consumer units.

The pure exchange cart system requires the periodic replacement of the supply cart in the consumer unit with a cart fully stocked to PAR level, and then the return of the partially used supply cart to the distribution room for inventory and restocking. A key difference between

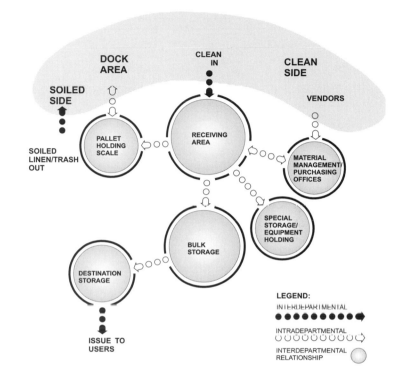

these systems is the redundant cart holding space needed in the distribution room in the exchange cart system. Today's computerized inventory systems facilitate instant information to support the replenishment approach.

Because of their value or special storage requirements, specialty goods, such as imaging film supplies, lab reagents, and cath lab catheters, may be stored entirely within the consumer department. These goods are received by materials management and moved in bulk directly to the consumer departments.

Relationships with other departments

Materials management must be directly accessible from the exterior via a receiving dock area. In planning this department, its activities should be kept away from

▲ A materials management interrelationship diagram.

GENERAL SPACE REQUIREMENTS, MATERIALS MANAGEMENT			
Room	Suggested Area per Station (net square feet)	Optimal Dimensions	Necessary Adjacent Support Spaces
General Storage (combined bulk storage, clean/sterile distribution, decentralized holding rooms)	20 per inpatient bed minimum	12 ft height	
Receiving dock	225–280	12 ft wide x 16 ft deep per bay	Medical gas cylinder holding Hazardous materials holding Flammable supply holding

circulation routes for the public, ambulatory patients, and most staff traffic. However, easy access to all consumer departments for distribution is desirable. The routes of such access should be separate from public thoroughfares. Central sterile processing should be located nearby for expedience in daily restocking. For operational reasons—often driven by preferences of surgery managers and physicians—CSP may be separate from or integrated with surgery.

Key spaces

State and local building codes sometimes address the general space needs and design criteria within materials management or "general stores," as it is often labeled in code references. These codes should always be reviewed for minimum standards necessary for plan approval. Best practice standards within the healthcare industry, including some generations of the AIA *Guidelines for Design and Construction of Hospital and Health Care Facilities*, suggest guidelines for selected operational spaces, as shown in the table above.

Key design considerations

The design of the materials management area should address the following considerations:

- Direct dock access for receiving, with staging space for checking deliveries prior to storage or distribution

- Breakdown area for unit of issue stock, with convenient waste management pathways (box bailer or access to trash compactors)

- Capability to segregate flow of clean and dirty activities at the dock (complete separation is not necessary); ability to move trash, hazardous waste, and soiled linen to holding areas or transport vehicles without conflicting with clean incoming goods

- Clear and adequate circulation pathways for materials movement equipment such as forklifts

- Exterior access for selected materials storage in dedicated, code-compliant rooms, such as for flammable or hazardous substances and portable medical gas cylinders of various sizes.

Special equipment and furniture requirements

Special equipment requirements may include dock levelers, in-floor industrial scales, 36 to 42 in. deep pallet or deep carton storage, forklifts or pallet lifts, 24 in. deep shelving for unit of issue supply holding (in fixed or movable high-density storage systems), and replenishment or exchange carts (typically 24 by 60 in.).

Supporting spaces

In addition to basic storage and distribution areas, materials management should include support areas:

- Staff lounge, lockers with showers and changing areas, and toilets

- Administrative offices

Special planning and design considerations

Special design considerations include the following:

- Service traffic must be separated from patient vehicle traffic.

- Weather protection and environmental control should be available at the portal to the receiving dock.

- Life safety codes require rated enclosures for certain types of storage, as well as minimum ceiling or sprinkler head clearance vertically above the top levels of stored materials

- A pneumatic tube station within the or distribution room should be provided.

- Various other types of automated conveyance systems may be considered, but most are typically too costly to justify. Often, 6 in pneumatic tube transport systems are effectively used for immediately needed items not in stock on the user unit, and a station for this system should be provided in the distribution area (unless provided in adjacent CSP).

Trends

The centralization of materials management services will continue or increase, in order to serve greater numbers of facilities within a system. Various approaches and applications of "just in time" delivery of supplies will continue to minimize inventory and requirements for storage space in healthcare facilities. Automation of processes for inventory, ordering, and restocking will be increased in an effort to minimize staffing requirements for materials handling. Distribution of supplies to the points of care will continue to be an expedient way to maximize use of clinical human resources. In addition, new ideas on achieving care goals without increasing material management staff requirements will be explored.

Pharmacy

The pharmacy department provides prescription medications, intravenous (IV) solutions, and investigational drugs for clinical research, as well as other related products for patients. There are three primary services of the hospital pharmacy:

1. Receipt and preparation of prescriptions

2. Dispensing

3. Clinical consulting

Pharmacists receive orders or prescriptions from physicians. These prescriptions are prepared and dispensed to the patient by the pharmacist. In the hospital setting, medications may be dispensed in a variety of ways. They may be prepared in a central or satellite pharmacy and delivered to the patient care unit for administration by a physician, nurse, or other caregiver.

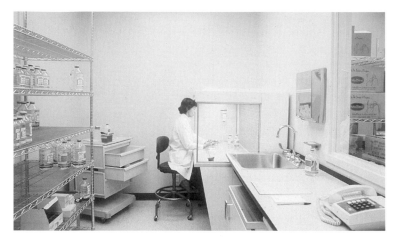

▲ A laminar flow room at Texas Scottish Rite Hospital for Children in Dallas, Texas.

▶ A interrelationship diagram of the pharmacy department.

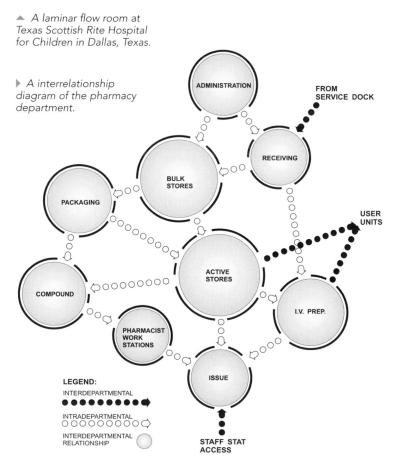

Moreover, automated vending systems may be positioned as satellites in high-use areas such as critical care, emergency, and similar locations. A vending system allows the caregiver to administer physician-directed medications and drugs using pharmacy-prestocked products in a high-use area. Pharmacists are commonly encouraged to consult clinically with the patient on the administration of a medication. This assists the patient in learning the risks and possible effects of the medicine.

Settings

An inpatient pharmacy is typically located near material management functions for convenience in receiving bulk items. It can also be located near inpatient care units for dispensing medications or at a central location, such as near elevator banks. Outpatient dispensing is provided in the hospital for outpatients requiring discharge medications and prescriptions. Outpatient dispensing should be conveniently located for serving departing patients. Most states require separate inpatient and outpatient pharmacy licensing.

Operational considerations

The pharmacy department should have secure access control. Entry points should be limited, if possible, to receiving and dispensing. Ideally, both entry points are under the pharmacist's visual control. Space should be available to allow separate work flows for the preparation of prescriptions and IV solutions. Dispensing and storage areas must be located near these two work-flows areas. The IV preparation area and fume hood should be near the bulk storage area and IV dispensing. Satellite pharmacies are integral to critical care, surgery, and other

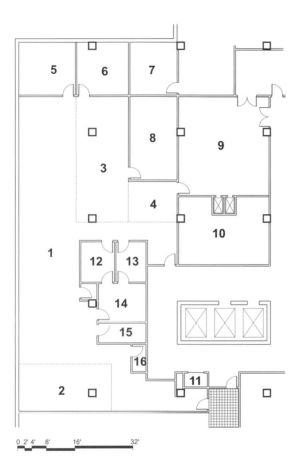

◀ *A pharmacy floor plan at Winchester Medical Center in Winchester, Virginia.*

1 MANUFACTURING, PACKAGING,& STORAGE
2 BULK STORES
3 UNIT DOSE
4 BREAK OUT
5 IV ADMIX
6 IV STORAGE
7 LOCKER LOUNGE
8 COMPUTER SYSTEM
9 CART DISPATCH
10 MECH
11 NIGHT LOCKER
12 DIRECTOR'S OFFICE
13 OFFICE
14 SECRETARY/ WAITING
15 CONFERENCE
16 NARCOTICS LOCKER

0 2' 4' 8'   16'   32'

areas. Automated materials movement systems, such as pneumatic tube stations, are desirable and efficient. A 6 in. pneumatic tube system is ideal for moving larger items, such as IV bags.

Space determinants include the kind of drug distribution system—either centralized or decentralized—as well as the work load generated by the patients. The patient work load may include both inpatient and outpatient demands.

Space needs
According to the AIA *1996-1997 Guidelines for Design and Construction of Hospital and Health Care Facilities,* local agencies having jurisdiction over the pharmacy should be consulted prior to planning. The pharmacy has certain designated spaces and support requirements, which include following:

Dispensing

Pickup and receiving area

Reviewing and recording area

Extemporaneous compounding area

Work counters

Staging of carts area

Security for drugs and personnel

Manufacturing

Bulk compounding area

Packaging and labeling

Quality control area

Storage

Bulk storage

Active storage

Refrigerator storage

Volatile fluid storage

Narcotics and controlled drugs storage (two locks and alarm)

General supplies and equipment storage

Administration

Quality control/cross-checking

Poison control and information center

Pharmacist's office, filing, and resource books

Patient counseling and instruction

Education and training (area may be shared)

Hand washing

Convenient toilet and locker access

Special planning and design considerations

Flexibility within the pharmacy is paramount, especially during a facility's growth and change. Modular casework provides the flexibility of configuration and layout that is desirable in any pharmacy. Lighting should be adequate for reading small labels and finding medications in banks of shelves. Fume hoods, to provide a sterile work environment for the admixtures and IV preparations, should include a nonhydroscopic filter rated at 99.97 percent high efficiency porticulate air (HEPA), as measured by (DOP) tests. A pass-through window, required for walk-up medication dispensing, must be secured. Key pad locks at all entrances are necessary.

Trends

Pharmacists are becoming active in the clinical administration of prescription medications in the inpatient and outpatient settings. With this responsibility, pharmacists are more likely to support a decentralized service encouraging their availability to the patients. Staffing remains a critical issue in cost control; thus, many facilities still prefer a single, centralized pharmacy, augmented with automated pharmaceutical vending machines that are decentralized throughout the hospital.

▲ University of Chicago Hospitals,
Duchossois Center for Advanced Medicine,
Chicago, Illinois (Tsoi/Kobus and Associates).

The atrium provides a central focus, with clinics on one
side, and diagnostic and treatment functions on the other.

▲ New England Medical Center, Patient
Care Center, Boston, Massachusetts
(interiors: Tsoi/Kobus and Associates).

Waiting room.

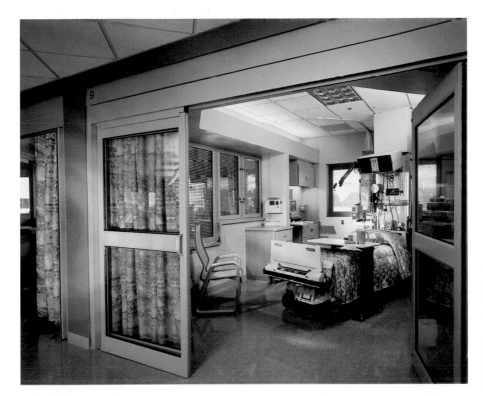

◀ *St. John's Regional Medical Center, Oxnard, California (HKS Inc.).*
Intensive care room.

▼ *Yuma Regional Medical Center, Yuma, Arizona (HKS Inc.).*
Bed unit.

▲ Valley Children's Hospital, Madera, California (HKS Inc.).

An interplay of geometric forms.

▶ HealthPark Medical Center, Fort Myers, Florida, (HKS Inc.).

Children's waiting area.

▲ Valley Children's Hospital,
Madera, California (HKS Inc.).

Exterior view.

▲ UCLA/Santa Monica Hospital
Medical Center, Santa Monica,
California (BTA).

Patient tower with outpatient
services building in the foreground.

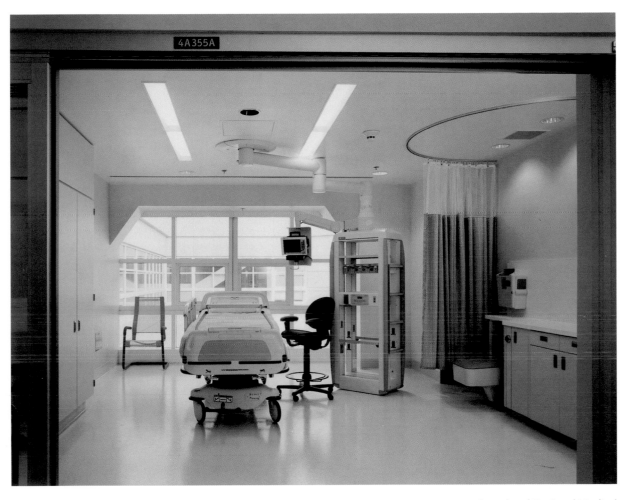

▲ Arrowhead Regional Medical Center, San Bernardino County, California (BTA).

Intensive care room.

▲ Daniel Freeman Memorial Hospital,
Inglewood, California (BTA).
Courtyard.

▶ UCLA/Santa Monica Medical
Center Women's Center,
Santa Monica, California (BTA).
Fifth floor courtyard.

▲ *St. Luke's Medical Center,
Milwaukee, Wisconsin (BTA).*
Entry courtyard.

◀ *Arrowhead Regional Medical
Center, San Bernardino County,
California (BTA).*
Nursing tower.

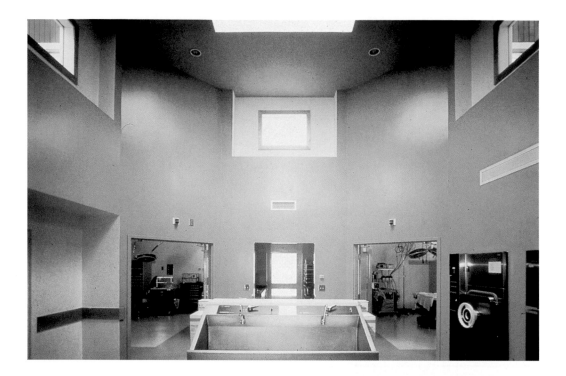

▲ *Athens Regional Medical Center Surgicenter, Athens, Georgia (Payette Associates Inc.).*

Operating rooms, clustered around a single sterile core.

▶ *Athens Regional Medical Center Surgicenter, Athens, Georgia (Payette Associates Inc.).*

Indirect overhead natural light in the recovery room lends a bright atmosphere, protects privacy, and prevents glare.

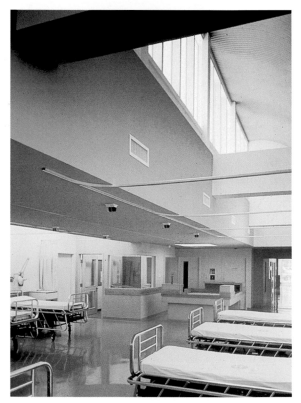

▲ Massachusetts General Hospital,
Northeast Proton Therapy Center,
Boston, Massachusetts (Tsoi/Kobus
and Associates).

Entrance rotunda represents the
cyclotron.

▲ *Massachusetts General Hospital, Northeast Proton Therapy Center, Boston, Massachusetts (Tsoi/Kobus and Associates).*

Upper-level lobby.

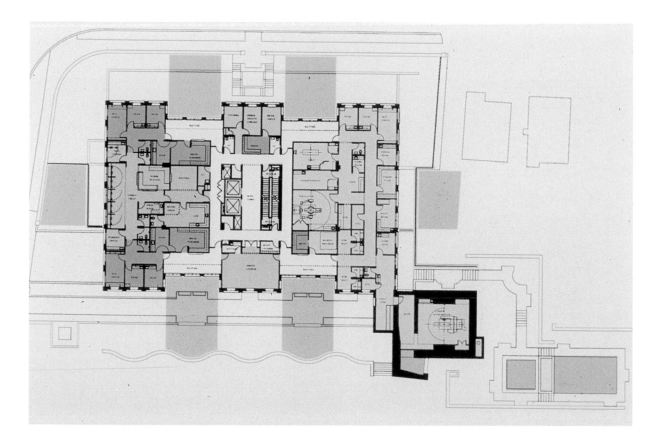

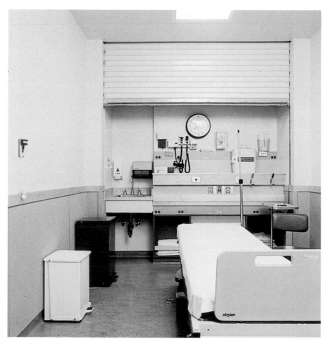

▲ Greenwich Hospital Cancer Center, Greenwich, Connecticut (Payette Associates Inc.).

Grouping spaces by function allows multiple disciplines in one facility to share resources while protecting patient privacy.

◀ The Cambridge Public Health Alliance, The Cambridge Hospital, Emergency Department, Cambridge, Massachusetts (Payette Associates Inc.).

An automatic rolling door controlled from outside the room provides quiet room security.

▲ *Saints Memorial Medical Center,*
Outpatient Dialysis Unit, Lowell
Massachusetts (Payette Associates Inc.).

Television sets built into a soffit above
the nurse's station entertain patients
without sacrificing close supervision
during treatment.

INPATIENT CARE FACILITIES

MICHAEL BOBROW AND JULIA THOMAS *Bobrow/Thomas & Associates*

INTRODUCTION

It is easy to lose sight of the calming influence that sensitive design can have on the emotional state of the patient, as well as family, visitors, and staff. Going to a hospital is stressful enough; there is no reason for the patient's physical surroundings to amplify that aspect of the experience. We can learn from the admonition to physicians "to do no harm" while trying to heal. The architect and hospital staff need only step back and visualize the most comfortable experiences and settings they have experienced and try to capture the poetry of those moments.

Nowhere is the opportunity to do this as great as in the patient room—whether for acute or intensive care, pediatrics, or women's services—and in the nursing unit. The patient room should be designed with the sensitivity one would desire for his or her own bedroom at home, and the floor environment should be as easy to use and understand as in the best of the great small hotels.

Clearly a calming environment can affect the emotional state of the patient. A patient and a family can better cope with their hospital experience if they have a greater sense of control over their stay. Such a supportive environment includes ease of wayfinding, privacy and ease of communications, control of light, sound, and temperature, as well as the opportunity to commune with nature in a calm and beautiful landscape.

Recognizing this, hospitals and architects have made a concerted effort to raise the level of awareness concerning the hospital environment and to create a greater sense of control for the family. This is reflected today in the training of hospital staff in sensitivity to the psychological needs of the patient and family and in the foregrounding of these issues in the planning and design of any building project.

There has been a growing body of research that documents the role of light, gardens, and control of the environment in the healing process. More information can be found through the AIA Academy for Health Care Design, the Planetree Organization, and the Symposium for Health Care Design. Each sponsors research and public meetings and documents findings for the architectural and healthcare communities.

We urge readers to internalize these humanistic concerns, and so create facilities that are not only highly efficient inpatient units but also restful, inviting refuges for the healing process.

BACKGROUND

The hospital is one of society's most important civic buildings. It is most often where we are born and where we die. In between, it is also a place of much emotional turmoil and much joy. The architecture of the hospital must respond to both this emotional context, of hope and tragedy, and the functional requirements of treatment and technology. Unfortunately, the design process is often overwhelmed by the functional needs of medical science, and too often the psychological needs of the patient and the family are overlooked while the body is treated.

Nowhere is a balance more critical than in the inpatient setting of a nursing unit, where the greatest amount of time is spent by patient and family. Today the patient room is seen as a place of sanctuary, privacy, and safety—the place where the patient and family are in control of their lives and environment. The patient room can now house the family, if necessary, and can be designed as an extension of the daily life of the patient, with total access to the world through the full range of communications tools such as phone, fax, and Internet.

The nursing unit is seen as a continuation of this environment, providing a family support system where spaces for family and staff are made as accessible, user-friendly, and important as the functional needs for nursing care. Hospital support services can now cater to the individual needs of the patient, through food selection and concierge-type services.

The original models for considering the hospital as healing architecture were Aalto's early work at Paimio, Finland, and Mendelsohn's work in Haifa and Jerusalem. This line was continued in the early studies of the role of architecture in enhancing the experience of family and patient by architects such as Edward Durell Stone at the Community Hospital of the Monterey Peninsula, Caudill Rowlett Scott (CRS) at Samaritan Hospital in Tempe, Arizona, and Bobrow/Thomas and Associates at Daniel Freeman Memorial Hospital in Inglewood, California, among others, and through research at the University of California at Los Angeles, Columbia, and Texas A&M graduate schools of architecture's programs in hospital design.

Further exploration of these concepts grew out of the concern of Planetree—an organization that developed a model for healthcare that supports and nurtures healing—for patients' sense of control of their experience, and in response to families' increased demands for a say in the care of patients, as well as new indications from marketing that distinction in architecture and service, as provided by the best hotels, can improve the success of a hospital in its community.

Finally, these ideas and practices have been stimulated and tested by the recent development of the Symposium for Health Care Design and its publication *Aesculapius*, which focuses strictly on ways in which architecture can influence a patient's experience. The concept has been formally tested in recent studies in which environmental factors of the kind we have been considering have been found to have a positive impact on the outcome of the patient's visit and on recovery time.

The success of early experiments with integrating gardens and providing a view from each room, offering single-bed accommodations, using warm, incandescent light, and providing family support space have created magical opportunities for further experimentation in designing units that integrate the power of evocative architecture into the healing process.

NURSING UNIT EVOLUTION AND TRENDS IN DESIGN AND PLANNING

Historically, the nursing unit has been the core of the hospital. Its purpose has been to house patients requiring care, often for long periods of time. Interestingly, because early hospitals were born out of the assumed responsibilities of religious orders, hospital design resembled the open bays and structures of church naves, a pattern that was repeated for centuries until the evolution of nursing care required new forms.

As technology and healthcare evolved over the centuries, so did the role and form of the nursing unit. The design of nursing units has responded to the needs of the era in which they were built, and many operating hospitals still have elements of these building forms and patterns. A discussion of the evolution of nursing unit design is therefore useful in understanding their potential roles and uses in the future.

The forces of their times are evident in the earliest unit designs. The layout of the hospital nursing unit underwent few changes in basic plans from the thirteenth through the nineteenth century. It was essentially a long, open space with beds located on the exterior walls.

The design of the earliest nursing units was primarily determined by construction methods and limits. These included dominant forces such as the maximum practical structural span available for buildings and the need for natural ventilation.

Because the nursing units were part of an abbey, the surrounding grounds were often used for agricultural purposes, particularly hospital herb gardens. Elements of this pattern have reappeared in recent times with the contemporary integration of landscape and hospital. Over the years, the size of hospitals grew, particularly in major cities. Existing examples are Brunelleschi's Ospedale Santa Maria Nuova in Milan and the Santo Spirito in Rome.

Nursing units evolved over time to reflect patterns of care. In the Hotel-Dieu in Paris, which spanned the Seine, there were often four patients to a bed. Significant advances in development occurred with the Nightingale Plan,

▲ Hotel-Dieu, Beaune, France, 1443.

▼ Patient beds, Hotel-Dieu, Beaune, France.

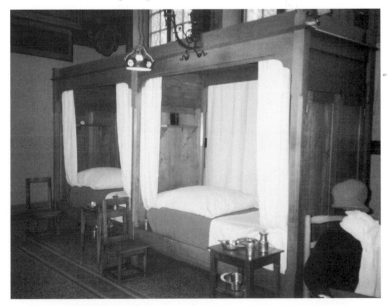

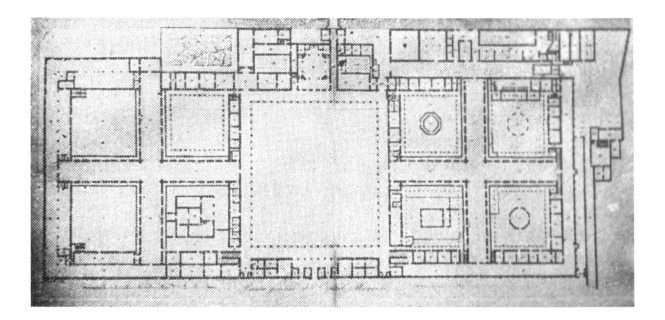

which became the standard in hospital planning for many years. This open plan, with through ventilation and a nurses' station at the entry, proved to be highly efficient in providing care. During the Crimean War, with the need for rapid deployment of treatment facilities, mobile hospitals were designed by Brunel and established a plan that is used by architects today, with open-ended growth patterns laid out as part of the plan.

The main technological changes affecting nursing unit design were effected by the introduction, in the late nineteenth century, of long-span steel construction and elevators and, in the mid twentieth century, air-conditioning. These three developments had a major impact on the evolving role of the hospital in the realm of medical and nursing care and the treatment of disease.

Nursing units could be stacked and connected by elevators at the same location at the support base of the

▶ Brunelleschi's Ospedale
San Maria Nuova,
Milan, Italy.

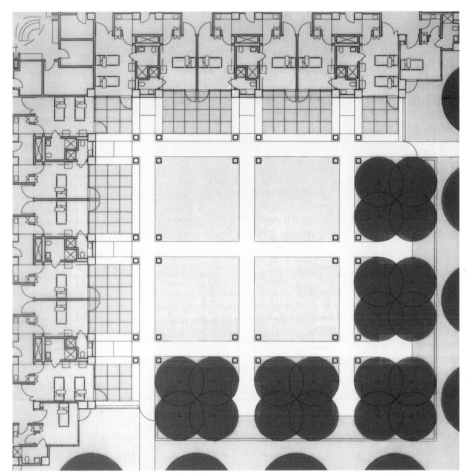

City of Hope National Medical Center patient pavilion plan and gardens (BTA).

Santo Spirito, Rome, Italy.

hospital to produce a single vertical circulation system. This provided greater efficiencies than in hospitals that grew by adding wards to wards in a longitudinal, horizontal pattern, taking up large areas of land and creating great walking distances for support staff and families.

The introduction of air-conditioning allowed the nursing unit to be moved away from locations that provided natural ventilation, a traditional configuration that had often limited the widths of buildings to from 45 to 60 ft. Units could now be designed to follow functional and organizational demands, allowing for the creation of more efficient nursing units. These units often became so wide, however, as to confuse patients' and families' sense of orientation in the building.

With the increased use of hospitals owing to advances in research and medicine, nursing care evolved as well. The need for efficiency in operation became paramount, and this pressure yielded highly functional units. However, with this move toward efficiency, many hospitals lost their focus on the patient's

135

▶ *Hotel-Dieu, Paris, France.*

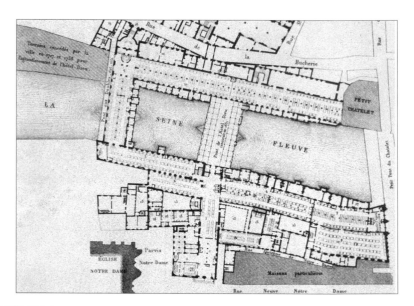

▼ *Hospital Renkioi on the Dardanelles, 1855–1856.*

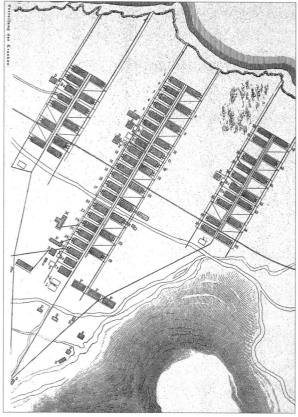

and family's emotional needs, and the role of architecture in serving those needs.

PLANNING FOR EFFICIENT OPERATION

In 1875, at the hospital for the Johns Hopkins University of Baltimore School of Medicine, some bold new concepts emerged. Hospitals since the thirteenth century had had beds lining the exterior walls. Now new configurations were tried, including compact circular, square, and octagonal shapes, with all patients being visible from the central nursing desk. This allowed for direct observation, and the ability to care equally for all patients. This conceptual model was the basis for the circular units of the 1950s.

Although these early studies did not have a general effect on nursing unit design until three-quarters of a century later, progress was made in other important areas. Large, open wards came into disfavor. They were noisy, allowed patients little or no privacy, and made it virtually impossible to isolate infected patients.

The open ward was gradually replaced by smaller rooms off a double-loaded central corridor. Because the design of accommodations for fewer patients per room necessarily increased the area and corridor length generated for each patient room, nurses reconciled themselves to miles of daily walking as they went about their duties.

Evaluation of the Functional Plan

The increase in nurses' travel raised an important design issue, still addressed in all nursing unit designs today. How does the architect design for a balance between the need for individuals' privacy, or for added support space, and the size of the total unit and the goal of close nurse-patient access? Many units were built that were excessive in size and, therefore, very labor-intensive.

At the first American Hospital Association Institute on Hospital Planning held in Chicago in 1947, architect Lewis J. Sarvis stated, "Investigation indicated that nurses spend at least 40 percent of their time walking." A major goal in planning thus became the reduction of nurses' travel in order to increase direct nurse-patient contact.

A revolution in hospital planning occurred involving a wide range of plan organizations and forms. With the fortuitous introduction of the Hill-Burton Act after World War II, every community was given the opportunity to create a local hospital that reflected the latest trends. Unfortunately, many of them followed recommendations published by the U.S. Public Health Service as guidelines rather than standards, and many old patterns of planning were perpetuated. However, others were experimental, and a number of consultants and architects made major contributions to the evolution of the nursing unit, including Sidney Garfield, MD, the founder of the Kaiser Permanente System; Gordon Friesen, hospital consultant to many large orders of Catholic hospitals, and Jim Moore, a California architect.

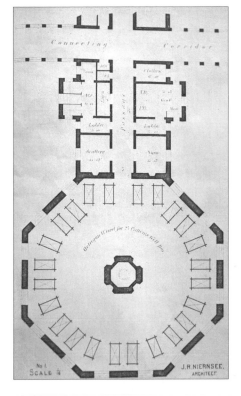

◀ *Johns Hopkins Design Competition 1875—octagonal plan.*

Yale University Studies on Nursing Unit Efficiency

In the late 1950s, John Thompson and Robert Pelletier of the School of Public Health at Yale University developed the "Yale Traffic Index," which studied traffic patterns in many types of existing hospitals. The researchers identified 14 traffic links that made up 91 percent of nursing unit traffic. They then evaluated units in the light of these patterns.

The use of this tool gave architects an early method of evaluating the impact of design on hospital costs of operation. But the limitations of that survey emerged in another study in the mid-1960s. As Jan Koumans of the Netherlands pointed out, *The distance from patient room to service room is important only when this service room will be used with a constant frequency. A change of organization could make this service room disappear altogether, which will make any comparison with another nursing unit organized along different lines impossible. The points of contact should be chosen at the beginning and at the end of a certain kind of activity, which must be performed regardless of any change in the organization of the unit.*

This is particularly noted in later designs of nursing units that dispersed supply centers outside of each patient room.

A more recent study of nursing unit efficiency was made by Delon and Smalley at the Georgia Institute of Technology and the Medical College of Georgia. The investigators not only compiled *frequency* of travel in a typical hospital, but interpolated a factor representing cost of employee travel time

and another financial factor: the prorated cost of construction. This indirectly led to today's important analysis of the per diem cost of construction, a very effective way of evaluating the relative insignificance of construction costs over the lifetime of a building.

MPA/BTA Nursing Unit Analysis Model, Plans and Technique

At Medical Planning Associates (MPA), and subsequently at Bobrow/Thomas and Associates (BTA), a simpler method was developed that does not require advanced mathematical analyses, although its results closely match those of the earlier methods. Its advantage as a design tool lies in its simplicity and convenience. It produces a useful indicator of the travel characteristics of nursing unit design— that is, the distance-to-bed factor, which is simply a summation of distances from nursing work centers to beds divided by the number of beds, and which serves as a proxy for more complex modelling.

This method recognizes one or more "nursing work cores" as centers of nursing activity containing the elements most used and most critically needed by the nurse. Measurements from these centers of nursing activity to each bedside are tallied and averaged for comparison. In previous years, a single work core often served an entire floor of beds. More recently, the work core was subdivided so that it could be located closer to patient room clusters and convenient to each nursing team. Figures indicate a range of 12 to 16 patients per individual team. Indeed, in some plans currently in operation much of the support space is adjacent to each individual patient room.

In planning, a clear recognition of each unit's organizational pattern is necessary.

YALE UNIVERSITY TRAFFIC INDEX FACTORS	
PERCENT OF TRAVEL TIME	NURSING STAFF TRAFFIC LINKS
19.1	Patient room to patient room
16.7	Nurses' station to patient room
14.1	Utility room to patient room
9.8	Nurses' station to utility room
6.1	Nurses' station to elevator
5.8	Nurses' station to medical clinic
4.6	Patient room to pantry
3.7	Patient room to elevator
4.8	Medication room to patient room
2.5	Utility room to elevator lobby
2.8	Utility room to medical clinic
0.7	Utility room to pantry
1.1	Utility room to janitor closet
1	Nurses' station to pantry

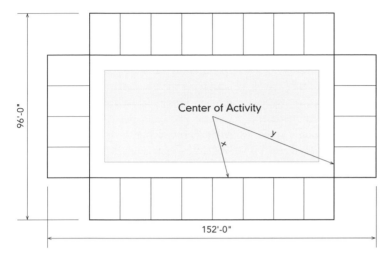

Number of Beds per Floor	24
Number of Beds per Cluster	6
Shortest Distance from Center (x)	29
Greatest Distance from Center (y)	60
Total Corridor Length	304
Perimeter Length	336
Total Area	12,993 sf
Center Support Area	3,840 sf
Available Bed Area	6,720 sf
Corridor Area	2,432 sf
Percent of Support Area	29%
Perimeter to Total Area	1 : 38
Total Area/Number of Beds	360 sf
Distance to Bed Factor	19

▲ Nursing unit analysis format (MPA/BTA).

One of the most critical aspects is the variation in size, location, and makeup of the staff during all shifts. A scheme with support space fully dispersed, with a close patient-nurse link during the day shift, may be very inefficient with a reduced staffing of the night shift and a consequent repositioning of the nurses to a location accessible to a larger number of beds.

Maximum and minimum travel distances from the center of activity are as important as the average distance. With great distance variations, some patients may receive more nursing observation than others. Analysis of the maximum distance between patient rooms is an indicator of the inefficiency generated during lower staffing hours.

Current trends have eliminated inpatient care for patients who ten years ago would have been admitted to the hospital. This means that patients who are admitted are in far greater need of observation. Therefore, the primary goal is to minimize distance—the average distance of travel, the range of distance

between the nearest and farthest patient rooms and the nurse work core, and the distances between all patient rooms. These distance calculations must be tempered by a factor relating to the number of beds per unit.

PLAN TYPES

The efficiency rankings of the general plan types are surprisingly consistent. A more compact, substantially concentric plan is generally more efficient; however, the exterior shape is less an indicator than the internal core organization and layout. Recently, very efficient plans have been established with groupings of concentric pods, and with the evolution of bedside computer charting and digitized imaging, as well as advances in distributing supplies and drugs from carts or dispersed support areas located adjacent to patient rooms, many of the reasons for travel between patient room and nursing stations are diminished.

Planners have tried many plan configurations with the goal of achieving efficient activity patterns; the following

1900s: Double-Loaded

1940s: Race Track

1950s: Compact Circle

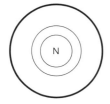

1930s to 1950s: Cross Shape

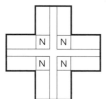

1950s: Compact Square

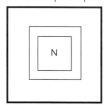

1970s: Compact Triangle

▲ *Generic plans of common nursing unit forms.*

discussion shows key points in the evolution of the compact inpatient care unit.

The typical double-loaded corridor was the standard design for many years because of the need for cross-ventilation and natural lighting. However, it made for very long distances between the nurses' station and the end rooms of the unit.

Double Corridor (Race Track) Plan

Holy Cross Hospital in Los Angeles, designed in the fifties, reflects the freedom possible with economical air-conditioning and changing codes. This design demonstrated a far more efficient unit than the single corridor plan: it placed the nursing support area between two corridors in what has been called the "double corridor" plan. The core still contains space unrelated to nursing (elevator space) and is thus less compact than it could be.

This unit also shows a combination of one central work core with dispersal of some support functions in the form of a pass-through "nurseserver" adjacent to the door of each room to provide patient supplies for the convenience of staff. This concept, developed by hospital consultant Gordon Friesen, became a common element in the "Friesen" hospitals that emerged in the 1950s and 1960s. Although this design was highly efficient during the day, the distances from the ends of the floor created problems when staffing was limited at night.

Compact Rectangular Plan

The compact rectangular unit of Providence Hospital in Anchorage, Alaska (1950s), is much more flexible than the

circular unit in terms of the ratio of patient rooms to amount of support space, because of the ease of changing the exterior dimensions on each side while maintaining the same bed count. Most compact rectilinear plans have an efficiency rating close to that of the circular plans and provide a higher degree of flexibility in planning the units.

Compact Circular Plan

In its first phase of construction, Valley Presbyterian Hospital in Van Nuys, California (1956), developed a compact circular unit with elevators removed from the center and located where they could also serve additional nursing towers in the future.

All 34 beds were arrayed around the nursing support space, and both average distance and range of distance to work cores were minimal. Another means of reducing nurse travel was to provide redundant circulation—that is, more than one route from point to point. This was recognized by the Yale evaluations as the most efficient plan designed to date in the study.

Working within a circle has a built-in problem, because the number and sizes of patient rooms dictated by program requirements controls the diameter of the circle. Codes often limit the number of beds per nursing station to 35, imposing yet another parameter. It is strictly a coincidence when the space in the center provides the area programmed for nursing support.

However, when the bed count and the support areas are in balance, as in Valley Presbyterian's Phase II tower (1960), the circular unit can be the most efficient model. In this second tower the diameter was increased from 88 ft to 96 ft to provide balanced support space for 19 two-bed rooms.

A larger-diameter third tower with 32 single-bed rooms was added in 1969. As discussed earlier, the nursing core was forced to be much larger than needed to accommodate all single-bed rooms. Consequently, efficiency dropped and patient observation was obscured.

This was a seminal project in the history of hospital planning, because it provided an early rational method for hospitals to grow and, at the same time, maintain organizational order. Designed by architect Jim Moore, this strategy has been applied countless times in the development of subsequent hospital plans.

Prior to the development of this plan, nursing units were added adjacent to one another, with their own separate elevator cores, creating disorienting circulation patterns for the visitor and staff searching for the right bank of elevators. Much of the work of recent years has been focused on clearing up this confusion of circulation caused by ill-thought-out patterns of nursing unit growth.

All towers are served from the same expanded elevator core. There is no compromise in nursing activities caused by the removal of the elevators from the nursing core. On the contrary, efficiency in the entire hospital's operation is higher because of the clear, simple circulation system. The Valley Presbyterian Hospital has grown from 63 beds to 360 beds in less than 15 years, maintaining the same efficient circulation system by adding elevators adjacent to the original core.

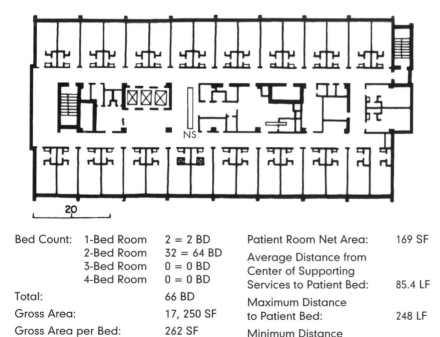

◀ Double corridor (racetrack) plan. Holy Cross Hospital, Los Angeles, California (Architects: Verge & Clatworthy. Consultant: Gordon Friesen.)

Bed Count:	1-Bed Room	2 = 2 BD		Patient Room Net Area:	169 SF
	2-Bed Room	32 = 64 BD		Average Distance from Center of Supporting Services to Patient Bed:	85.4 LF
	3-Bed Room	0 = 0 BD			
	4-Bed Room	0 = 0 BD			
Total:		66 BD		Maximum Distance to Patient Bed:	248 LF
Gross Area:		17, 250 SF			
Gross Area per Bed:		262 SF		Minimum Distance to Patient Bed:	52 LF
Supporting Services Area		2,650 SF			
Circulation Area		4, 605 SF		Distance-to-Bed Factor:	1.29

▶ *Compact rectangular plan. Providence Hospital, Anchorage, Alaska. (Architect: Charles Luckman Associates. Consultant: MPA.)*

NS

20

Bed Count:	1 Bed-Room	0 = 0 BD	Patient Room Net Area:	143 SF
	2 Bed-Room	13 = 26 BD	Circulation Area:	2,384 SF
	3 Bed-Room	2 = 6 BD	Average Distance from Center of Supporting Services to Patient Bed:	53.6 LF
	4 Bed Room	2 = 8 BD		
Total:		40 BD	Maximum Distance to Patient Bed:	68 LF
Gross Area:		8,360 SF	Minimum Distance to Patient Bed:	32 LF
Gross Area per Bed:		209 SF	Distance-to-Bed Factor:	1.34
Supporting Services Area:		1,230 SF		

▼ *Compact circular plan. Valley Presbyterian Hospital Phase I, Van Nuys, California. (Architect: Pereira and Luckman.)*

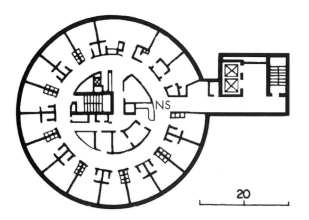

NS

20

Bed Count:	1-Bed Room	0 = 0 BD
	2-Bed Room	15 = 30 BD
	3-Bed Room	0 = 0 BD
	4-Bed Room	1 = 4 BD
Total:		34 BD
Gross Area:		7,068 SF
Gross Area per Bed:		2,078 SF
Supporting Services Area:		954 SF
Circulation Area:		1,958 SF
Patient Room Net Area:		170 SF
Average Distance from Center of Supporting Services to Patient Bed		49.5 LF
Maximum Distance to Patient Bed:		60 LF
Minimum Distance to Patient Bed:		44 LF
Distance-to-Bed Factor:		1.43

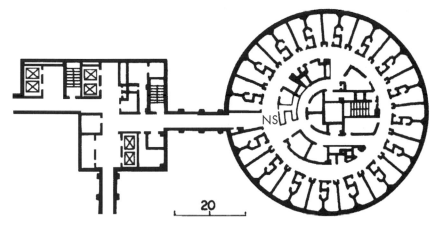

◀ *Valley Presbyterian Hospital Phase III, Van Nuys, California. (Architect: Charles Luckman Associates. Consultant: MPA.)*

Bed Count:	1 Bed Room	32 = 32 BD
	2 Bed Room	0 = 0 BD
	3 Bed Room	0 = 0 BD
	4 Bed Room	0 = 0 BD
Total:		32 BD
Gross Area:		10,607 SF
Gross Area per Bed:		3,211 SF
Supporting Services Area:		1,797 SF

Circulation Area:	3,146 SF
Patient Room Net Area:	110.8 SF
Average Distance from Center of Supporting Services to Patient Bed:	65 LF
Maximum Distance to Patient Bed:	84 LF
Minimum Distance to Patient Bed:	32 LF
Distance-to-Bed Factor:	2.03

▼ *Valley Presbyterian Hospital at full growth.*

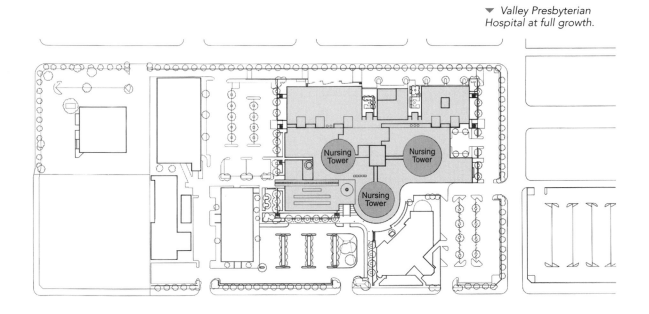

◀ A recent adaptation of the compact circular plan at Brigham and Women's Hospital, Boston, Massachusetts (TK&A).

1 Single Patient Room
2 Single Patient Isolation Room
3 Anteroom
4 Nurses' Station
5 Patient Nurses' Station
6 Clean Utility
7 Soiled Utility
8 Physicians' Workroom
9 Office
10 Staff Conferencce Room
11 Elevator Lobby
12 On Call Area
13 Lounge
14 Procedure Room
15 Prep
16 Galley
17 Rehabilitation Gymnasium
18 Trash Room

MULTIBED VERSUS SINGLE-BED ROOMS

Patient accommodation had progressively moved from total openness and sharing of space with multiple patients in open wards, as in the Nightingale Plan, down to eight-patient, six-patient and four-patient wards, with toilet and bathing facilities often shared by a group of patient rooms. In a radical shift, the norm after World War II became the two-bed room with shared toilet. Shared showers and toilets between rooms still exist in many hospitals.

Surprisingly, the idea of providing private bedrooms in hospitals has been considered for years. In 1920, Asa S. Bacon, then the superintendent of Chicago's Presbyterian Hospital, published an article entitled "Efficient Hospitals" in the *Journal of the American Medical Association*. Bacon made a strong plea for the private room—from the standpoints of both the patient's privacy and comfort and the hospital's goal of maximum occupancy. He noted that the serious problem of contagion was greatly mitigated, and that the physician or nurse could give better examinations and take more complete histories in the single room.

Although Bacon's ideas were virtually ignored for almost a half century, the concept of the all single-bed room hospital is now widely accepted. In recent years most hospitals planned to update their facilities in favor of maximizing single-bed rooms.

There are other advantages to single-bed-per-room nursing units. The patient can rest undisturbed by a roomate's activities. A patient can become ambulatory earlier when the toilet and shower are in the room, and such rooms can be used for many types of isolation. Because patients in single-bed rooms are rarely moved, medication errors are greatly reduced. Moreover, the hospital realizes some economies by the elimination of patient moves. In units with multibed rooms the number of daily moves has averaged six to nine per day, at a significant cost (in added paperwork, housekeeping, patient transport, medication instructions, etc.).

UCLA/Santa Monica Medical Center

The design of a hospital with only single rooms is not without its problems, however. If the single room is designed along the lines of the conventional patient room (with corridors running approximately 12.5 feet per room), the corridors can become too long, increasing nurses' travel distances. To overcome this problem, there are plans that overlap or stagger groups of three or four rooms

▼ *Asa Bacon plan proposal for single-bed room.*

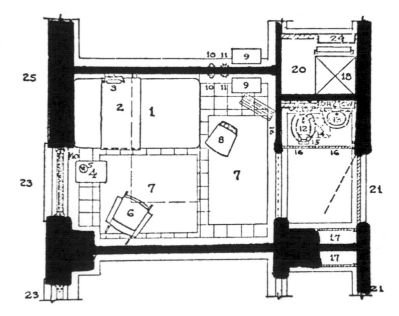

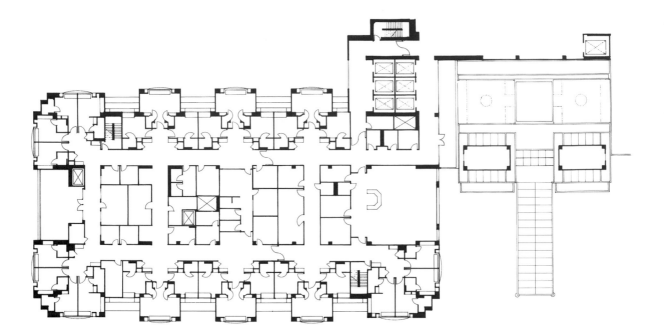

▲ *Third floor plan, UCLA/Santa Monica Medical Center, Santa Monica, California (BTA).*

around alcoves, such as at the UCLA/Santa Monica Hospital Medical Center and at the Motion Picture and Television Fund Hospital, often made possible by providing nursing substations with computers.

In planning the single room as an alternative to the semiprivate room, the room must be made highly efficient. Early experiments by architect Jim Moore and nursing consultant Nina Craft, RN, showed that the room could be effectively compressed if the bed was located diagonally instead of parallel to the corridor. This reduced the corridor run per room by more than 25 percent, without compromising the function of the space. Many hospitals were designed with this innovative plan in the 1960s and 1970s, which proved to be highly efficient. Placing the bed at an angle created an uninviting bedroom, many designers felt. Unfortunately, over time

these smaller rooms have proven inflexible to changes such as increased bed length and more staff and equipment congregated around the patient.

A compromise solution, developed in several hospitals by Rex Whittaker Allen, FAIA, provided two-bed rooms divided by a movable partition. These partitions are often closed (at patients' preference). However, it has been found that some patients do enjoy the ability to converse with another person and still have control over the sliding door. Variations of this combination are being planned today.

Providence Hospital, Medford, Oregon

The preference for privacy was borne out by several surveys of patients. At Providence Hospital in Medford, Oregon, one of the first all single-bed room hospitals (built in 1965), a survey showed that 92 percent of the doctors and

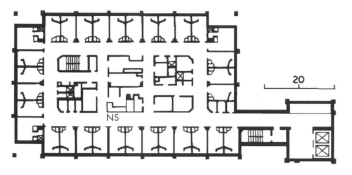

▲ Providence Hospital, Medford, Oregon. (Architect: Edson & Papas. Consultant: MPA.)

Bed Count:	1-Bed Room	32 = 32 BD
	2-Bed Room	0 = 0 BD
	3-Bed Room	0 = 0 BD
	4-Bed Room	0 = 0 BD
Total:		32 BD
Gross Area:		12,153 SF
Gross Area per Bed:		380 SF
Supporting Services Area:		1,848 SF
Circulation Area:		4,470 SF
Patient Room Net Area:		115 SF
Average Distance from Center of Supporting Services to Patient Bed:		70 LF
Maximum Distance to Patient Bed:		100 LF
Minimum Distance to Patient Bed:		36 LF
Distance-to-Bed Factor:		2.19

hospital employees believed that their work was easier when patients were housed in single rooms, and 95 percent of the patients indicated that if costs were equal, they would select a single room for any future hospitalization.

Hospitals have realized further cost benefits from utilizing single rooms. Even with higher unit costs based on construction, furniture, maintenance, housekeeping, heating and ventilation, linen changes, and nursing, units with single rooms can match the per diem cost of multibed rooms because of the very high occupancy factors possible. Occupancy of multibed rooms generally reaches a maximum of 80 to 85 percent, whereas single-bed rooms can reach 100 percent occupancy. This allows for the provision of fewer beds to take care of the same size population. For example, an 80-to-85-bed, all single-bedroom hospital can care for the same number of total patients as a 100-bed hospital with 2-bed rooms.

Kaiser Foundation, Panorama City, California

The Kaiser Foundation Hospital in Panorama City, California (1960s) was

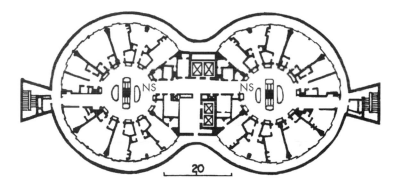

▲ Kaiser Foundation Hospital, Panorama City, California. (Architect: Clarence Mayhew. Consultant: Sidney Garfield, MD.)

Bed Count:	1 Bed Room	6 = 6 BD
	2 Bed Room	12 = 24 BD
	3 Bed Room	0 = 0 BD
	4 Bed Room	4 = 16 BD
Total:		46 BD
Gross Area:		15,850 SF
Gross Area per Bed:		345 SF
Supporting Services Area:		1,811 SF
Circulation Area:		7,246 SF
Patient Room Net Area:		198 SF
Average Distance from Center of Supporting Services to Patient Bed:		47.5 LF
Maximum Distance to Patient Bed:		60 LF
Minimum Distance to Patient Bed:		24 LF
Distance-to-Bed Factor:		1.03

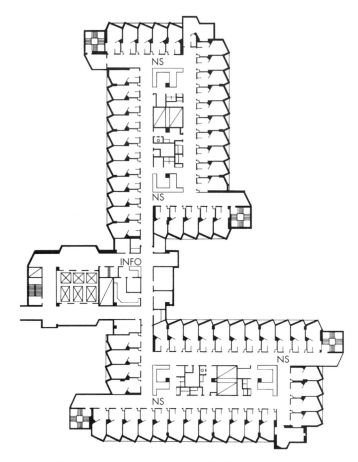

▲ *St. Vincent's Hospital, Los Angeles, California (DMJM, MPA, and BTA).*

Bed Count:	1-Bed Room	32 = 32 BD
	2-Bed Room	0 = 0 BD
	3-Bed Room	0 = 0 BD
	4-Bed Room	0 = 0 BD
Total:		32 BD
Gross Area:		10,643 SF
Gross Area per Bed:		332 SF
Supporting Services Area:		3,128 SF
Circulation Area:		2,688 SF
Patient Room Net Area:		120 SF
Average Distance from Center of Supporting Services to Patient Bed:		45.5 LF
Maximum Distance to Patient Bed:		60 LF
Minimum Distance to Patient Bed:		24 LF
Distance-to-Bed Factor:		1.42

also a landmark building, conceptualized by its founder Sidney Garfield, MD. It was notable for several developments in the evolution of the compact unit.

Although it provided two-bed rather than single-bed rooms, the design shows an intent to provide only necessary functions near the patient and to remove all spaces and equipment not required for direct patient care from the center to the unit. These spaces have been relocated in the link connecting the two 23-bed units on each floor. Thus, although the nurses' station was completely open in the center of the unit for optimum visibility between the station and the patient rooms, it did not realize all of the benefits of the open plan because many of the beds were hidden behind the toilet rooms located inboard on the corridor side of the patient rooms.

A significant feature of the plan is the separation of visitor and staff traffic, with visitors routed from a control point near the elevators, around balconies on the outside of the nursing towers. This was replicated in several projects in more temperate climates, such as in Hawaii. Today's codes often do not allow the openness of this plan, however, because of requirements for fire separation and appropriate exiting, and these units, when undergoing upgrading to meet today's standards, are often forced to eliminate this innovation.

St. Vincent's Hospital, Los Angeles, California

To maximize the patient-nurse link, St. Vincent's Hospital in Los Angeles (1973) eliminated all noncare functions from the nursing unit and relocated them in a central freestanding service core adjacent to the unit.

The architects further reduced the nursing core area by sharing functions among the 16-, 32-, and 64-bed modules of each floor.

For the module of 16 beds (St. Vincent's established 16 as the number to be effectively served by one nursing team) the shared items included doctors' and nurses' charting, dictation, medications, clean/sterile supply, and linen (the last three items on carts).

The following items were shared between two 16-bed modules: nurses' lounge and toilet, clean/sterile supply backup, soiled utility, and a nourishment unit.

The following items were centralized to serve a 64-bed nursing floor (four modules): space for the floor's administrative manager; reception; nursing service office; floor pharmacy; visitors' lounge; consultation, examination, and conference rooms; and tub rooms.

As patients have been drawn away from the acute hospital to other types of facilities by the forces of managed care and improvements in outpatient capabilities, the level of acuity (the degree of illness and the corresponding level of care needed) in general hospital patients has risen; so have the numbers of staff and the need for closer patient observation and monitoring. As a result, the number of beds per 1,000 population (a standard industry measurement) has dropped drastically, and the design of today's nursing units has moved closer to that of intensive care and step-down units—a unit providing a level of care between intensive care and normal patient care.

St. Luke's Medical Center, Milwaukee, Wisconsin

At St. Luke's Medical Center in Milwaukee, Wisconsin (1991–1999), two alternative experimental designs were recently mocked-up and evaluated, testing new precepts of plan organization. The plan compared a typical contemporary compact unit (Scheme A) with internal patient/visitor access, to one that provided a perimeter family and patient solarium–living room surrounding the beds (Scheme B). Nursing stations were placed in this zone, but all service activities were taken out of public view within an interior service zone with separate access to each bedroom.

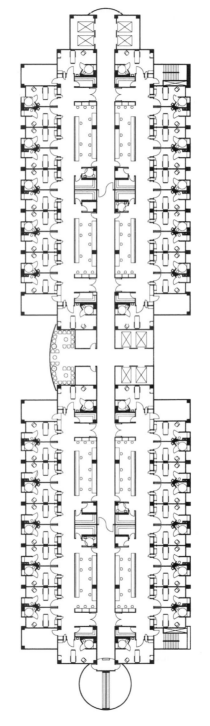

◀ Scheme A: Prototypical nursing unit, St. Luke's Medical Center, Milwaukee, Wisconsin (BTA).

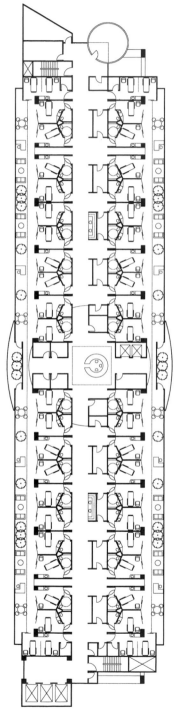

▶ *Scheme B: Prototypical nursing unit, St. Luke's Medical Center, Milwaukee, Wisconsin.*

Flexibility of Room Use/Bed Reductions

As discussed previously, hospitals have realized cost benefits from utilizing single rooms. Because single-bed rooms can be virtually 100 percent occupied, whereas multibed rooms have maximum censuses of 80 to 85 percent, fewer beds can be provided to handle the same daily census and greater efficiency in nursing unit staffing can be achieved.

Aside from the need for fewer beds, flexibility is a key factor in the new design equation, as it can provide maximum utilization of space. For example, designing patient rooms that can be easily converted from general acute care to highly acute care or even critical care rooms will provide maximum flexibility and utilization, particularly given the trend toward increasing inpatient acuity levels and the resultant need for higher staff ratios.

Single-bed rooms have also become an important marketing tactic for hospitals in their attempts to create a "noninstitutional" environment. Patients prefer the privacy of a single-bed room, the ability to control the environment (light, sound, view) and to have accommodations for family.

Whereas in the past patient rooms were designed as highly specialized for particular diagnoses and acuity levels, today's designs include "universal rooms," which can be easily converted to accommodate a range of acuity levels. This is accomplished by designing single-occupancy patient rooms large enough to accommodate increasing numbers of complex bedside treatments, providing electronic service cores to allow for changes in patient monitoring, and by situating rooms to allow for maximum patient visibility by the nursing staff.

Larger Single-Occupancy Rooms

In some instances, larger single-occupancy rooms have been included in a hospital plan. For example, at City of Hope National Medical

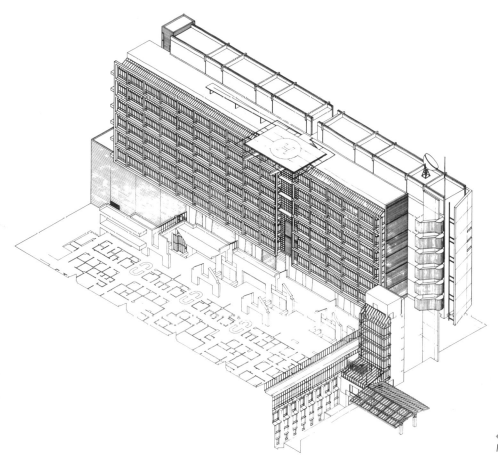

◀ *St. Luke's Medical Center, Milwaukee, Wisconsin.*

Center in Duarte, California, nursing units were designed with four 8-bed pods. Two 32-bed units, constituting one nursing floor, were then able to share such support services as physical therapy, treatment rooms, and multiple staff offices.

For purposes of a more detailed exploration of the design of nursing units, a recently designed hospital has been chosen as a case study. Although many innovations have been applied here, the design should be considered only as one in a line of design evolutions in the de-

velopment of the nursing unit. Only time will tell whether its innovations will last.

Case Study: The San Bernardino County Arrowhead Regional Medical Center Nursing Units

As hospitals continue to reduce the number of beds in operation to match changing utilization patterns, the conversion of multibed rooms to larger single-occupancy rooms has become the norm. The trend toward the single-occupancy room is epitomized by the Arrowhead Regional Medical Center, the $470

151

million, 1 million sq ft replacement facility for San Bernardino County, California. Completed and occupied in 1999, it is the first instance of a county facility planned for all single-occupancy rooms.

The county of San Bernardino is the largest county in the United States. With major responsibility for both highly specialized tertiary and community care for a dispersed population, in a location close to three active seismic faults and with existing buildings failing to meet current standards, the county made a bold

decision to invest in a totally new facility.

The charge to the design team (Bobrow/Thomas and Associates, Executive and Design Architects with Associate Architects Perkins and Will) was to create a state-of-the-art facility that would be most efficient to operate, offer maximum flexibility, and provide a healing environment for families and patients in a technology-intense facility.

The planning of this medical center, and specifically its nursing units, provides an insight into the considerations and criteria for design and the decisions that were made. The charge to create the most efficient nursing unit possible led to a detailed analysis of the optimal floor size for economic efficiency and the choice among plans that would allow high nurse-to-patient visibility, flexibility in bed assignment, and efficiencies through all shifts of hospital operations.

Flexibility in nursing units was achieved through the design of multiple "pods" of patient rooms, enabling the size of the units to respond to such variables as occupancy count, patient types, and models of nursing care.

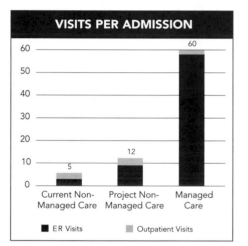

VISITS PER ADMISSION

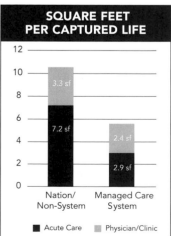

SQUARE FEET PER CAPTURED LIFE

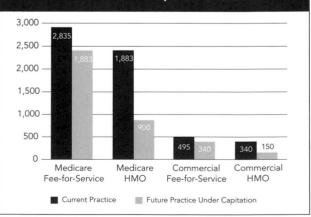

INPATIENT DAYS PER 1,000 ENROLLMENTS

After research on staffing efficiencies for various nursing and support disciplines and analyses of plan alternatives, the final plan was designed as a cluster of units connected by a continuous band of beds on the perimeter to allow for flexibility in assignment to individual nursing stations.

The floor is organized around three 24-bed nursing units, which share an adjacent common support and vertical circulation core. Each nursing unit has three nursing substations each with a general assignment of eight beds, all visible from the station. With substations providing small charting areas, medications, and supplies, the nursing staff is "freed" from the central nurses' station.

This efficiency in turn creates economies of scale, which can allow for specialized support spaces on each nursing floor, such in as the previously noted St. Vincent Hospital. Based on the MPA/BTA model, the average distance to each bed is 19 feet at Arrowhead Regional Medical Center. This allows the nursing unit to house the most intensely ill patients.

The use of single-bed rooms accommodates changing acuity levels and increases

▲ City of Hope National Medical Center, rendering of patient nursing unit (BTA).

in bedside treatments and provides maxi-mum flexibility in assigning patients to rooms as occupancy levels fluctuate. This concept is enhanced by the use of comput-erized charting stations for patients' med-ical records, located at bedside and in nurs-ing substations situated within each pod.

The floor plan is also notable in that several other contemporary concepts have been applied. The grouping of three units connects at a central service core, which allows for a single point of floor control. Banks of elevators separately assigned for the public, service, and patients are given separate floor lobbies to allow for the appropriate separation of traffic and con-nections to other portions of the hospital. Common shared areas are clustered at the center, such as reception, waiting and administrative, and support spaces.

Each corridor partition for each patient room was designed to be glazed or solid, depending on the needs for observation. The partitions can be modified quickly by the hospital's own staff.

◀ City of Hope National Medical Center, rendering of single-bed patient room.

▶ *Diagram of monitored care.*

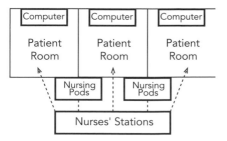

In a departure from the normal mechanical servicing of floors, which is accomplished through vertical shafts, to maximize flexibility all vertical ducts were eliminated from the nursing floors by the creation of separate mechanical service rooms on each floor. Air distribution is achieved through a ceiling plenum space, with floor-to-floor heights of 17 ft, and as a result the floors are totally free to be modified over time within the constraints of the floor plan's configuration.

To further this concept, the patient room was designed to place all vertical services at the periphery of the building. This was accomplished by locating all patient toilets and showers on the external band of the building. This feature became part of the energy-efficient design of the hospital by providing an extra zone of insulation from the desert heat and the western exposure.

Finally, this placement of patient room elements allowed the patient to be viewed directly from the corridor for ease of communication with the nursing staff, thus reducing the use of nurse call systems.

Functional Issues

A number of major contemporary functional issues were addressed and satisfied in the design of the Arrowhead plan:

Larger, single-bed patient rooms
- Ability to convert medical/surgical beds to intensive care beds, including monitoring capabilities
- Provision of space for charting and procedures in room
- Continuity of care on each floor

Shared common services and spaces
- Procedure room/treatment room in acute patient areas
- Physical therapy/treatment room on the floor
- Decentralization of nursing stations

▼ *Nursing unit alternative analysis.*

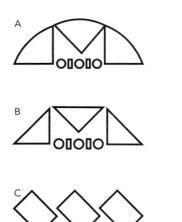

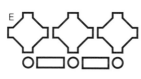

Nursing Unit Option	Total Area (3 Units)	Area per Bed	Average Distance of Bed to Nursing Station	Bed Continuity	Easy Hierarchical Orientation	Shared Support	Natural Light Introduced at Intersections
A	34,860	484	19'	X	X	X	X
B	37,575	521	19'		X	X	X
C	40,455	561	30'				
D	35,100	487	19'		X	X	
E	41,775	580	27'				
F	35,100	487	19'	X	X		X

ANALYSIS OF NURSING UNIT ALTERNATIVES

		24 Series						28 Series						30 Series						32 Series						36 Series					
		A-24	B-24	C-24	D-24	E-24	F-24	A-28	B-28	C-28	D-28	E-28	F-28	A-30	B-30	C-30	D-30	E-30	F-30	A-32	B-32	C-32	D-32	E-32	F-32	A-36	B-36	C-36	D-36	E-36	F-36
A	Number of Beds per Floor	24	24	24	24	24	24	28	•	•	28	28	•	•	30	30	•	•	•	32	•	•	32	32	32	36	36	36	36	36	•
B	Number of Beds per Cluster	6	8	8	6	6	8	7	•	•	7	7	•	•	10	10	•	•	•	8	•	•	8	7	•	9	12	12	9	9	•
C	Shortest Distance from Center (x)	29'	10'	26'	42	42	45	35	•	•	51'	49'	•	•	44'	32	•	•	•	42	•	•	55'	56'	•	49	49	38'	63'	49'	•
D	Greatest Distance from Center (y)	60'	28	68'	54'	74'	82	59	•	•	64'	77	•	•	75'	88'	•	•	•	78'	•	•	74'	90'	•	87'	91'	108'	84'	94'	•
E	Average Distance from Center	47	19'	41.5	48'	54'	67	55	•	•	56'	59'	•	•	55'	56'	•	•	•	63'	•	•	64'	68'	•	71'	66'	76'	71'	67'	•
F	Total Corridor Length	304'	294'	288'	304'	303'	583'	360'	•	•	360'	448'	•	•	689'	383'	•	•	•	416	•	•	416	504'	•	472	462	476	472	504'	•
G	Perimeter Length	336	336	336	336	336	336	392	•	•	392	392	•	•	420'	420	•	•	•	448	•	•	448	448	•	504'	504'	502	504'	504'	•
H	Total Area (Square Feet)	12,992	12,151	11,522	13,776	15,731	21,410	16,660	•	•	17,444	19,396	•	•	16,887	16,338	•	•	•	20,720	•	•	21,504	23,452	•	25,172	22,301	21,794	25,966	22,084	•
I	Center Support Area (Square Feet)	3,840	3,076	2,498	4,624	4,608	6,198	5,940	•	•	6,724	6,704	•	•	5,459	4,869	•	•	•	8,432	•	•	9,216	9,193	•	11,316	8,521	7,930	12,100	6,704	•
J	Available Bed Area (Square Feet)	6,720	6,720	6,720	6,720	8,045	7,141	7,840	•	•	7,840	9,165	•	•	8,400	8,400	•	•	•	8,960	•	•	8,960	10,285	•	10,080	10,080	10,050	10,080	11,405	•
K	Corridor Area (Square Feet)	2,432	2,344	2,304	3,032	3,077	4,686	2,980	•	•	2,880	3,525	•	•	3,028	3,068	•	•	•	3,328	•	•	3,328	3,973	•	3,776	3,700	3,813	3,776	3,973	•
L	Percent of Support Area	29%	25%	21%	29%	29%	29%	45%	•	•	38%	34%	•	•	32%	29%	•	•	•	40%	•	•	42%	39%	•	75%	38%	36%	46%	30%	•
M	Perimeter of Total Area (G:H)	1:38	1:36	1:34	1:41	1:46	1:63	1:42.5	•	•	1:44	1:49	•	•	1:40	1:39	•	•	•	1:46	•	•	1:48	1:52	•	1:50	1:44	1:39	1:51	1:43	•
N	Total Area/# of Beds (H/A) (Square Feet)	360	506	506	574	655	892	595	•	•	623	692	•	•	703	544	•	•	•	647	•	•	672	692	•	699	929	605	721	613	•
O	Distance to Bed Factor (E/A)	1.9	1.84	1.73	2.0	2.25	2.75	1.9	•	•	2.0	2.1	•	•	1.85	1.86	•	•	•	1.9	•	•	2.0	2.1	•	1.97	1.85	2.1	1.9	1.87	•

▶ *Fourth floor nursing unit at Arrowhead Regional Medical Center (BTA/P&W).*

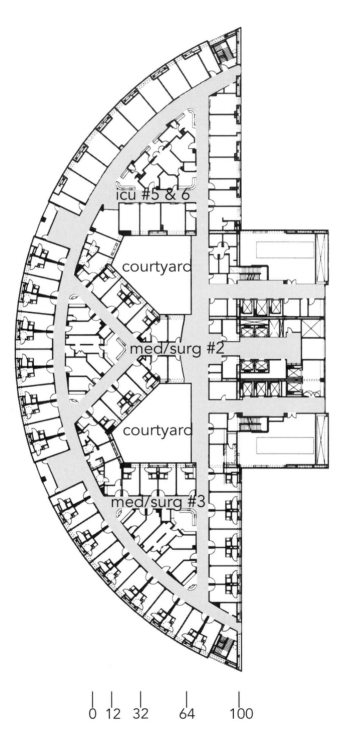

icu #5 & 6

courtyard

med/surg #2

courtyard

med/surg #3

0 12 32 64 100

- Unit flexibility for occupancy and nursing practices/swing capability
- Digital imaging stations for image viewing on units

Patient environment
- Space for family and visitors in the room
- Provision of education, lounges, consult areas for patients/family
- Views of nature and/or outdoor access, natural light
- Enhanced control of environment by patient, such as lighting, noise, television, views, and visitors
- Patient view of corridors
- Reduced noise levels

The search for the appropriate nursing unit for each hospital evolves from a careful study of the critical design issues at each institution and its particular site. The evolution of the plan for this unit is an example of that process at Arrowhead Regional Medical Center. The specifics of each new project will dictate a new solution, benefited by the research and analysis of plans developed earlier.

INTERIOR CONSIDERATIONS AND ARCHITECTURAL DESIGN ISSUES

Contemporary design of interior spaces in hospitals is based on creating welcoming environments, with the goal of making the inpatient hospital a friendlier, more responsive place. Within the limitations imposed by codes, economics, and maintenance issues, the change in the "look" of hospitals over the past ten years reflects the recognition that they must be sensitive to patients' needs for comfort, control, and other psychological requisites. Models for this change have derived primarily from hospitality (hotel) industry designs as applied to hospitals.

There is still room for improvement in applying these concepts to the traditional separation between the "back of the house" and "front of the house" mentality whereby hospitals are perceived strictly as functional machines and systems. Designers and hospital managers are becoming aware that the entire hospital must be designed to increase its comfort, appearance, and efficiency for patients, family, and visitors, as well as for physicians, nurses, and all hospital staff members.

Daylighting
One of the chief improvements in the design of interior spaces has been to incorporate natural light into the hospital, particularly in areas that are programmatically dense. An early example can be found at Daniel Freeman Memorial Hospital in Inglewood,

▼ Hospital lobby at Arrowhead Regional Medical Center.

▲ *The dining room at Arrowhead Regional Medical Center.*

▼ *Single-loaded corridor at Arrowhead Regional Medical Center.*

California (BTA), where courtyards tie together three levels of the hospital, including the basement, with lush landscaping. Located along one side of the main corridors and at major intersections, the courtyards provide orientation for visitors and staff (a concept further developed at many hospitals, including Arrowhead).

Where natural light is not available, or to supplement it, a variety of contemporary fixtures are available that mimic daylight or incandescent light, creating a far warmer experience than that provided by standard cool fluorescent fixtures.

Configurations

Most intractable to significant change (with the exception of the progress made in women's centers) is the standard patient room. With the gradual conversion of most hospitals to all single rooms, a more comforting environment for patient and family is provided. Too often, however, the designs of these rooms center on the placement of the bed, the head wall, and visual access to nursing staff, rather than the needs of the patients and family. The introduction of a second bed as a window seat allows a family member to stay overnight with the patient, normalizing the patient's experience and, in fact, relieving nursing staff of many simple nonnursing activities.

The earliest experiments in this area occurred in women's services. Two landmark projects set the pace in this market-driven, highly competitive niche of healthcare. At Cottonwood Hospital in Salt Lake City, KMD architects set a standard for the design of women's centers. At UCLA/Santa Monica Hospital Medical Center, BTA evolved the concept to include courtyards where new mothers could enjoy candle-lit dinners with their husbands, celebrating their experience, and lay windows were designed to include a sleeping area for fathers.

Breakthroughs came early in the design of labor/delivery/recovery/postpartum rooms. In these rooms, concern for family needs, and reconception of the birthing experience as one shared with the family, has led to homelike settings. Such a room may include a view to an outside garden, a sleeping area for the husband in the form of a window bed, or a double bed for both parents.

Opportunities to apply these ideas throughout the hospital are now being explored further. An early experiment at Daniel Freeman Memorial Hospital created a gathering place for patients, staff, and visitors around a small kitchen area, known as the "Village Pump," which the book *Pattern Languages* described as the equivalent of the meeting place at the water pump in European villages. Corridors were made wider than the required 8 ft to allow for ambulation and further congregation.

A second concept tried at Daniel Freeman was the use of a freestanding circular table that served as both a nurses' charting area and a place for patients to congregate and discuss care plans with staff. This nonthreatening circular table removed a significant barrier to the humanizing of the patient and family experience.

Hospitals developed recently by the Planetree organization follow these precepts and take the humanizing of the design to greater levels of detail, with each hospital building on the experiences of those preceding it.

Finishes and Floor Treatments

Although the choice between carpets and no carpets is still an issue for some hospitals (for reasons relating to cleanliness and infection control), there are many opportunities to use floorings that create attractive solutions to problems of maintenance and cost.

Arrowhead mandated stringent requirements for durability and maintenance of all of its interior finishes. The hospital lobby illustrates the culmination of months of testing finish materials. This is an area of very high traffic, which may be subjected to abuse and vandalism. Although all the finishes, terrazzo floors, and limestone and slate walls were selected to withstand extreme wear, they also

City of Hope National Medical Center patient living room (RTA)

City of Hope National Medical Center patient living room.

INPATIENT CARE FACILITIES

▶ *Entry to UCSF Stanford Health Care, Center for Cancer Treatment and Prevention/ambulatory care pavilion (BTA).*

▼ *Clinic waiting area at UCSF Stanford Health Care, Center for Cancer Treatment and Prevention/ambulatory care pavilion.*

are beautiful, providing a tactile experience and an air of permanence, and allow natural light to penetrate deeply into the spaces.

The corridors at Arrowhead Regional Medical Center are adjacent to interior courtyards, which allows natural light to enter and provides a layer of light patterns that change throughout the day. The use of an impervious panel up to the wainscot, and above that an applied textured hard wall coating, provides a durable and washable surface as well as a contrast to the gloss of the terrazzo floors. These materials were thoroughly tested in mock-up rooms over the years of design development before final selection.

Color has long been recognized as a tool for wayfinding; different colors can be used to delineate departments and buildings or to call out an area of importance, such as a nurses' station.

The dining room at Arrowhead Regional Medical Center is a place where families, patients, and staff can gather and enjoy a

◀ *Atrium Lobby at UCSF Stanford Health Care, Center for Cancer Treatment and Prevention/ambulatory care pavilion.*

departure from the clinical experience. Although it is located in a subterranean space, natural light enters through skylights in the soaring ceilings. Planters and dramatic color, commonly used in hospitality design, are appropriate here as well. The art program features historical photographs of the region and people instrumental to the development of the original San Bernardino County Hospital (now Arrowhead Regional Medical Center).

The current trend in patient room design is to provide opportunities for personalizing space with tackable surfaces and shelves for photographs, flowers, or books. Window seats can be used for contemplation as well as sleeping space for spouses. The patient rooms at City of Hope National Medical Center were designed to maximize garden views, and access to operable windows allows the patient a feeling of control over the environment—scent, sound, and light.

It is important to design gathering spaces for patients and family members outside the patients' rooms. These spaces can be designed to resemble a living room, with finishes such as wood, carpeting, and stone. A fireplace and intimate areas for conversation create a unique respite from the conventional hospital experience.

SPECIALIZED INPATIENT NURSING UNITS AND THEIR UNIQUE PLANNING ISSUES

There are a variety of units designed to handle special groupings of patients, the most common of which are the acute medical/surgical unit, the critical care unit, the obstetrics/gynecological unit, and the pediatric unit. As the size and role of an institution increases, there may be additional specialty units.

In large tertiary or teaching hospitals and in specialty hospitals there can be a further level of distinction based on the need to cluster similar patients to care for them effectively. Other types of units include rehabilitation, psychiatric, and many variations of critical care units. For purposes of this general volume on hospital design, we will discuss briefly the most common types of units and one recently developed specialty unit. All of these units share certain common planning patterns; variations in design respond to the type of patient and the care needed.

Intensive and Coronary Care Units

Early intensive care and coronary care units closely resembled the postanesthesia recovery areas from which they evolved. Beds were lined up in open wards with little space between them and no provisions for patient privacy other than cubicle curtains. More recent units provide privacy while maintaining high visibility from the nursing station. These units have evolved permutations, most comprised of single-patient rooms, with maximum visibility, flexibility of bed location, and complex utility support.

Gases, air, vacuum, and electronic monitoring are often provided from a movable service column. These rooms now are much larger than standard patient rooms to allow for the many staff needed during an emergency.

Maternity and Women's Health

Specialty care units can provide valuable marketing opportunities for the hospital, not only through the services they provide but through their design as well. Maternity units constitute one of the most popular marketing "niches" of today. Maternity (i.e., obstetrical) units can be designed with a strong emphasis on "high touch," with a homelike, noninstitutional ambiance.

Large single-patient rooms utilized for labor, delivery, and recovery (LDR) are designed as cozy bedrooms, with obstetrical equipment hidden away. These rooms quickly convert to high-tech procedure rooms as delivery progresses, simply with the necessary equipment and lighting pulled in. Although the trend

▶ *Women's Health Services Building, West Allis, Wisconsin (KS/BTA)*

The living room area, immediately adjacent to the main entry, serves as the heart of the Women's Health Services Building. Careful attention was given to the space to create a residential character. Here patients and visitors can congregate, sit by the fireplace, or read in the library.

◀ One of the highest priorities in the design of the Women's Health Services Building was to bring light and nature into the building as far as possible. The Cafe Bookstore, opening onto a healing garden, is one of several public areas where visitors are encouraged to sit or to wander and browse. Current information on women's health issues is available at the bookstore. In this store, reflecting the trend in bookstore design, visitors can read while having a beverage or something to eat.

until recently was to use these rooms as postpartum beds as well, this practice has changed because of several issues: inefficiency in room utilization, difficulties with nurse cross-training, and patient preferences to continue recovery in a quieter setting. Consequently, many postpartum beds are located adjacent to LDR areas, in their own quiet rooms, frequently with newborns rooming-in with their mothers and with double beds provided for the fathers.

Postpartum rooms, as well as many other inpatient women's services areas, are now designed to include many comforts that enhance the patient's recovery and positive experience with the hospital. These amenities may range from lounges located on the floor (for patients and families) to small reading areas, sitting rooms with computers, and access to an electronic library (including books

and items available from the hospital gift shop).

Similar design concepts are being applied to other women's nursing units, with various services (gynecology, cancer,

▼ There was a definite desire at West Allis for the postpartum patient area to have a strong literal connection with the birthing floor, and this was provided with an open mezzanine and connecting stair.

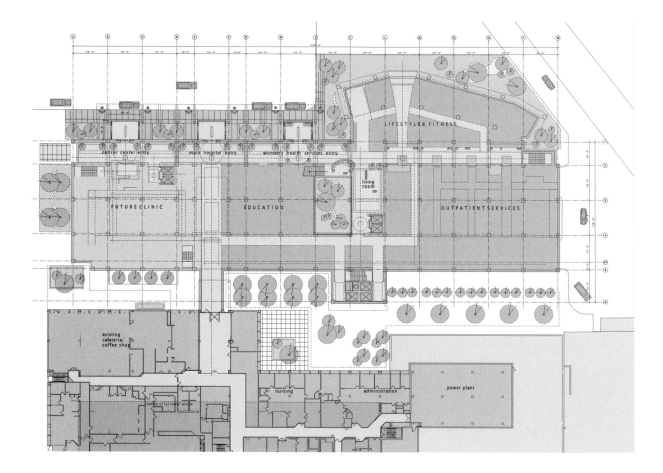

LIFESTYLE & FITNESS

living room

cancer center entry   main hospital entry   women's health services entry

FUTURE CLINIC   EDUCATION   OUTPATIENT SERVICES

existing cafeteria/ coffee shop

outline of (e) floor above

nursing   administration   power plant

▲ The first-floor plan of the Women's Health Services Building illustrates the organization of the outpatient services. Exercise and alternative treatments are located "in the garden," with an indoor/outdoor component to their programs. Clinic functions are located so as to maximize shared support spaces.

and urology, for example) consolidated into a single specialty unit. The ambiance in these units is one that promotes healing and tranquility, the antithesis of institutional environments of the past.

The West Allis Women's Health Services Building (KS/BTA) in West Allis, Wisconsin, is an excellent example of how the evolution of care has now holistically blended the inpatient and outpatient experience. The design was based on several visioning sessions used to establish the appropriate feelings the center should evoke and the physical elements that would support them.

Pediatric Patient Units

A pediatric unit is one of the most specialized inpatient units, with obvious requirements for children. How can a pediatric patient unit be designed to reduce the fear and anxiety inherent to hospitalization for children? Attention must be paid not only to the needs of the children but to the needs of their family members as well.

Pediatric nursing units require design of appropriate scale for children. Designing rooms that contain nooks and crannies, areas in which the child can play, hide, and feel secure, can help to allay fears and

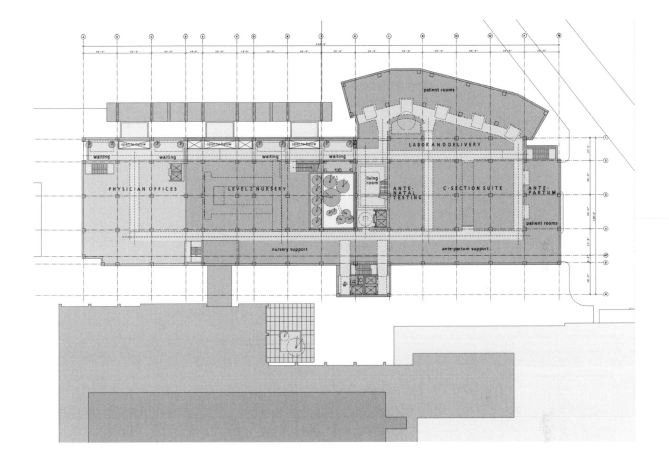

reduce boredom. Views of the outdoors, scenes of nature, and various colors enhance healing and feelings of well-being for the child, as well as for the parents.

Pediatric patient rooms must also include amenities to make children and parents feel as comfortable as possible. Providing pull-out beds or other furniture to allow for rooming-in enables parents to become active caretakers, thus reducing their anxiety. One of the most overlooked areas of pediatric unit design is the impact on care providers. Nursing staff, for example, must have the ability

to keep patients both entertained and quiet; both needs are affected by design. Providing nursing staff with the necessary visibility to pediatric beds is critical, as it is on many specialty adult units.

The highly stressful nature of pediatric nursing also requires planning for staff areas that enable caregivers to "regroup." Providing nursing staff with areas that have access to the outdoors or to views of nature is a highly effective means of ameliorating stress and reducing burnout.

Several questions typically arise in designing pediatric units, which are often

▲ *The second floor houses LDR rooms, the caesarean section suite, and the Level II nursery, departments that have critical functional adjacencies in order to provide the highest level of care during the birthing process. The LDR rooms are situated so as to take advantage of garden views.*

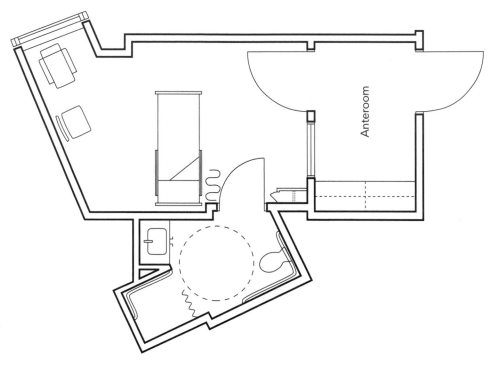

Anteroom

▶ *Patient isolation room at Arrowhead Regional Medical Center.*

answered by the specific hospital. These include the question of private versus shared patient rooms, as children often benefit from peer companionship, and questions concerning pediatric unit designations. For example, should pediatric intensive care be a separate unit, part of the pediatric unit, or integrated into adult intensive care? And should pediatric bed distributions be categorized according to age or diagnosis?

These questions often require a great deal of thought by a variety of user groups within the hospital to determine the most appropriate decisions, based on nursing models, market trends, and competitive factors. Each, however, will influence the design of the pediatric nursing unit, again reaffirming the need for overall flexibility in hospital design.

AIDS/HIV, Cancer, and Infectious Disease

In the 1980s, when acquired immunodeficiency syndrome (AIDS)/human immunodeficiency virus (HIV) became recognized as an epidemic, there was a rush to create not only AIDS inpatient units but specialized AIDS hospitals as well. However, as patients were increasingly treated in outpatient settings, the need for these units began to decline and those requiring hospitalization were admitted to various inpatient units pending the manifestations of their disease.

One of the most significant needs of these patients when they do require hospitalization is for appropriate safeguards for their often compromised immune systems.

"Immunocompromisation" is a condition experienced not only by patients with AIDS, but by many cancer patients as well, particularly those undergoing intensive chemotherapy.

Such patients are universally at risk of becoming infected by "general" contagion, let alone by increasingly common instances of infectious disease. Consequently, inpatient unit design must provide a small percentage of rooms with positive air exchanges in order to protect at-risk patients. Positive airflow means that the air pressure in the patient room is positive in relationship to the air pressure in adjacent rooms. Thus, air flows from the protected area, reducing the chances of infection not only from airborne illness but also from certain environmental elements inherent to buildings, such as mold and aspergillus, a frequent byproduct of building construction.

Other rooms requiring special air-handling mechanisms include those for patients with infectious disease. These rooms have a negative airflow (opposite to the positive airflow of the rooms described earlier), which is exhausted directly to the outside of the building. Many healthcare futurists believe that an onslaught of infectious disease, with increasing drug-resistant bacteria, may appear in the not-too-distant future and travel to and from third-world and other distant countries. We are already seeing increases in drug-resistant staph and tuberculosis, not to mention the potential for Ebola and other viruses.

To contain the spread of infectious disease, particularly in hospitals, where patients are already so vulnerable, patient units should contain rooms with negative airflow, as well as with anterooms for

visitors/staff to change clothing. In the future many rooms may be designed with the ability to be adjusted to both positive and negative pressure, allowing for flexibility but adding significantly to their costs. This will require the cooperation of code authorities and the careful attention of hospitals to the day-to-day operation of mechanical systems.

FUNCTIONAL AND SPACE PROGRAMMING ISSUES

As the forces of change continue to have an impact on healthcare delivery, the design of the hospital's inpatient areas will continue to be affected. Whereas "bigger is better" was the mode until the 1980s, reduced inpatient capacity, higher intensity of care, efficiency, and flexibility have become the new design drivers.

Hospitals designed in the 1970s and earlier have proven to be highly inefficient in the new environment of healthcare delivery. Consequently, many recent design projects have consisted of retrofitting hospital facilities in order to deliver outpatient care efficiently. The majority of today's design projects reassess initial planning assumptions, which often results in a reduced number of patient beds.

As more medical treatment was delivered on an outpatient basis, the need for inpatient beds continued to decline drastically. Overall reductions in patient lengths of stay, dictated by the more stringent reimbursement policies of managed care, furthered this decline. Managed care drove a nearly 50 percent reduction in bed need, with demand decreasing from 927 beds per 100,000 population in 1992 to 498 per 100,000 in the year 2000.

BTA's work with Cook County

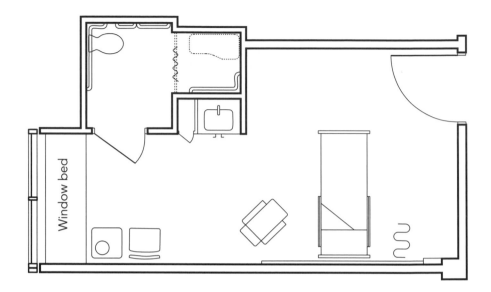

▶ *Universal patient room at Arrowhead Regional Medical Center.*

Window bed

Hospital in Chicago, Illinois, resulted in a reduction of beds in the proposed new facility from 900 to 464. The Arrowhead project reduced beds from 500 to 373, and in Salinas, California, Natividad Medical Center's replacement facility reduced beds from 219 to 163.

To promote flexibility and address the need for nursing units with increased staffing levels, patient rooms can be designed to accommodate a range of acuity levels and diagnoses. This is accomplished by designing single-bed patient rooms, sufficiently sized to accommodate increasing numbers of bedside treatments, by providing appropriate wiring for patient monitoring capabilities, by situating rooms to allow for maximum patient visibility by nursing staff, and by placing toilets on the exterior wall of the rooms. All of these elements enable patient rooms to be easily converted from general medical/surgical beds to more acute, monitored, critical, or intensive care beds.

Single-Patient Occupancy

An additional advantage to the flexible, "universal" room design is its focus on single-patient occupancy. While bed numbers have been decreasing nationwide, census rates have been increasing as the availability of beds declines. Single-bed patient rooms provide the ability to increase room utilization—from a 75 to 85 percent average to, theoretically, 100 percent. This is due to the elimination of patient "incompatibility" factors such as differences in sex, diagnoses, and disease communicability.

Furthermore, single-patient rooms enable more treatments to be administered at bedside, thus reducing the need to transport patients to procedure rooms off the unit, and can accommodate changing levels of care to be provided in one location, rather than transferring patients to different nursing units.

Finally, single-bed patient rooms give

TYPICAL DEPARTMENTAL SPACE ALLOCATION TABLE

Code	Room Name/General Quantity Component	Room Name/Specific	Quantity	Area	NSF Comments
22 General Patient Care					
22 General Patient Care - Unit 9					
22K. 10A.1	Private patient room		6	212	1,272
22K. 12A.1	Semiprivate patient room		7	250	1,750
22K. 15A.1	Isolation patient room		4	212	848
22K. 77A.1	Toilet	Patient (M/F)	17	54	918
22K. 87A.1	Anteroom		4	40	160
22K. 56A.2	Nurse substation		2	172	344 1 per 12 beds
	2 Charting				
	1 Medication				
	1 Nourishment				
	1 Sink alcove				
	1 Supply/linen				
22K. 56A.1	Nurse station		1	327	327
	6 Charting				
	1 Monitor				
	2 Viewing station				
	1 Crash cart				
	1 Pneumatic tube				
22K. 70A.2	Conference room	Team	1	140	140
	7 Conference seats				
22K. 61A.2	Workroom	Resident/student	1	120	120
22K. 83A.1	Storage	W/C stretcher	1	80	80
22K. 83A.2	Storage	Equipment	1	120	120
22K. 91A.1	Soiled utility		1	185	185
	Total Subdepartment NSF				6,264
	Total Subdepartment GSF	(conv. factor) 1.55			9,709

hospitals a competitive edge, providing more desirable "private" patient rooms, which can be personalized and offer "move in" space for patients' visitors and family members. Patient rooms increasingly include family amenities, such as pull-out beds or reclining areas for overnight stays. This has had a beneficial effect on the demands on staff. The appeal of such rooms is further enhanced by the provision of small kitchen areas, located on the nursing floors, specifically for the use of visiting family members or friends.

Design that fosters the image and delivery of "high-tech" services is countered by a new, strong focus on human elements, the classic "high-touch" counterpart to technology. Inpatient design now seeks to facilitate the creation of noninstitutional environments, fostering healing according to the concept of holistic treatment of the individual—that is, treatment of mind, body, and soul. These factors have a subtle but significant impact on space programming.

Bed Projections/Bed Need Analysis/Inpatient Support Services

Before the advent of managed care and the surge in outpatient care delivery, projections of the number of beds required were not only critical to determining the sizes of nursing units, but essential to determining the sizes of most other hospital departments as well. Today this priority has changed drastically; beds have become almost ancillary to the space required for hospital services. Department sizing is now highly dependent on outpatient visits, as well as the role of the hospital within its system

or community and its unique service demands and requirements.

Inpatient bed projections are, however, necessary to determine the anticipated sizes and types of inpatient units, again with an emphasis on flexibility, in order to accommodate changing acuity and service needs. Bed projections are derived from patient-day estimates, based on trends and demographics, market and system share, physician referrals, annual admissions, and average lengths of stay. Patient days are divided by both the total days per year and anticipated occupancy factors, determined by the type of bed (acuity level/diagnosis) and patient room type (private versus shared).

Although patient bed projections are no longer the major indicators of many ancillary department space needs, they are relevant to the requirements of certain support services, such as dietary services, admissions, housekeeping, materials management, autopsy/morgue, and certain laboratory and pharmacy requirements.

The size and type of nursing unit will determine the need for certain satellite facilities, such as a pharmacy, food heating and delivery systems, supply distribution, patient records and charting, transport systems, and imaging systems, as well as the size and shape of nursing stations and substations.

Finally, bed demand will strongly determine the role of the inpatient component of the hospital. Will demand suffice to create separate inpatient and outpatient service areas/locations for a specific service, creating sufficient work loads to justify service replication or redundancies? Will future bed demand point to new groupings of inpatient beds, creating new types of units yet to be seen?

Certainly, if we look at demographic projections pointing to significantly longer life spans and envision technologies we have not even dreamed of, the potential for new and creative inpatient unit design is remarkable.

Programming Steps

Prior to designing any nursing unit, several predesign steps must be accomplished. One of the most detailed of these steps is the development of the department space program. Space programming is a process in which the specific requirements of a department are identified, including such elements as specific room requirements and dimensions, descriptions of the department's operations and unique functional requirements, and departmental adjacency requirements as they affect operational flow.

Frequently, this phase of work also includes a preliminary cost analysis—providing an assessment of the completed project cost or costs for various options that may be developed—block floor diagrams, and work load analyses, used to determine the sizes, numbers, and types of rooms required in the future. A work load analysis ensures that the space program is created to address future needs, so that it will be able to fulfill the hospital's requirements at the time of construction completion, well in the future. Supplemental information required includes typical room layout and room criteria sheets identifying basic room layouts and requirements, an equipment inventory, and special code analyses.

A department space table is developed to identify the specific rooms and spaces required for efficient departmental

operations, based on anticipated future demands. The process is both statistical and judgmental, inasmuch as each institution is different. Space tables, developed through discussions with department managers and medical and nursing staff, should be aligned with the strategic directives of the hospital. When possible, staffing and operating simulation are utilized in planning the unit.

The space tables are organized by room/space type and function and include the specific net square foot (NSF) requirement for each room, a total NSF for all rooms constituting the department, and a department-specific conversion factor that accounts for circulation through the department.

Circulation/conversion factors average about 40 to 50 percent for most inpatient departments. Once the conversion factor is applied to the total departmental NSF, a departmental gross square footage summary (DGSF) is derived.

Total building gross square footage (BGSF) is computed for the entire building, consisting of structure, mechanical/electrical, and circulation factors, with a typical conversion factor of 25 percent added to the total DGSF of all departments.

At all hospitals a functional program is developed to describe the functional operation of the proposed facility. A functional program identifies a department's functional requirements, often including an overview of planning and design issues, relationships between departments and within each department, staffing requirements and work load/volume projections. In addition, descriptions of departmental operation and flow, along with flow diagrams, are provided.

The functional program serves as a narrative for both the architect and the future user, describing how the department is planned to operate, what constraints or directives were inherent to the planning of the department, and what the operational and work load assumptions were at the time of program development. This document is particularly important in planning nursing units, owing to the impact of critical assumptions on design. These may include, for example, assumptions regarding bed demand and utilization, types of nursing models and nurse: patient ratios, implementation of computers or other types of electronic patient monitoring, and the future role of the hospital itself within its system or specific market (i.e., tertiary hub, community hospital, teaching/research facility).

An extracted example of a recent functional program of a major teaching hospital follows.

TYPICAL FUNCTIONAL PROGRAM

General Patient Care

General patient care units provide general acute nursing care to all hospital inpatients. These units will serve all medical and surgical specialties and subspecialties, adult and pediatric. The following discusses specific operational requirements for general patient care units.

Currently, general acute care beds are dispersed throughout the hospital. The majority of general patient care beds (acute care) are located in multibed wards, designated by specialty and separated by sex. This results in reduced utilization rates, insufficient isolation

capacities, and limited flexibility to accommodate changing patient acuity levels.

Continued trends in the patient population indicate increasing inpatient acuity levels and continued high incidence rates of contagious diseases such as tuberculosis, both of which render the current configuration of patient beds insufficient for providing appropriate care. In addition, many beds within the hospital are currently utilized for observation purposes. The new hospital will contain dedicated observation beds for stays of less than 24 hours. These beds will not be located within nursing units, but in locations more proximal to their related services.

To attain maximum utilization of patient beds in the new hospital, maximum flexibility of beds is required. This will be accomplished by: (1) creating patient units that are generic rather than specially configured per specialty; (2) providing patient beds with the ability to be utilized for a range of acuity levels, via provision of adequate space and wiring for telemetry; and (3) providing sufficient numbers of single and isolation patient beds to accommodate increasing patient acuity, immunocompromization, and communicable diseases.

Intermediate care will be provided either in general patient care units or intensive care patient units. The degree of care will be determined by the type of monitoring and nursing care required. General patient care units used as intermediate care units will utilize bed telemetry monitors and can increase nurse to patient ratios to provide a higher level of care.

Pediatric patient care will be provided a distinct identity within the hospital and will include special pediatric amenities and support. The pediatric patient care units will be separate from adults units and should have good access to pediatric intensive care units and pediatric emergency.

In addition to providing flexibility, patient units should provide maximum efficiency for staff and optimum care and comfort for the patient. Consequently, nurse travel distances should be minimized, including distances from nursing stations and supply areas to patient rooms; efficient supply delivery and sufficient storage/holding areas should be provided; traffic within the patient care unit should be minimized and controlled; and patient travel off the unit should be reduced whenever possible. To achieve these objectives, the following key concepts should be implemented:

- Patient care units should be decentralized into smaller bed clusters or "pods," with two to three clusters constituting a larger unit. Each cluster will contain decentralized nursing substations, providing increased visibility of patient beds and reduced congestion at the central nurse station appropriated for the larger unit. Computerized charting will further the efficiency of this configuration, reducing the need for paper charting in the nursing station.
- A nurse server should be provided adjacent to or within each patient room in order to provide immediate access to nursing supplies. Nurse servers will be replenished by materials management staff, who will stock them from a central exchange cart holding area on each patient unit.

- Traffic on the unit should be reduced through the provision of supply holding areas adjacent to service elevators, and through the provision of sufficient space within patient rooms to accommodate multiple family members and staff. In addition, dedicated visitor waiting areas will be located central to each patient floor, reducing the number of visitors in corridors and at nursing stations.
- Providing space on patient units for frequently utilized ancillary and support services will reduce patient transport off the unit. Patient floors consisting of two to three patient units should provide sufficient space for utilization of certain ancillary and support services, such as rehabilitation therapy (PT/OT) and patient education. These "multi-purpose" rooms should be generic and utilized as needed.

Patient/work flow

The flow of patients and work must deal with the following concerns:

- The majority of patients will come to the patient care unit directly from Admitting/Bed Control. Certain patients will come to the patient care unit from Emergency, or less frequently, the Trauma Department. These patients either will have been admitted by Admitting staff located in the Emergency Department or will have been transported directly to a patient bed and admitted directly on the floor. Transfer patients (from other hospitals) will be admitted directly on the patient unit. A smaller segment of patients will be unscheduled, admitted directly on the unit from various outpatient ancillary procedure areas or observation areas.

- Once a patient is admitted to a bed, the patient's travels off the unit should be limited. Although transport to certain ancillary services will be required, many services will be provided directly on the unit, either at bedside or in general multipurpose rooms. Single-patient rooms and more spacious semiprivate rooms should enable many procedures to be provided within the patient room.

- Patient transport off the floor should be provided by a dedicated patient transport elevator.

- Visitors should be directed from the information area on the first floor of the hospital to the appropriate patient floor. A clerk/reception station on the floor will direct them to the patient rooms or to the visitor waiting area located on each floor.

- Clean supplies should be delivered via service elevator to clean utility rooms on each patient floor. An exchange cart system will be utilized, stocked on the floor by materials management staff, who will then replenish nurse servers located adjacent to patient rooms.

- Linen should be delivered by materials management staff daily, and should be collected daily from soiled utility rooms, centrally located on each patient floor.

- Trash and waste should be collected by environmental services staff from soiled utility rooms located near service elevators, central to the patient floor.

- Dietary carts will be transported to a dietary rethermalization kitchen, centrally located on each patient floor.

- Pharmaceutical supplies will be provided by pharmacy staff. An automated dispensing cart should be located on each patient unit. Stat. pharmaceutical supplies should transported via pneumatic tube.

- Laboratory specimens should be transported via pneumatic tube. A tube station should be located in each central nursing station on the unit.

- Patient records are anticipated to be fully electronic, accessed via computer.

Adjacency requirements

Space adjacencies have a major effect on the efficiency of patient care.

- Functionally similar patient units should be located adjacent to each other, or on the same floor, to accommodate shifts in census, accommodate overflow, and share equipment and staff if necessary.

- All general patient care floors should be vertically contiguous for enhanced flexibility as well as operational efficiency (i.e., supply transport).

- All general patient care units should have direct access to patient transport elevators and key ancillary services such as inpatient surgery and inpatient diagnostic imaging.

Key functional requirements

The hospital's general patient care floors should comprise three key functional areas. Patient bed clusters of approximately 10 to 12 beds should be aggregated into a standard patient care unit (20 to 24 beds), which should, in turn, be aggregated into a patient floor

(60 to 72 beds). A hierarchy of necessary support spaces should be provided at each functional level.

Patient bed clusters should be effective for the majority of nursing models and should work effectively with most general acute care nursing ratios. Patient rooms should be distributed as follows: 25 percent isolation rooms, 75 percent single-patient rooms. This distribution is planned to accommodate rising patient acuity levels as well as the increasing incidence of communicable disease. Each patient cluster should contain the following:

- *Patient room (single).* Each patient room should be sufficiently sized to accommodate increasing amounts of bedside treatments and staff administering them. Rooms should also contain sufficient space for family members or other visitors. Each patient room should contain a dedicated toilet and shower. Each room should contain a closet for patient belongings. In anticipation of increasing inpatient acuity levels, each bed should be capable of telemetry wiring in order to be used as an intermediate care bed if necessary. Visibility into the room should be provided from nursing substations outside the patient room. Because of the anticipated use of portable renal dialysis machines, special plumbing requirements should not be needed in patient rooms.

- *Patient isolation room.* Patient isolation rooms should provide the same amenities and space accommodations as general patient rooms; however, each room should contain an anteroom to the outside for contamination control. Rooms should be equipped with special air handling to prevent the spread of communicable disease. Access to the isolation room should be provided through the anteroom, following gowning procedures which will occur there. Linens and nurse servers should be located in the anteroom, allowing for supplies to be accessed without exiting the room. When not required for isolation, this room type may be used for nonisolation patients.

- *Support areas.* Each bed cluster should contain a nurse substation with space for charting, medications, nourishment, supply/linen, and hand washing. In addition, nurse servers should be provided for each patient room.

Each *patient care unit* should comprise two to three patient bed clusters and should contain the following support components:

- *Nurses' station.* A central nurses' station should include telemetry viewing if beds are monitored, pneumatic tube station, staff charting, and crash cart holding.

- *Staff support areas.* Staff support areas located on the immediate patient care unit should include dictation/viewing, team conference, resident/student workroom, and a small teaching/education room.

- *Storage/utility.* Storage areas should be provided for wheelchair/stretcher holding and general equipment. A soiled utility room should also be located on each patient care unit.

Each *patient care floor* should consist of two to three patient units and should include support that can be shared by all units on the floor. Floor support should consist of the following:

- *Waiting reception.* Visitor waiting, as well as family consultation rooms, should be centralized on the general patient care floor. Reception, information, and public flow should be controlled at an adjacent reception/clerk area.

- *Staff offices/work areas.* Staff offices for nurse managers and attending physicians should be located in a central administrative area. A multidisciplinary staff workroom should accommodate other staff participating on the care team, including social workers, dietitians, therapists, and those of other disciplines.

- *Staff support areas.* Central staff support areas should include a staff lounge, locker rooms, on-call rooms, and a teaching/education room.

- *Storage/utility.* Centralized floor storage should be provided for additional equipment and supplies. A clean utility room and a central holding room for hazardous, medical, recyclable, general waste, and soiled linen holding should be provided.

- *Multipurpose/rehabilitation therapy room.* A multipurpose room should be accessible from all patient care units on the floor for physical and occupational therapy that cannot be conducted in the patient room.

- *Kitchen.* A large kitchen for rethermalization and dietary cart holding should be located central to the floor.

Intensive/Critical Care

The intensive/critical care units include all medical and surgical specialties accommodated in coronary, medical, pediatric, surgical, neurology, burn and trauma, and neonatal intensive care units. The existing units, dispersed throughout the hospital, require additional isolation room capacity to accommodate increasing incidence of contagious and immunocompromised patients.

As with general patient care units, intensive care unit (ICU) configurations should remain consistent among units to maximize flexibility and allow for future census changes. Intermediate levels of care will be provided in either general patient care units or in intensive/critical care patient units. The degree of care will be determined primarily by the type of monitoring and nursing care required. Intensive care units should accommodate intermediate care by reducing nurse-to-patient ratios on the unit.

In addition to providing flexibility, intensive care patient units should provide maximum efficiency for staff and optimum care and comfort for the patient. Pediatric intensive care should be a distinct unit, segregated from adult areas. Pediatric intensive care units should have direct access from general pediatric patient care units, and from the pediatric emergency room.

Patient and work flow

- Patients will come to the unit either from inpatient admitting, the emergency department (including transfers), the trauma department, general or intermediate patient care units, or other ancillary services—such as surgery or cardiac catheterization departments. Because of the high acuity level of many of these patients, admission directly on the unit will be frequent, with admitting staff going to the patient room.

- Because of the acuity of these patients, transport off the unit should be limited. Any required transport will be through a dedicated patient transport elevator, equipped with emergency code buttons.

- Visitors should be directed from the information area on the first floor of the hospital to the appropriate inpatient floor. A clerk/reception station on the floor will direct them to the patient room or to the visitor waiting area centrally located on each floor.

- Clean supplies should be delivered via service elevator to clean utility rooms on each patient unit. An exchange cart system will be utilized, stocked on the patient floor by materials management staff. Materials management staff will distribute supplies from exchange carts to nurse servers located adjacent to each patient room.

- Linen should be delivered by materials management staff daily via vertical lift, and should be collected daily from soiled holding rooms.

- Trash and waste should be collected by environmental services staff from soiled utilities located near service elevators, central to the patient floor.

- Dietary carts should be held and food reheated by dietary staff in rethermalization kitchen located central to each patient floor. Carts will be transported via service elevator.

- Pharmaceutical supplies will be provided by pharmacy staff. An automated dispensing cart should be located on each patient unit.

Emergency pharmaceutical supplies should transported via pneumatic tube.

- Laboratory specimens, including those for blood gas analysis, should be transported via pneumatic tube. A tube station should be located in each patient unit nursing station.

- Patient records are accessed via computer.

Adjacency requirements

- Intensive care patient units should be located in the same area in the hospital. Functionally similar units should be located adjacent to each other or on the same floor, to be utilized for overflow and to share staff and equipment, if necessary.

- The majority of intensive care units should be directly accessible to the emergency department.

- The burn ICU should be directly adjacent to inpatient surgery for access from the burn operating room.

- The trauma ICU should be directly adjacent to trauma resuscitation for shared nursing staff.

- If possible, the trauma ICU and burn ICU should be adjacent or proximal to each other for shared staffing and to accommodate overflow.

Key functional requirements
Each intensive care unit should contain single-patient rooms, including one to two isolation rooms provided for contagious or immunocompromised patients. Each unit should contain the following:

- *Intensive care room.* Intensive care rooms should be single-patient rooms with good visibility from the nursing station. The use of breakaway glass doors should increase visibility, with curtains used when privacy is required. Rooms should contain either showers/toilets or pullout toilet. Further studies entailing mock-up rooms will be made to determine the most desirable type of toilet; to create ultimate flexibility for a "universal room" concept, consider showers. Room entrances should be sufficiently large to immediately accommodate emergency equipment and mobilizers. Because of the anticipated use of portable renal dialysis machines, special plumbing should not be needed in patient rooms.

- *Patient isolation intensive care room.* Patient isolation intensive care rooms should contain the same amenities and space requirements as general intensive care rooms, but should also contain anterooms for contagion control. Nurse servers, linen, gown, and masks should be located in the anteroom, where gowning should occur prior to entering the room. Appropriate air-handling systems should be provided.

- *Support areas.* Each patient room should contain a nurse server located adjacent to the patient room.

- *Nurses' station.* A central nurses' station should include staff charting, telemetry viewing, remote diagnostic image viewing, pneumatic tube station, and crash cart holding.

- *Staff support areas.* Staff support areas on the unit should include dictation/viewing, team conference, family consultation, staff lounge, and offices.

- *Storage/utility.* Storage areas should be provided for wheelchair/stretcher holding, general equipment, general supply, and portable X-ray (alcoves). Clean and soiled utility rooms should be provided on each unit.

Each patient care floor should consist of two to three patient units and should contain support that can be shared by all units on the floor. Floor support should consist of the following:

- *Waiting/reception.* Visitor waiting should be centralized on each patient care floor. Reception, information, and public flow should be controlled at an adjacent reception/clerk area.

- *Staff support areas.* Central staff support areas should include a staff lounge, locker rooms, on-call rooms, and a teaching/education room.

- *Storage/utility.* Centralized floor storage should be provided for additional equipment, including PT/OT and respiratory therapy equipment. Janitor closets, a clean utility room, and a soiled utility room for hazardous, medical, recyclable, and general waste should also be provided.

- *Rethermalization kitchen.* A large kitchen for meal rethermalization and dietary cart holding should be located central to each floor.

- *Burn unit.* The burn unit has special requirements, including special air handling (positive air exchange or laminar airflow), to prevent infection. In addition, this unit should contain a hydrotherapy area and gowning rooms for all staff and visitors. Rehabilitation requirements on this unit are more extensive than on other units and include additional equipment storage for physical and occupational therapy.

INTERDEPARTMENTAL RELATIONSHIPS AND DEPARTMENTAL GROUPINGS

The location of nursing units is driven by their need for support from diagnostic and treatment facilities, the link to the emergency room, the need for service and support, and the possible clustering of many units together.

As a rule, nursing units are stacked to allow for economies of construction through a simplified structure and stacking of mechanical, electrical, and plumbing systems. Complexities in stacking arise when the units are of different sizes and special studies are necessary to ensure compatibility.

The other major variables affecting location are the size of the units and the position of the nursing function in the master plan. Studies of recent units indicate that for a variety of reasons, primarily economic, nursing units of this era tend to be larger, creating "superfloors" (i.e., floors of 70–120 beds) of many nursing units.

Often the design of a nursing unit or tower of units is severely affected by the master plan. Because hospitals continue to evolve and are always to considered incomplete, the ability to simply tie into a single vertical service core is critical. Hospitals can look at the strategy developed at Valley Presbyterian Hospital, which allowed it to grow from 63 to 360 beds with three towers in a 15-to-20-year period (see pages 142–143).

INTERNATIONAL CHALLENGES

The variations in international culture, economy, governmental role in healthcare delivery, insurance, technology, service, and demography make the design of inpatient units difficult in countries outside the United States. Although most nations aspire to the levels of design of contemporary American hospitals, one can see similarities only in the most economically developed countries. In these countries variations are minor, with the exception of the use of single-bed rooms. Most of these countries still

OPTIMAL STAFFING/SERVICE RATIOS										
Position / Service										Annual Cost / Unit*
Nursing team (11.5 FTEs)	$10,000/bed		$10,000/bed							$348,714
Clerk		$640/bed								23,500
Nurse manager		$1,040/bed								50,000
Pharmacist					$1,000/bed					80,000
X-ray technician				$625/bed						37,500
Phlebotomist			$790/bed							39,500
Therapist		$880/bed					$630/bed			39,500
Food service										19,000
Supply distribution										23,000

	20	30	40	50	60	70	80	90	100	
		Maximum utility		Number of beds Optimal Range						*1997 data

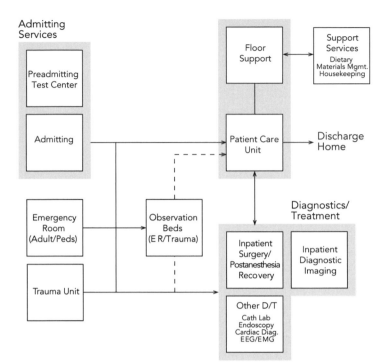

Admitting Services

Preadmitting Test Center

Admitting

Emergency Room (Adult/Peds)

Observation Beds (E R/Trauma)

Trauma Unit

Floor Support

Support Services
Dietary
Materials Mgmt.
Housekeeping

Patient Care Unit

Discharge Home

Diagnostics/ Treatment

Inpatient Surgery/ Postanesthesia Recovery

Inpatient Diagnostic Imaging

Other D/T
Cath Lab
Endoscopy
Cardiac Diag.
EEG/EMG

▲ Interdepartmental relationship diagram (BTA).

provide care in multibed settings.

In the economically developed countries, notably in western Europe and parts of Asia and the Middle East, the factor that differentiates them most is the ability to provide service (and maintenance) for complex technological systems.

In many developing cultures, economic concerns may keep design at a level experienced in this country earlier in the twentieth century. Cultural differences are also evident. In some countries the role of the entire family must be accounted for in the development of space for nursing units. Families often stay with sick relatives, cook in their rooms, and provide much of the care to support the understaffed facilities. Thus, spatial requirements must be adjusted.

In countries where air-conditioning is not possible, the design of the units reverts back to long, narrow wings to allow for through ventilation.

In many Islamic countries, separation of the sexes must also be accounted for, not only in providing separate accommodations but in preventing views from wing to wing.

The ability to provide immediate backup support for technological elements is a further challenge to the designer. Many projects built in the Middle East were unusable in their early development until they had backup systems and staff to service the complex technology.

DETAILED TECHNICAL ISSUES

Structural Issues

In California, because of the recent Loma Prieta and Northridge earthquakes, a new replacement policy has been established for all structures housing inpatients. To be phased in over 30 years, this will require all facilities to remain operational after an 8.0 earthquake. The only large hospital designed to that standard and operating at the time of publication with that technology is San Bernardino County's Arrowhead Regional Medical Center, designed by Bobrow/Thomas Associates, Executive and Design Architects in association with Perkins and Will.

Building structure

In considering the structural system for a facility devoted to inpatient care, it is important to select a column grid that will accommodate the narrow dimension of the patient room. A 30 ft square module will typically allow two patient rooms between column lines. For some

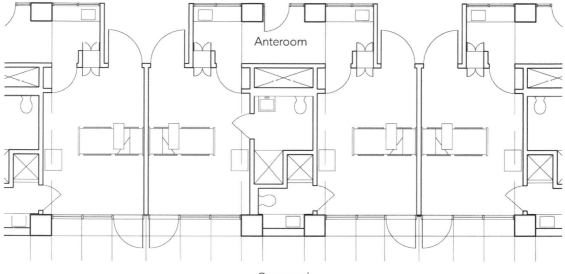

Anteroom

Courtyard

rooms (LDRs, for example) a slightly larger module may be better, dictating this grid throughout the building. Alternatively, LDR rooms can be oriented differently, with the long dimension against the outside wall.

The building structure, typically, is steel frame or reinforced concrete. Steel frame construction, fireproofed, is most common in seismically active areas. A steel frame can be either moment resisting or braced. For braced frames, the plan layout will have to contend with location of cross-bracing, which limits future flexibility. For moment-resisting construction, special welded connections are required at beam-to-column intersections. Moment frame construction is therefore more expensive.

Concrete construction is also common throughout most of the country. Concrete construction may also consist of moment-resisting frames or, more commonly, may include shear walls,

which, like cross-bracing, will limit flexibility. Floor construction may be flat slab or may include concrete joists.

Because of the need to withstand seismic forces and remain operational after a major earthquake, some inpatient facilities are now being designed with base isolation. This relatively new technology places isolation media between the columns of the building and its foundation, diminishing the effect of ground movement. Base-isolated buildings suffer less internal shaking in a major earthquake, lessening damage to buildings systems.

Designed on 380 base isolators with horizontal viscous dampers, as well as other technology to allow for a movement range of 8 ft, the Arrowhead Center is a model that will be studied for future projects. Although California is far ahead with seismic design, other parts of the country along the Pacific plate and in the Midwest may find this a driving force

▲ Bone marrow replacement therapy room at City of Hope National Medical Center.

in redesign. This is an opportunity for many hospitals to change the structure of future facilities into a contemporary model where ambulatory care is a dominant component and inpatient care is reduced but far more intense in services and care.

Safety Issues

Even as hospitals change, the inpatient component must still be licensed. The design of hospitals, including the inpatient components, is among the most code regulated of any building design type. Because these buildings directly affect the health and welfare of people, they are licensed by each state and must meet minimum requirements for both operation and construction. Designers must comply with the individual state licensing regulations.

In addition, the inpatient facility is considered to be an "essential building," which must be able to continue in operation despite local disasters. Therefore, it must meet higher standards for structural safety and for preventing the interruption of mechanical and electrical services. In California, for example, the structural resistance of essential facilities to the ground motion of earthquakes must be significantly stronger than that required for conventional buildings. There are specific code requirements for provision of emergency power supply, as well as priorities for electrical services that must be on emergency power.

Inpatient units must also meet life safety requirements, which are conditioned on the presumption that bedridden patients may not be able to exit the building on foot. Codes require that floors occupied by patients

be divided approximately equally into two or more separate smoke compartments, which are sealed off from each other with fire-rated smoke partitions including combination fire/smoke dampers in the HVAC ducts. In the event of fire, patients from one smoke compartment can be wheeled, in hospital beds, into the adjacent smoke compartment to await rescue. Because of the prospect of moving patients in beds, corridors are required to be a minimum of 8 ft in width, and cross-corridor doors between smoke compartments are required to allow passage in either direction.

Because inpatient facilities treat patients who receive reimbursement under Medicare, they must meet federal government standards in addition to state and local requirements. If accredited, they must also meet the standards of, and are subjected to, inspections by the Joint Commission on the Accreditation of Healthcare Organizations (JCAHO). Generally, the federal government, through the Healthcare Finance Administration (HCF), and JCAHO refer to the National Fire Protection Association (NFPA) model codes, including the *Standard for Health Care Facilities (NFPA 99)* and the *Life Safety Code (NFPA 101)*.

Another essential source for understanding the code requirements for inpatient units, and an excellent design reference, is *Guidelines for Design and Construction of Hospital and Health Care Facilities*. Published every two years by the American Institute of Architects Academy of Architecture for Health, with assistance from the U.S. Department of Health and Human Services, the *Guidelines* is referenced directly by many states as a model code. For states that publish a stand-alone code, such as California, the organization of the code sections that apply to inpatient units is similar to that of the *Guidelines*. It is essential, however, to understand the state and local codes that apply to a particular site, to acknowledge from the outset of design that there will be conflicts between the various codes that apply, and to proactively work with code authorities to seek clarification.

In addition to the codes that govern health and life safety, the Americans with Disabilities Act (ADA) also affects the design of inpatient units. The accessibility guidelines included in the ADA acknowledge the special nature of hospitals by not requiring universal access. For general purpose hospitals, psychiatric facilities, and detoxification facilities, the guidelines indicate that 10 percent of patient rooms and adjoining toilets must be accessible. For long-term care facilities, 50 percent of patient rooms and adjoining toilets must be accessible, and for hospitals and rehabilitation facilities that treat conditions affecting mobility, 100 percent of patient rooms and toilets must be accessible. Other than the exceptions indicated for patient rooms and adjoining toilets, an entire inpatient facility must be accessible, in accordance with the ADA guidelines.

Mechanical Systems

Heating, ventilation, and air-conditioning (HVAC) systems must be designed to achieve patient comfort and energy efficiency. They must also accommodate the heat loads produced and environmental conditions required by sophisticated medical equipment.

Because inpatient units are usually within large structures and are often part of a larger campus of healthcare facilities, services are frequently provided from a central plant. Systems that utilize hot water or steam from central boilers and chilled water from central absorption refrigeration units are usually more energy-efficient than those that include boilers and chillers in dedicated spaces for particular buildings. The decision on whether to have a central plant directly affects the amount of space required in either the central plant or a new building and has implications for cost and master planning for routing piping throughout the campus.

Air for heating, cooling, and ventilation is supplied via supply and return ducts from air-handling units. Codes require ducted return in order to control exhaust and filtration. Variable air volume (VAV) boxes are permitted as a means to control air distribution to individual registers, as long as a supply of air is always provided in inpatient areas to meet minimum ventilation standards.

The location of fan rooms is a design issue that relates to building flexibility. Placement of air-handling units in fan rooms on each floor, as was done at Arrowhead Regional Medical Center, allows changes to be made on one floor without affecting the entire building. Air-handling units, potential sources of noise and vibration, should be placed on isolation pads, and the rooms in which they are placed require acoustical treatment.

For most spaces in inpatient facilities, air return is via a common path of connected air ducts returning to the air-handling unit for filtration (using 90 percent efficient HEPA filters for most spaces and 99.97 percent efficient HEPA filters for protective environment rooms) and recirculation. Outside air, to meet minimum requirements, is also introduced into the system at the air-handling unit.

With increased concern for patients with compromised immune systems and patients with contagious diseases, recent code changes have required the creation of protective environment rooms and airborne infection isolation rooms. In a protective environment room, the pressure relationship to surrounding rooms is positive, and air entering the room is protected with 99.97 percent efficient HEPA filters. In an airborne infection isolation room, the pressure relationship to surrounding rooms is negative, and all air is exhausted directly to the outdoors.

The design of rooms for these patients involves the use of an anteroom, which functions as an airlock between the patient room and the surrounding spaces. The proposed plan for patient rooms at the City of Hope National Medical Center, where patients undergo bone marrow replacement therapy, illustrates the use of one anteroom shared by every two patient rooms. The pressure relationship of the patient rooms to the anteroom shared is positive, and all air is exhausted from the anteroom directly to the outdoors. The large doors leading directly into the patient rooms are used only when the patients are first admitted. Nurses and doctors enter and exit the patient rooms via the anteroom.

In designing the inpatient building, the location of outdoor air intakes must be carefully considered to avoid local sources of pollution (for example, heavy automobile traffic) and to separate intake and exhaust fans. Indoor air quality should be a major determinant in the

architectural design, as well as in the design of the HVAC systems. Materials should be selected to avoid products that give off unacceptable levels of volatile organic compounds (VOCs).

In addition to special HVAC requirements, mechanical design includes special plumbing requirements, which involves the provision of piped medical gases. These normally include oxygen, vacuum, and medical air. In surgery nitrogen (for running equipment) and nitrous oxide (for anesthesia) are normally used as well. Because the anesthesia gases used today are not explosive, there is no longer a requirement for nonconductive flooring in the operating room. Medical gas systems will have to be zoned, with zone alarms near nurses' stations or other normally staffed locations. Zoning allows the isolation of portions of the system if there is a fault, without taking down the whole system. Medical gas systems are subject to testing and certification during construction by an independent testing agency, as a cross-check to make sure that outlets are installed correctly. With the use of gases in surgery comes the requirement for separate exhaust of waste gases, to protect operating room personnel. This is accomplished through the use of a scavenger system—a vacuum system that exhausts waste anesthesia gas when the patient exhales. It keeps the breath of the patient from infecting medical staff and/or keeps anesthesia gases out of the general atmosphere of the operating room.

Vertical transportation is also a key mechanical design element for inpatient facilities. Elevators should be grouped for efficiency and located in cores that work together with the overall circulation scheme to allow separation of visitor, patient, and staff/service circulation. The location of the elevator core should also take into account future expansion, wayfinding, and other master plan issues.

Special elevators outside the main elevator cores are frequently necessary. Examples include oversized cars that connect surgery directly to emergency room trauma units or to intensive care units. Patients can be moved in these elevators while on stretchers, surrounded by medical staff, and connected to monitors, IVs, and medical gases. Special elevators or hoists (dumbwaiters) are also frequently used to connect central processing, where surgical equipment is sterilized, directly to the surgery suite. In this case there will usually be a "clean" elevator for sterile supplies and carts and a "dirty" elevator for soiled instruments and carts.

Pneumatic tube systems are frequently included in inpatient units. Pneumatic tubes, which were formerly used primarily for movement of forms and records, are now mostly used for pharmaceuticals and for blood samples. The recent development of "soft landing" pneumatic tube systems has made this practical, and increasing use of electronic media has made the movement of paper less critical.

Electrical/Communications Systems

Electrical systems for inpatient units are required to provide power to maintain critical operations even if the local power source is disrupted. Emergency power generation with an adequate supply of on-site fuel is required by code. In addition, in planning for hospital construction and expansion, redundant

supply from the power company on two separate feeders, ideally from two separate main transformer locations, is a good idea. In the event of a power failure, automatic transfer switches shift loads from the local power to generators in a manner of seconds. However, for some critical functions, such as physiological monitoring, an uninterruptible power system (UPS) may also be required.

The electrical code specifies which inpatient care services (the most critical) must be restored first, and which functions can be restored with some time lapse. Today's code does not require all functions to be on emergency power; however, the facility may elect to increase generator capacity to keep more services up and running. For example, it may be wise to put elevators on emergency power even if this is not required by the particular jurisdiction.

Communications systems in inpatient units include conventional voice (telephone, intercom), nurse call, data network, and many specialty applications such as picture archiving and communications systems (PACS) for the transmission of radiographic images. In addition to internal staff and patient communications, an inpatient facility also includes electronic systems that actuate controls for the HVAC and lighting systems and provide fire alarm, fire protection, and building security functions.

A recent trend in the design of inpatient facilities is the specification of the many electronic systems components with a standards-based interface so that they can electronically communicate with each other, electronically report to a building management system computer, and, most important, share a common networking infrastructure, or cable network backbone. This creates an integrated building system (IBS), which has the benefit of reducing the number of different types of cabling as well as the overall amount of cable. For the shared backbone to be successful, bandwidth must be adequate.

Currently, Category 5 copper wire can be used for most applications; however, fiber optics are required for high-volume uses, such as imaging. Anticipating the continued future growth in required bandwidth, one possibility is to install hollow tubes to future outlets. At any time in the future, fiber can be blown to the outlet locations (using liquid nitrogen). This has a first-cost premium but might be worthwhile for flexibility.

Another factor influencing flexibility is the sizing and location of communications rooms. These should not be combined with electrical rooms, and they should be large enough to allow for future expansion or should be located adjacent to soft space into which they can be expanded. Ideally, communications rooms should be stacked, one floor above the other, to minimize bends in fiber-optic trunks. The maximum distance from each communications room to a data outlet is today 300 ft. For large floor plates, this may dictate more than one communications room on each floor.

A growing amount of inpatient information is being assembled electronically. Currently, inpatient facilities are installing systems for the electronic retrieval of medical records and X-ray images. There is also a trend toward fully electronic charting, although currently a combination of paper and computer records is not unusual. Nurse call systems are also becoming more

sophisticated, including the use of remote paging devices that allow the nurse to receive calls and communicate away from the nurses' station. In addition, telemetry for physiological monitoring is also becoming routine. This allows an expectant mother, for example, to walk the corridors of the nursing unit while still in communication with a fetal monitor, instead of being confined to her room.

With the pace of technological change at its current rapid rate, and with the long development time (five to seven years) for a major inpatient building, it makes sense to defer some of the systems selection decisions until well into the development process. This requires the design of a system infrastructure that is flexible enough to adapt to the last-minute selection of systems, which in turn allows the inpatient unit to take advantage of advances in technology.

Special Equipment

Planning for the required medical equipment is a key part of the design of any inpatient unit. Equipment can range from major imaging and treatment devices, costing millions of dollars, to small rolling stock such as instrument carts in an operating room. Equipment planning usually groups individual items into categories: Group I, major fixed equipment; Group II, major movable equipment with electrical, mechanical, and electrical service requirements; and Group III, minor movable equipment such as carts, stands, and so forth, with no service requirements. Coordinating the budgeting, selection, and purchasing of equipment is a major task. Of particular concern to the architect is the assembly

MEDICAL CENTER: ENGINEERING ALTERNATIVES AND COSTS

Item No.	Description	In Current Plans	Area (sq ft)	Cost/sq ft	Current scope in base estimate	Current scope, new (not in base estimate)	Current scope, remodel (not in base estimate)	Potential additions or alternatives (not in base estimate)	Comments
	Building Scope:								
1.1	Reduction in shell space with increase in clinics/support	Yes	3,882	$80		$310,560			
1.2	Cardiac cath lab at former residents' sleep rooms, level 3	No	2,131	$90				$191,790	Without equipment
1.3	Physical therapy space at Extended Care	Yes	800	$169	$135,2C0				Did not increase building area
1.4	Resident's lounge/workroom at remodel area	Yes	1,300	$52					
1.5	Connector corridor to south of existing dietary	Yes	2,000	$110			$220,000		
1.6	New lobby and exterior stairs at conference entry	Yes	300	$90			$27,000	$67,600	
	Building Construction/Finish:								
2.1	Precast architectural concrete exterior @ Family Center	No	9,800	$16				$156,800	
2.2	Upgrade of architectural finishes:								
2.2.1	Sheet vinyl flooring in lieu of VCT @ Extended Care	No	8.68	$2				$17,360	
2.2.2	50% Vinyl wall covering in lieu of paint @ Extended Care	No	25,872	$3				$77,616	
2.3	Skylights at 2nd floor waiting areas	Yes	8	$1,000		$8,000			Per 4' x 8' unit
2.4	Higher precast walls at Central Plant	Yes	2,212	$25		$54,194			

of equipment information needed for engineering coordination.

For the largest equipment items, coordination usually occurs directly with the equipment vendor, who prepares the installation drawings. Linear accelerators, which are used for cancer treatment, require thick walls and ceilings for radiation shielding. These devices must also be located at the lowest occupied building level (ground floor or basement) to eliminate the need for (expensive) radiation shielding below the equipment. Magnetic resonance imaging (MRI) units require extensive radiofrequency shielding and a ground floor location. MRI units need controlled access to ensure that metal objects are not brought within the magnetic field.

Radiology departments require coordination of complex imaging equipment. Areas of technology that are currently undergoing great expansion include cardiac catheterization, electrophysiology, and interventional radiology. The line between diagnostic and interventional procedures is becoming less strict, with the prospect that traditional imaging rooms will take on some of the characteristics of surgery and surgical operating rooms will increasingly include imaging capabilities.

Acoustics

Acoustic control in the inpatient unit is important to the well-being of both patients and staff. Walls between patient rooms, as well as offices and examination rooms, should provide acoustic privacy. Partitions between these spaces should have a sound transmission class (STC) of 45. In addition, isolation of vibration from mechanical equipment and the prevention of noise from pipes, elevators, and other building services is essential.

For some areas within the inpatient facility, special acoustic standards apply. One of these areas is the neonatal intensive care unit, or special care nursery. Recent research in the developmental pattern of preterm infants indicates the importance of maintaining a quiet environment in the nursery. The noise level within these areas should never exceed 50 decibels.

Acoustic control will at times conflict with other requirements, including the cleanability of interior surfaces. Some areas will be required to have ceilings that are washable and, hence, not acoustically treated. Floors may have to be of sheet vinyl rather than carpet. The design and selection of components such as acoustic wall panels and furniture may in some cases be used to compensate for hard surfaces in the room.

Key Cost Factors

As in the design of any building, key decisions early in the project will have a great influence on the cost of the inpatient facility. Among these are selection of the site, including the extent to which existing buildings impede construction activity, the extent of demolition required, utilities that may have to be relocated, and soils and geologic conditions. Other key decisions include selection of the basic structural system, mechanical and electrical system types, and exterior envelope criteria.

Initially, the most important step is setting an appropriate quality level for the project. This will require discussions with the client concerning the budget target as well as the client's own preconceptions about what the building should be. Healthcare construction costs vary by

MEDICAL CENTER: BUDGET RECAPITULATION

Budgeted Line Item	April 30, 1999 Master Plan	Adjusted Total Budget Aug. 27, 1999 BTA	Preliminary Schematic Estimate Sep. 17, 1999	Schematic Estimate Oct. 5, 1999 BTA	DRAFT Design Dev. Estimate Jan. 27, 2000 BTA
1 Construction cost	$38,642,169	$45,149,000	$44,629,567	$45,584,023	$48,961,027
2 Site development	$2,773,000	$2,773,000	$4,500,000	$4,644,442	$4,859,450
3 Design contingency	$6,212,275	$2,575,000	$1,785,183	$2,009,139	$1,942,441
4 Subtotal (1+2+3)	$47,627,444	$50,497,000	$50,914,750	$52,237,604	$55,762,918
5 Escalation (June 2000)	$4,411,444	$1,800,000	1,740,806	1,828,316	1,123,626
6 Site construction cost (4+5)	$52,038,888	$52,297,000	$52,655,556	$54,065,920	$56,886,544
7 Furniture, fixtures & equipment (F.F.& E)	$7,961,545	$7,960,000	$7,419,944	$7,960,000	$7,960,000
8 Construction contingency (3%)	$0	$2,345,000	$2,345,000	$2,345,000	0
9 Owner Contingency (2% of line 1)	$0	$2,265,000	$2,265,000	$2,265,000	$2,448,051
10 Subtotal (7+8+9)	$7,961,545	$12,570,000	$12,029,944	$12,570,000	$10,408,051
11 Subtotal construction + F.F. & E. (6+10)	$60,000,433	$64,867,000	$64,685,000	$66,635,920	$67,291,497
12 Permits/Testing/OSHPD/I.O.R.	$1,088,000	$1,088,000	$1,088,000	$1,088,000	$1,088,000
13 Fees (A&E, A&E Reimb., CM, CM Reimb.)	$6,717,833	$5,630,000	$5,630,000	$4,920,688	$5,100,000
14 Subtotal (12+13)	$7,805,833	$6,718,000	$6,718,000	$6,008,688	$6,188,000
15 Subtotal grand total (11+14)	$67,806,266	$71,585,000	$71,403,500	$72,644,608	$73,479,497
16 Site development bldg. relocation	$6,225,000	$3,745,000	$3,745,000	$2,045,000	$2,045,000
17 Total cost (15+16)	$74,031,266	$75,330,000	$75,148,500	$74,689,608	$75,524,497
18 Family Center	$1,275,000	$1,050,000	$1,231,500	$1,690,392	$1,673,439
19 Financing	$7,093,733	$6,020,000	$6,020,000	$6,020,000	$6,020,000
20 Total project cost (17+18+19)	$82,400,000	$82,400,000	$82,400,000	$82,400,000	$83,217,936
20A - Total project cost overage - to be reduced:					$817,936

Addendum - medical office building:	Concept 12/9/99
21 Construction cost with contingency & escalation	$5,117,171
22 Site development	$200,000
23 Fees (A&E, A&E Reimb.)	$270,000
24 Contingency (10% of Line 51)	$511,717
25 Total cost, MOB (21+22+23+24)	$6,098,888
26 Grand total project cost (20+25)	$89,316,824

Medical center areas (Building gross sq ft)

	April 30, 1999 Master Plan	Adjusted Total Budget Aug. 27, 1999 BTA	Preliminary Schematic Estimate Sep. 17, 1999	Schematic Estimate Oct. 5, 1999 BTA	DRAFT Design Dev. Estimate Jan. 27, 2000 BTA
New hospital building (OSHPD) T1	173,635	179,048	186,844	184,435	186,468
Existing hospital renovation (OSHPD)	23,400	20,855	23,136	23,136	23,136
Outpatient - serv. (non-OSHPD)T2	40,000	57,902	68,109	69,000	69,000
Administration/support (non-OSHPD) T2	31,161	35,853	30,000	31,200	29,952
Extended Care/rehab (OSHPD) T2	25,413	23,540	22,933	23,847	24,545
Generator building					3,437
Subtotal area	293,609	317,198	331,022	331,618	336,538
Family Center	7,000	7,319	9,852	13,365	13,802
Total Area	300,609	324,517	340,874	344,983	350,340

region, with a premium for inpatient unit construction in seismically active areas. Currently, construction costs range between $200 and $300 per square foot, depending on the complexity of space provided and the quality level selected.

In managing an inpatient facility project, the architect must keep in mind that construction cost is one component of the overall project cost. It is useful to establish with the client and/or construction manager a cost budget for all categories. Once the cost budget is

established, it can be monitored, with updated estimates at each design phase, and adjustments made to keep the overall project cost in line. An example of the cost budget by categories for a recent inpatient facility project is shown in the table on page 189. As of the most recent phase, a budget shortfall has been identified. To bring the project in on target, value engineering ideas were offered to the client, as shown in the table on page 187. Only by closely monitoring costs at each stage of design can budget control be maintained.

TRENDS, INCLUDING REUSE AND RETROFIT

Health System Trends and Indicators for Inpatient Design

With the rapid changes in healthcare delivery, the impact on inpatient care is significant and constantly evolving. The following are some of the trends and indicators affecting nursing unit design today:

Increasing levels of care for patients

Increasing utilization of home health/subacute care/skilled nursing units

Increasingly elderly population with multiple diagnoses/illnesses

Increasing utilization of computerized/bedside charting

Increasing provision of treatments at bedside

Increasing integration of family members as caregivers

Increasing focus on patient education/information

Increasing focus on patient ambulation

Increasing utilization of ICUs for surgical recovery, bypassing postanesthesia recovery

▼ *California State University, Channel Islands (BTA; formerly the Camarillo State Developmental Hospital).*

Increasing potential for infectious disease and/or immune-compromised patients

Questionable success of cross-training

Questionable success of patient-centered care approach to increasing ancillary services on the patient unit

Changing types of nursing care/support (decreasing licensed vocational nurse/registered nurse levels)

Increasing utilization of electronic information and delivery (e.g., tube systems and digital radiography)

Increasing emphasis on patient-focused care and treating the person vs. the disease

Adaptive Reuse of Hospitals

The reuse of hospitals for purposes other than healthcare is the subject of increasing discussion, given the overbedding of hospitals and unnecessary duplication of hospital facilities. This becomes increasingly important as inpatient utilization declines and more procedures are done on an outpatient basis in clinics and doctors' offices.

There have been a multitude of suggestions for the reuse of hospitals. Actual transformations to other uses have included an art college on the East Coast, the reuse of a psychiatric long-term hospital as a state university in California, and a number of hospitals converted to single-room-occupancy housing.

SUMMARY

Because change is a constant force in design, today's designs must acknowledge that what is built for today is not permanent and will at some point become a candidate for reuse, retrofit, or removal. Therefore, the need for a comprehensive master plan that provides an "arrow" into the future is necessary. Hospital planning at its highest level recognizes this open-ended indeterminacy and creates a conceptual structure for this change.

It is to be expected that inpatient care will change and in many cases disappear. There is a need to create nursing units today that are adaptable to major change through the use of flexible long-span structures, with vertical service systems pulled out of the core to leave the floor plate as free as possible for change.

Trends indicate that virtually all patients in the future who are housed in acute care hospitals will require a level of care close to intensive care, with sophisticated monitoring. The rooms must be designed today as "universal rooms" to allow for this evolution.

Although construction of replacement nursing units is often questioned because of initial costs and the difficulty of financing, the solution to that dilemma is in the design of an efficiently staffed unit. The cost of construction is but a small part of the cost of the daily operation of a hospital. Over the lifetime of a building, construction costs have averaged only 6 percent of operating expenditures. It can be demonstrated (in todays dollars) that the savings of one nursing staff member or equivalently salaried employee can save one million dollars in construction costs. The reductions in staff possible with new construction of efficient units can often pay for the unit.

Thus, the challenge to architects and hospitals is to create nursing units that are most efficient for today's operation, are flexible enough to adapt to the unknown needs of tomorrow, and provide a humanizing architecture that can be a positive contributor to the healing process.

CHAPTER 4

AMBULATORY CARE FACILITIES

THOMAS M. PAYETTE *Payette Associates Inc.*

INTRODUCTION

At the turn of the century, Charles and William Mayo developed concepts for healthcare delivery involving interdisciplinary physician cooperation for comprehensive care. Their vision laid the foundation for the ambulatory care industry that is thriving today. Combining the centralization of resources found in traditional hospitals with the individualized attention of a country doctor's practice, the Mayo Clinic gained renown for systematically and sympathetically dealing with patients and their various aliments. Patients would come from around the country to the clinic with the assurance that their problems could be diagnosed and treated better at the Mayo Clinic than at any local facility. The influence of this system has reached far beyond the clinic's earliest treatment rooms in Rochester, Minnesota; it has shaped healthcare delivery around the world.

The Mayo Clinic and the other ambulatory facilities that followed drew strongly on the practice of the clinics traditionally affiliated with medical schools, in which prospective doctors gained experience by applying the diagnosis and treatment methods learned in their classes through treating the poor. Though amenities in these facilities were few, their appeal was that patients could have many of their healthcare needs addressed in one place, and the clinics could spare the expenses incurred by private practices (where examination and treatment rooms were suited to a single doctor's preferences and procedures).

With the advent of the health maintenance organization (HMO) and the centralization and sharing of resources it fostered, the demand for such facilities grew. The HMOs, which were conceived as a method of providing total healthcare for the beneficiaries of large corporations (such as the Kaiser group, whose HMO Kaiser Permanente is still widely used in the western United States), were understandably interested in efficiently providing quality care for a variety of needs and clientele. Since the companies were investing in all of their workers' health, managed care dissolved many earlier distinctions in care between rich managers and poorer laborers. As a result, the basic clinics were gradually enhanced to provide greater privacy and comfort to the patients while retaining an interdisciplinary approach to patient care.

This history has greatly influenced the design decisions for ambulatory care facilities. The success of these new centers in a highly competitive healthcare industry depends on design that is both cost-effective and innovative enough to attract and retain customers. Increasingly, architects are asked to structure spaces for effective staffing and the particular medical requirements of individual centers, as well as for aesthetic appeal. While each example chosen for inclusion in this chapter illustrates specific design solutions relevant to its respective focus, there are numerous design implications inherent in all facilities. The following are key factors facing the design of today's ambulatory care centers:

Site Planning

Though ambulatory care centers are intended to serve ambulatory patients—those who can arrive and leave with little or no assistance—there is still a wide range of mobility among the patients. Access and convenience factors such as the following are therefore important in the siting and layout of these facilities.

- Convenient parking and drop-off are essential to a successful ambulatory care center.
- Patients should not have to endure lengthy traveling time in and out of a building.
- Drop-off areas should be covered.
- Handicapped access should be provided.

Relationship to hospitals

Because ambulatory care centers are often located on hospital campuses, care should be taken in siting to meet the needs of the entire hospital community. The following are overall design considerations:

- Ancillary services at the hospital, such as lab and radiology, should be in close proximity to the ambulatory care center.
- Physicians should be able to travel between inpatient and outpatient environments with ease.
- Provision should be made for ease of access for staff and patients to both inpatient and outpatient areas.

Circulation

Physician offices

Ambulatory care centers often include physician offices. These should be grouped so that they are accessible to both patients and clinical departments. The less time a physician spends traveling between clinical areas and offices, the greater the cost efficiencies and the better the patient service.

Staffing operations

Efficient staffing operations are critical to the delivery of patient care, as well as to cost containment. Work areas need to be laid out to accommodate staff utilization. For example, nurses' stations can be designed to handle periods of high patient volume and multiple shifts. They should be oriented with sight lines to patients to monitor treatment and recovery. Operating, recovery, and treatment rooms should be standardized so they can be used by all staff and physicians for the full range of treatment. They should be equipped with appropriate instruments and supplies and designed with staff efficiency as a guiding principle.

Patient/family education

An important aspect of ambulatory care is providing patients and families with information about diagnosis and treatment. Many ambulatory care centers now house educational resource areas, including books, videos, and accommodation for seminars. These resources can translate into large program requirements such as libraries, conference rooms, and telecommunications wiring. Educational resource areas may be integrated into other existing spaces, such as lobbies or waiting areas.

Support services

Comprehensive ambulatory care centers may include services not directly linked to clinical procedures. Complementary services, such as pharmacies, day care, medical equipment and fitness retail areas, and dining facilities, may be included in the building program. Placement of such services should correspond with use; central lobbies, corridors, or atriums are good choices.

Wayfinding

Easily finding his or her way once inside the building helps the patient overcome fear and anxiety. Consider the following in planning an ambulatory care center:

- Place registration and/or information desks close to the front door for immediate visibility.

- Provide thorough signage in lobbies, at corridor intersections, and at elevator lobbies.

- Use natural light to give patients a sense of bearings. Visitors will remember naturally lit areas, whether clerestories, windows overlooking nature, or simply areas with borrowed light.

- Other amenities, such as water (aquariums, waterfalls, fountains), artwork (sculpture, paintings, display cases), donor recognition walls, and architectural details, all serve as good interior landmarks, helping patients to find their way through the typical myriad of corridors, departments, and waiting areas and thus increasing patient comfort.

HVAC/Electrical Considerations

The primary concerns in designing for climate control are patient and staff comfort, energy efficiency, and cost. Consider the following steps in designing HVAC/electrical systems:

- The exterior building skin should be designed to prevent the outside heat

and cold from reaching the interiors. A concern in hot climates is mildew from condensation on the interior of heavily cooled spaces. Sun shading of openings is cost-effective. In cold climates, heated vestibules should be located at main building entries.

- Recirculate air where allowable.

- Zone the building according to environmental requirements, grouping, for example, heavily conditioned/filtered spaces together. Perimeter corridors offer a double buffer zone, providing privacy and protection from undesired environmental factors.

Interior Design

The interiors of ambulatory care environments play a key role in providing patient comfort and reducing anxiety and help differentiate them from typical inpatient facilities. The following considerations should be made in designing interior spaces:

- Furnishings and finishes should carry a nonclinical tone.

- Furnishings should be placed to accommodate patients and families and afford privacy.

- Furnishings, finishes, and fixtures should be easy to maintain and durable.

- The use of color is important to enliven spaces.

- Provide natural light and views to nature.

- Incorporate artwork in public and treatment spaces for visual relief.

- Special features, such as music and water, help visitors to find solace during periods of stress.

Cultural Considerations

The local culture may be an important consideration in the design of healthcare buildings, especially in international contexts. Common issues include:

- Historic development of the locale, which may influence building type (high rise towers, freestanding clinics, commercial integration).

- Privacy.

- Separation of male and female spaces.

- Accommodation of families, entourages and retainers.

- Variations in medical practice, depending upon physicians' background and training.

- Indigenous diseases, which may require larger facilities to accommodate a high volume of patients.

Anticipating the Future

Healthcare delivery is rapidly changing. As the shift to ambulatory care continues, architecture will need to respond to the following likely developments:

- new, advanced methods of healthcare delivery

- new technologies

- changes in healthcare reimbursement

- changing social and environmental issues

Specific architectural requirements may be imposed by the following developments:

- The use of patient "smart cards" and bedside computers for patient records, necessitating special cabling and code conformance (trenches in floors or ceilings).

- Teleconferencing among hospitals, ambulatory care centers, and research institutions, requiring specialized equipment and building infrastructure.

- New medical equipment requiring additional space for use, storage, circulation, and maintenance.

- Healthcare reimbursement continuing to shape costs. Attention should be paid to designing for improved staff utilization and patient service. The cost-effectiveness of facilities will continue to be important.

- New security systems and window and door screening to respond to higher levels of crime.

- More stringent environmental regulations, including waste treatment and disposal, traffic, zoning, building heights, wetland protection, and land conservation. Environmentally sustainable building materials and methods will become more standard.

- Siting limitations spurring the growth of ambulatory care centers in residential neighborhoods. Building massing, scale, materials, traffic patterns, and landscaping will be increasingly important.

AMBULATORY SURGERY CENTERS

In the last decade, much of surgery has moved out of the costly inpatient hospital setting into a freestanding ambulatory surgery environment, found most often in the form of the ambulatory surgery center. This is largely due to changes in hospital reimbursement policies that have evolved to favor ambulatory care. All but the most complex surgical procedures, such as transplants, can now be performed in the outpatient setting. The average length of stay for patients ranges from a few hours to one day.

Athens Regional Medical Center Surgicenter

Athens, Georgia

Architect: Payette Associates, Inc., Boston, Massachusetts

Completed: 1986

The Athens Regional Medical Center Surgicenter is a 20,000 sq ft addition to a 1910 hospital-owned residence, the Talmadge House. The house and most of its pecan grove and landscaped grounds were preserved and restored. The house now serves as the welcoming entrance to the Surgicenter. A barnlike addition houses the clinical portion of the building. Clerestories bring natural, indirect light into the operating rooms (ORs), as well as the recovery, prep, and dressing rooms and support work areas.

The new operating suite aligns with the main floor of the house. The land slopes down, allowing covered parking for staff and patient loading areas below the new addition. Cars are screened through the use of wood trellises.

Restored and renovated, the spacious ground floor rooms to the left of the entrance hall of the Talmadge House serve as the reception and waiting area. The rooms to the right of the hall house preregistration, medical examinations, and laboratory tests. The upstairs is used for development offices; the center is often used after hours for receptions.

The design of an ambulatory surgical center, where over 90 percent of the procedures are surgical, requires that all the equipment and amenities of a hospital surgical wing be incorporated into a smaller space that also functions as a walk-in clinic. The following are unique considerations in the planning and design of an ambulatory surgery center (or surgicenter, as they have come to be known).

▲ *The existing structure and landscape set a welcoming tone for the facility.*

Programming issues

- Determine the number and kinds of procedures that are going to be performed (the case mix). Most surgical procedures can be completed on an outpatient basis except for long, very invasive cases, e.g., transplants.

- The number of surgical procedures, together with the number of hours the facility is open (including weekends and evenings) will determine the number of operating rooms and types of equipment needed. Once the number and types of ORs are identified, the rest of the program can be determined, including preoperative rooms, postoperative rooms, and staff dressing and support areas—cleaning, sterilizing, supplies, etc.

- Make sure there is one-way patient flow. Patients entering the facility should not encounter those leaving.

- Prevent contamination by maintaining three zones of sterility:
  Off the street
  Within the suite
  Within the room

Additional design concerns

- Environment—Patients are ambulatory before and after surgical procedures. Most often they are awake (if somewhat sedated) during the procedure and aware of their surroundings, including light, view, sound, smell, and temperature.
- Privacy—Patients desire privacy versus contact with the outside world.
- Clothing—Patients arrive dressed for the outside world. They need a suitable place to change and store their clothes and the ability to retrieve them when preparing for departure.
- Companionship—Surgery is a group effort for both patients and staff. Friends or family can help during both pre- and postoperative periods. Waiting areas and public spaces should be able to accommodate large numbers of patients and supporting friends and family.

Circulation/space planning

- At the Athens Surgicenter, patients travel in a clear circuit from preparation room to operating room to recovery room to dressing room and second-stage recovery.
- Dressing rooms and prep rooms are adjacent, allowing access from both areas to lockers so that clothes do not have to be moved. From the preoperation zone, patients enter one

of the four operating rooms. After the operation, they are transferred to a recovery room and then to dressing rooms to retrieve their clothes.

- From second-stage recovery, patients leave the facility. Handicapped access is by an elevator at the section joining the old and new buildings.
- Operating rooms are clustered around a single sterile core. This allows the circulating nurse to cover four ORs easily. Surgeons can readily observe or assist each other. The number of sterilizers and warming cabinets can be halved, in comparison to the number needed in conventional suites. The sterile core is the hub of intercommunication between procedures.

Site planning, parking, access

Ordinarily, patients are not allowed to come to a surgicenter alone. The patient parking area must be convenient to both the entrance and the exit to minimize disorientation. Drop-offs and somewhat remote parking are acceptable if walkways and the building benefit from a pleasant setting.

Compliance with codes and the Americans with Disabilities Act (ADA)

- Life safety is critical in a surgicenter, although not as demanding as in a hospital OR. Procedures are of shorter duration and less invasive. Operations can be halted, if necessary, thus requiring less stringent codes.
- Universal design is essential for a surgicenter—people of every size, age, and condition are arriving for operations.

- Ample-sized seating, with room for people in wheelchairs and on crutches, should be provided.
- Handrails must be provided.

Structure

- Large bays (30 ft plus) in at least one direction allow flexibility and change in layout. There is increasingly more equipment in an OR on the ceiling and around the patient.
- Ducts and pipes may fight for space in the ceiling with mounting frames for surgical lights, gas columns, and imaging devices. The ceiling zone is as critical to the layout as the floor plan; a plenum of 3½ ft is recommended.

Mechanical systems

- The location and size of air-handling units—the spaces for vertical and horizontal runs and the ducts themselves—have a major impact on building cost. Shafts and horizontal runs must be woven into the plan for efficiency.
- Access to controls and filter boxes is important.
- Piping for medical gases is the critical plumbing item. The piping must be ultraclean; joints must be smooth inside and free of pinhole leaks.

Electrical/communications components

- Emergency power must be sufficient to stabilize patients and shut down the center.
- An uninterrupted power system (UPS) in the ORs bridges the short interval between the loss of normal power and activation of the emergency systems.

- The communication/data room needs to be a centralized, climate-controlled location with electrical and backup systems for all computer and communication equipment.
- Normal and emergency power panels should be separated, so as to avoid accidents.
- Since ambulatory care centers are small, relatively accessible buildings, the security systems must afford protection to patients, medications, and valuable equipment.
- Closed circuit TV needs to be provided for video imaging, which is a part of many surgical procedures.

Materials

The design challenge is to use materials that are easily cleaned and disinfected, can withstand hard use, yet are pleasing to the eye and touch.

Acoustics

Mechanical equipment should be isolated to avoid noise and vibration. Sound transmission through the ductwork should be prevented. Sound transmission between socially sensitive areas, such as staff lounges and patient waiting or dressing rooms, should be prevented by adjacencies or insulation.

Lighting

- Direct sun and glare from fixtures and surfaces matter, because staff and patients are most often in fixed positions, unable to move away from harsh light.
- Natural light and access to pleasant views, without compromising privacy within the building, are desirable.

AMBULATORY CARE FACILITIES

▶ *Main floor plan and roof plan denote patient circulation and the use of clerestories to bring in natural light.*

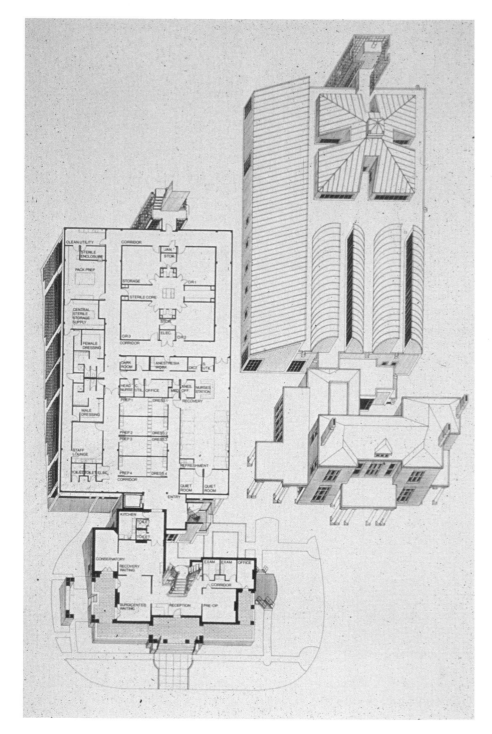

Natural light is most effective reflecting off walls, ceilings, and floors. Examples include clerestory or controlled top light, i.e., tinted-glass skylights, that bring light into the building, and windows screened by evergreen landscaping.

- Artificial lighting should define space and orientation but not create glare and bright spots.

Wayfinding

- Simplicity or understandability of circulation, plus orientations to the outside, are the keys to wayfinding.

- In ambulatory surgery centers, signage is an integral part of the architecture.

- Color, materials, and lighting are tools to reinforce the circulation systems, as well as to demarcate public, nonsterile, and sterile zones.

Renovation/restoration/ adaptive reuse

In evaluating an existing space for a new ambulatory surgery facility, the following points should be kept in mind:

- ORs, recovery, and central sterilizing areas are large rooms that are highly serviced by mechanical systems—air ducts, medical gas piping, waste systems, and so forth.

- The success of the center depends, in part, on the efficiency of its layout for the flow of patients, equipment, and material.

- In zones where stretchers are used, corridor widths should allow two patient stretchers to pass.

Athens Surgicenter used a historic building for low-tech functions and built a new addition for high-tech activities.

Operation and maintenance

A major component in good utilization is how quickly an OR can be cleaned and prepared for the next procedure. Space for surgical equipment, supplies, cleaning, and trash must be provided close to the ORs.

Key cost factors

There is a range of facilities costs across the United States. For a freestanding outpatient surgicenter, costs range from $200 to $300 per square foot, including full build-out and equipment, with medical equipment and mechanical, electrical, and plumbing (MEP) systems making up well over half of that cost.

Finances

Surgicenters are sponsored by physicians, businesses, and hospitals (private and public). They are financed by individuals, banks, investment groups, and, in the case of public endeavors, by grants.

OPHTHALMOLOGY CENTERS

Ophthalmology centers provide examination, diagnosis, and treatment of various eye diseases. They can be freestanding facilities or connected to larger healthcare complexes. Frequently, eye surgery facilities are constructed independently of large complexes and function autonomously as clinics devoted exclusively to the full range of ophthalmological services—from routine vision tests to laser keratotomy surgery, often including optical services as well.

University of South Florida Ophthalmology Center

Tampa, Florida

Architect: Payette Associates, Inc.
Architect of Record: Woodroffe Corporation Architects

Completed: 1996

The Ophthalmology Center at the University of South Florida is a reorganization of and addition to an existing building. As part of the reorganization, two separate institutions were to use the building, the Ophthalmology Center and the Cancer Center. Each required its own physical identity.

The Department of Ophthalmology comprises 28 examination rooms, related waiting areas, and a new entry cube, which gives the department its own identity. It is housed in a one-story building. The facility is accessible to all patients and is sited to provide convenient adjacent patient parking.

Twenty-four adult examination rooms have been placed in the new addition and are clustered together in groups of eight to form efficient working relationships. They are connected by staff corridors to offices and support areas within the existing building. The surrounding areas for patient access and waiting are open, with views to the outdoors. The examination rooms are enclosed, inasmuch as natural light is not desirable in performing eye examinations.

Four pediatric examination rooms are placed within renovated space of the existing building, with a separate pediatric waiting area. Shared toilets for both adult and pediatric patients are located between the two areas.

Treatment areas, including laser rooms, are placed between the adult and pediatric clusters for convenient access for both groups. Adjacent existing spaces include teaching facilities, laboratories, offices, and administration and staff support areas. For easy staff and physician access, the support area connects to the portion of the building used by the Cancer Center.

Programming

The needs and areas of specialization of the ophthalmologists and technicians, as well as the facility's hours of operation, determine the program. Ophthalmology centers require the following spaces:

- Preexamination rooms
- Examination rooms
- Procedure rooms
- Support space
- Waiting areas

Circulation

A good patient flow pattern includes the following steps:

- Check-in and waiting
- Move to an examination room for preexamination and/or pupil dilation
- Move to a smaller waiting area near the examination room
- Move to an examination/procedure room

Unique design concerns

In designing ophthalmology centers, it is best to assume that all patients are visually impaired. Consider the following points:

- Eliminate natural light from examination rooms.
- Provide natural light in waiting, circulation, and work areas.

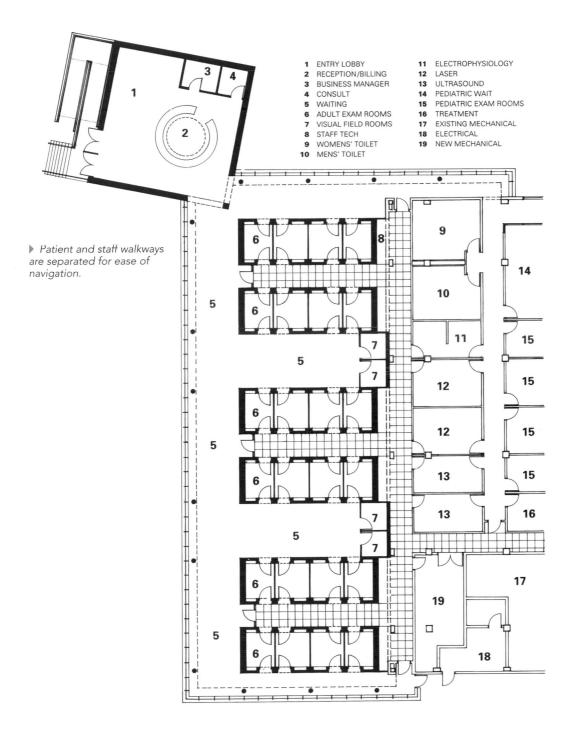

1 ENTRY LOBBY
2 RECEPTION/BILLING
3 BUSINESS MANAGER
4 CONSULT
5 WAITING
6 ADULT EXAM ROOMS
7 VISUAL FIELD ROOMS
8 STAFF TECH
9 WOMENS' TOILET
10 MENS' TOILET
11 ELECTROPHYSIOLOGY
12 LASER
13 ULTRASOUND
14 PEDIATRIC WAIT
15 PEDIATRIC EXAM ROOMS
16 TREATMENT
17 EXISTING MECHANICAL
18 ELECTRICAL
19 NEW MECHANICAL

▶ Patient and staff walkways are separated for ease of navigation.

- Place the general waiting area near the entrance.
- Place smaller waiting areas adjacent to examination room groupings.

Doctors should be able to control lighting and equipment from both their desks and the optical consoles behind patient chairs.

Site planning/ease of access

As in all ambulatory care facilities, convenient parking is important in an opthalmology center. Moreover, although friends and/or relatives often accompany eye patients, visual orientation requires extra clarity of design:

- Entrances should be clearly visible.
- Signage should be clear, with easy-to-read large and colored typography.
- The use of steps and raised thresholds should be minimized.
- Adequate lighting levels should be provided.
- A wide-ranging, contrasting, dark-to-light color palette should be used to express visual proportion and orientation.

Acoustic and sensory control

Visually impaired patients rely heavily on hearing and other senses. Special attention should be given to the following:

- Paging systems—attention should be given to placement and sound levels.
- Human voices—differentiate between areas relying on the sound of human voices, such as registration, and those that benefit from low voice levels, such as examination rooms.
- Floor and wall textures—varying textures can help in wayfinding.

- Handrails—can provide ambulatory support and guidance.

Lighting

Indirect lighting of walls and ceilings helps to define spaces. Visible light sources can act as beacons. In selecting lighting, consider the following factors:

- Quality of light—incandescent, natural, or fluorescent
- Control of light—ability to adjust lighting levels as needed
- Minimizing glare on both fixtures and building surfaces

Key costs

Typical costs for ambulatory eye centers range from $150 to $250 per square foot. Financial benefits can be gained through combining other activities with outpatient services:

- Coffee shop
- Cafe
- Optical shop
- Pharmacy
- Hospital supply store
- Newsstand

PROTON THERAPY CENTERS

Cyclotron proton therapy is an innovative treatment that uses a highly concentrated proton beam to irradiate certain cancerous tumors without damaging surrounding tissues, offering hope for patients with previously inoperable types of cancer.

Proton therapy centers are unique building types in that they:

- cost more than $300 per square foot, excluding equipment,
- require up to 100 percent additional design time, owing to their technical complexity, and

- incorporate experimental equipment for which no facilities have previously been designed.

Massachusetts General Hospital Northeast Proton Therapy Center

Boston, Massachussetts

Architect: Tsoi/Kobus & Associates, Inc., Cambridge, Massachusetts

Completed: 1997

The Northeast Proton Therapy Center at Massachusetts General Hospital is one of the world's first cancer treatment facilities to provide cyclotron proton therapy. Located adjacent to the hospital and a historic county jail, the site posed significant space constrictions, exacerbated by the need for building shielding and particle containment.

Programming issues

Having few precedents and no rules of thumb, the architect of a proton therapy center must apply rigorous study to the integration of building and equipment. Proton therapy centers have more exacting dimensional and programmatic requirements than other types of healthcare facilities, and there is no margin for error. At Massachusetts General Hospital, the following programming requirements were considered in the building's design:

- The cyclotron weights 200 tons and has a power output of more than 200 million electron volts.
- Gantries (devices by which the proton beam is aimed) rotate around one axis.
- The concrete floor is by necessity absolutely flat.
- Clearances for equipment access are less than an inch on this tight urban site.

Unique design concerns

Proton therapy centers, like many high-tech medical facilities, impose exceptional demands on the architect to accomplish certain objectives:

- Create a welcoming, reassuring patient care environment.
- Ensure safety against potentially harmful high-energy particles.
- Meet exacting dimensional and programmatic requirements.
- Enable servicing and future flexibility.
- Implement innovative project management methods.

At the Northeast Proton Therapy Center, the exterior rotunda symbolizes the heart of the facility: the cyclotron. The interior is encircled with a halo of clerestory windows. A bold mural depicts the energy peak of a proton beam as it strikes the heart of a tumor. For patients with life-threatening diseases, especially those undergoing high-tech procedures, it is important to provide a positive, uplifting environment. The architect can accomplish this through the choices of forms, materials, details, and color and the use of natural light.

Safety

All safety requirements must be fully understood before beginning design. The architect should work closely with the equipment manufacturer and shielding specialist throughout the design and construction process.

Safety requirements include the following:

- Designing 6 ft thick concrete walls surrounding the cyclotron and gantry (in patient treatment) room to protect patients and staff

▶ *Site Plan. Challenges included tight urban site, neighboring historic landmark, high water table, and sensitive adjacent uses (e.g., laser eye surgery center).*

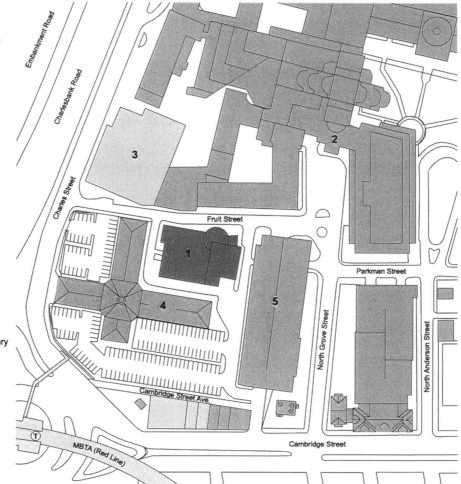

Site Plan

N

Legend
1. Northeast Proton Therapy Center
2. Mass. General Hospital Main Entry
3. Mass. Eye & Ear Infirmary
4. Jail
5. Garage

- Using earth around the building to absorb high-energy neutron particles
- Eliminating all line-of-sight penetrations that would otherwise allow errant particles to escape (e.g., by staggering the joints at concrete access hatches and incorporating double bends in electrical conduits)

Equipment serviceability and flexibility
Complex, innovative equipment can be finicky and difficult to service. To ensure serviceability, the following must be taken into account:

- The beam line (vacuum tube and magnets) must be fully accessible, with good clearances in all directions.

- Gantries must be accessible from catwalks.
- The machine shop should be located next to the cyclotron for accessible servicing.
- Removable shielding blocks and access hatches enable equipment replacement and removal.

To accommodate future growth and change, flexibility should be incorporated into the design for equipment upgrades and replacement. The design at Massachusetts General Hospital accommodates the possibility of a future additional gantry and ten-story addition above.

New project management methods
To date, the design and construction of proton therapy centers has involved only a select few architects, contractors, equipment manufactures, and healthcare providers.

Because the particle accelerator, gantry, and other highly specialized equipment used in the delivery of proton therapy are continually being improved, the building designer and equipment designer must work as one team. The need for close collaboration has favored design-build project delivery and innovative contractual arrangements.

Architects and contractors should have highly specialized medical expertise, with both national and international focus to aid the process of working with international equipment suppliers.

AMBULATORY PSYCHIATRIC FACILITIES
The United States model for mental health services is in the midst of significant change. Increasingly, healthcare providers are turning toward ambulatory treatment facilities to address the needs of patients with behavioral diagnoses. Ambulatory psychiatric care is not in itself a new phenomenon. Public mental health systems have been providing services for ambulatory patients (consumers) in day hospitals, psychosocial rehabilitation facilities, and other noninpatient treatment settings for 30 to 40 years, as economic and societal pressures initiated deinstitutionalization. However, the managed-care environment has created a need for a different kind of physical infrastructure for today's mental healthcare system. Hospitalization diversion strategies have resulted in the creation of a continuum of care between traditional outpatient (i.e., clinicians' offices) and inpatient treatment settings. These noninpatient facilities within the continuum are variously referred to as the following:

- Ambulatory behavioral healthcare facilities
- Partial hospitalization programs
- Outpatient psychiatric clinics
- Family resource centers
- Day hospitals

Hall-Brooke Hospital
Westport, Connecticut
Architect: Graham/Meus, Inc.
Completed: 2000
Located on a 25-acre site in Westport, Connecticut, this compact, 58,000 sq ft building will replace five nonconforming nineteenth- and early-twentieth-century structures. It is a two-story building that accommodates 60 inpatient beds in two flexible units on the upper floor, and partial hospitalization/outpatient

▶ *Site topography allows both a low-scale façade and full windows on the lower level.*

programs, administration, and support activities on the lower level. The new building takes advantage of the existing site topography to give the appearance of a low-scale, one-story lodge from the surrounding neighborhood, yet the lower level is at grade, providing full-height windows and a separate point of entry for the ambulatory psychiatric care wing that encompasses 12,400 sq ft on the north end of the building's lower level.

Programming issues

Ambulatory psychiatric facilities include the following programming components:

- Site planning/ease of access
- Flexibility
- Treatment program tracks

- Support areas
- Therapists' offices
- Central community room
- Other programmatic components

Site planning/ease of access

The in-and-out traffic feature of ambulatory care raises the following needs:

- For an identifiable and visible front door, particularly if the ambulatory care facility is on a hospital campus. The entrance of Hall-Brooke's psychiatric care building on the lower level has its own driveway, drop-off area, and parking lot.
- For specialized treatment and activity areas, accessible and in close proximity to each other.

- For a lobby with central control point and reception area, immediately inside the entry.
- For offices for admission/assessment and administration/finance, which should be located close to the entry.

Flexibility

Treatment programs utilize either group or individual therapy and therefore require highly flexible spaces and configurations. Flexibility is achieved by providing a variety of meeting places where one-on-one, small, and large groups can comfortably get together with little outside stimulation or disruption. These spaces should be designed to accommodate individuals and groups with differing requirements for human comfort. Basic requirements include the following:

- Neutrality—to provide comfortable environments for men and women of all ages
- Simplicity—to allow for different furnishings and equipment depending on the program
- Excellent acoustic isolation
- Flexible environment controls
- Controllable lighting

Treatment program tracks

The primary design element in an ambulatory psychiatric facility involves the concept of "tracks." Tracks are specific treatment programs for individuals with similar requirements, such as the following:

- Adult programs
- Women's programs
- Geriatric programs
- Child and adolescent programs
- Addiction treatment programs

- Dual diagnosis programs

The new Hall-Brooke ambulatory care facility provides program space for two adult tracks accommodating as many as 60 patients requiring partial hospitalization. A third track for as many as 20 children and adolescents operates independently in a school building that is also located on the Hall-Brooke campus. Treatment programs generally last from three to six hours and often include a meal or snack. The facility's programs include the following:

- Individual counseling
- Group therapies
- Social interaction

Track areas should be located to provide easy access to the following areas:

- Therapists' office
- Toilets
- Nurses' stations
- Medication distribution stations
- Reception
- Accounting

Each track includes a number of treatment areas:

- Large group therapy rooms for 12 to 18 people
- Small group therapy rooms for 6 to 10 people
- Individual counseling offices for one-on-one or small family meetings

Spaces should be comfortable, quiet, and private. Extra-wide corridors provide space for informal social interaction before and after sessions.

Support areas

Core treatment areas should provide clinical support to partial-hospitalization patients who require nursing services and medications in the course of their

▶ *Segmentation of space according to function provides flexibility and privacy.*

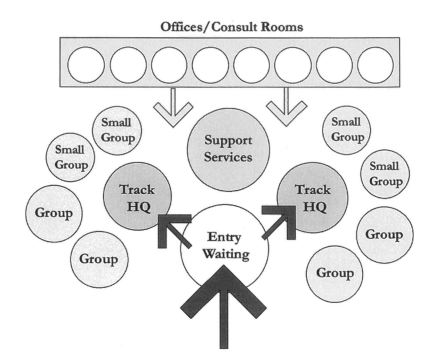

treatment program. These areas should be centrally located near the reception and nurse station area:

- Fully staffed nurses' station
- Glass-enclosed charting area
- Work area
- Medication room
- Small utility room
- Storage

Therapists' offices

Outpatient treatment and individual and family counseling are provided in therapists' offices. These areas have a number of requirements:

- Convenient access for administration personnel and clinicians to the track and specialty service areas

- A conference room for administrative and team meetings
- A design that promotes confidentiality and comfort

Central community room

The layout of the track area in Hall-Brooke involves a "neighborhood" concept, providing dedicated spaces for each track area while maintaining a separation between the patients in different tracks. Each track area is designed around a central community room/patient lounge. This space can be designed to serve a number of functions, such as the following:

- A place for socializing, meetings, breaks, and dining
- An arrival point

- A place for patient belongings
- A track headquarters
- A kitchen, with refrigerator, sink, and microwave oven

Other programmatic components

Although the modular track area is the basic building block in Hall-Brooke's ambulatory program, there are a number of other requirements:

- Public lobby/front door area
- A core of support functions
- Accommodations for clinical and administrative offices
- Certain specialty program areas

Circulation and planning

A number of points must be considered in planning a circulation system:

- The circulation system separates clinical functions from visitor, service, and administrative functions.
- A waiting area should be provided for outpatients to be seen in clinicians' offices.
- A direct path should be created from the lobby for tracked patients to their track headquarters.
- Inpatient and ambulatory services operate independently, yet should have access to all common resources such as rehabilitation programs and dining facilities.

Safety/security/durability issues

Although ambulatory psychiatric patients by definition do not pose a threat to themselves or others, provisions for safety, security, and control are given serious consideration in the design process. Safety, security, and durability features should be understated and seem natural in a pleasant, comfortable, and functional setting, using applications such as the following:

- Windows with panes of heat-strengthened glass
- Walls made of fiber-reinforced gypsum wallboard
- Solid gypsum wallboard ceilings in areas that are not always supervised
- Plumbing, electrical, and mechanical devices that are designed to be tamper-proof and to avoid "looping" hazards

Interior issues

The interior design of the Hall-Brooke Hospital and other mental health facilities is quite different from that of an acute care facility owing to the nature of the therapeutic environment, which is a synthesis between clinical programs and therapies and the physical setting. The philosophy underlying this synthesis requires careful attention to the selection and specification of every design element in the facility, to achieve a critical balance between the need for a noninstitutional, familiar, and comfortable setting with concerns for safety.

Ambulatory psychiatric facilities should be durable, controllable, flexible, and safe, yet also be sensitive to the emotional and spiritual needs of the patients and staff. The interiors of the Hall-Brooke ambulatory care wing are designed to support the therapeutic environment, using design elements such as the following:

- Soft, sound-absorbent materials, such as carpets in corridors and acoustical wall fabrics in therapy rooms

- Colors and materials that are neutral and coordinated to provide a soothing, calm atmosphere
- Wood casework, doors, and wall trim to offer warmth, durability, and a residential scale
- Indirect and dimmable lighting in corridors and therapy rooms

EMERGENCY DEPARTMENTS

Emergency departments are dedicated diagnostic and treatment areas intended for those patients urgently requiring medical treatment for injury or illness. Because of the location, convenience, and 24-hour operation of these facilities, nonemergency patients are also frequent users of emergency departments for more routine care or mild ailments. Current trends toward managed-care insurance have left the uninsured without "primary care physicians." These patients and disadvantaged people often find themselves in the public hospital emergency department—it is the primary care location of last resort. Emergency departments, known as EDs, are usually separated areas within hospitals, serving diverse population groups including adults, children, psychiatric patients, and prisoners.

Emergency departments should be easy to find for a first-time visitor and easily accessible by ambulance. They should have a clear reception and triage desk arrangement so that walk-in patients are quickly oriented. (Triage is a system whereby patients are quickly evaluated and directed to the appropriate caregiver and/or department.)

One of the foremost challenges in designing an ED in today's society is to make it sufficiently flexible to handle both high and low patient volumes and the variety of types of cases that come with a diverse population.

The Cambridge Public Health Alliance

The Cambridge Hospital Emergency Department

Cambridge, Massachusetts

Architect: Payette Associates Inc., Boston

Associate Architect: Warner and Associates; Boston, Massachusetts

Completed: 1999

The Cambridge Hospital Emergency Department is an 18-bed unit, built within renovated space in an existing hospital, as one phase of a larger ambulatory care expansion and renovation project. A number of design considerations evolved for this project:

- The extensive scope of the project suggested a larger restructuring and reorganization of the entire hospital and the reorganization of the entire campus.
- This finding led to the development of a new, relocated, main entrance lobby.
- The redesigned access to the hospital has reduced the number of doors to the hospital from six to one.
- The newly designed lobby is the single entrance point for all hospital patients and visitors, whether they require ambulatory, inpatient, or emergency services. The central lobby, with its directory, information services, central registration, and support areas, has become the hub of all hospital activities.

- The parking garage is located beneath the ambulatory wing, and its elevator brings visitors to the main lobby as well.
- This reorganization provides a single point of arrival, giving clarity to the design and easy wayfinding for patients, regardless of their needs.

Programming issues

In planning functionally efficient emergency departments, a number of key programming issues are worthy of consideration:

- Easy access and integration
- Zoning of service areas
- Flexibility of rooms
- Flexibility of staffing
- Security for staff and patients
- Patient privacy and safety

Access and integration

Connections between the ED and associated hospital functions, and the simplicity of those connections, are crucial for efficient functionality. The nontraditional integration of walk-in access from the main entrance allows simplified referrals between the hospital clinics and the express care service that may be provided within the ED. Because the hospital is located on a tight urban site, the old front entry from the street was converted into a covered ambulance bay. This has separated the ambulance bay from triage, in contrast to the recommended linkage.

The circulation plan guides the patient easily from the street into the glass-enclosed lobby and straight to the triage nurses' desk. The triage examination room and private consultation desk are directly adjacent to the triage desk for quick examination/assessment. The waiting area is directly opposite the triage desk. The separate waiting room alcoves for adults and children allow the triage nurse to guide a patient to the proper area in which to wait until central nursing directs the patient to a treatment room.

The unusual, triangle-shaped plan serves the three distinct populations of express care, adult care, and pediatric care.

Express care screens patients who either have minor ailments or who have come to the ED to receive primary care service after hours. Express care, which is at the front end of the triangular plan, comprises a nurses' station and two treatment rooms with a direct connection to the adult waiting area. Patients can rapidly receive treatment for minor injuries and ailments without interacting with adult emergency patients inasmuch as this area operates as a separately staffed examination suite.

The pediatric area, at the opposite end of the triangle, has its own nurses' station, toilet, and three treatment rooms. Pediatric patients can enter directly from the pediatric waiting area. The pediatric area is linked to the main nursing station through the doctors' charting area, which has an overview of the area through glass windows, but is acoustically separated from the adult area to maintain a calm, quiet atmosphere for children.

The adult care area is in the center of the triangle. The central nurses' station is in the middle of the floor, and the adult treatment rooms are arranged around it along the two legs of the triangle. The support rooms, such as medications, nourishment, laboratory, doctors' charting, and toilets, are interspersed between them.

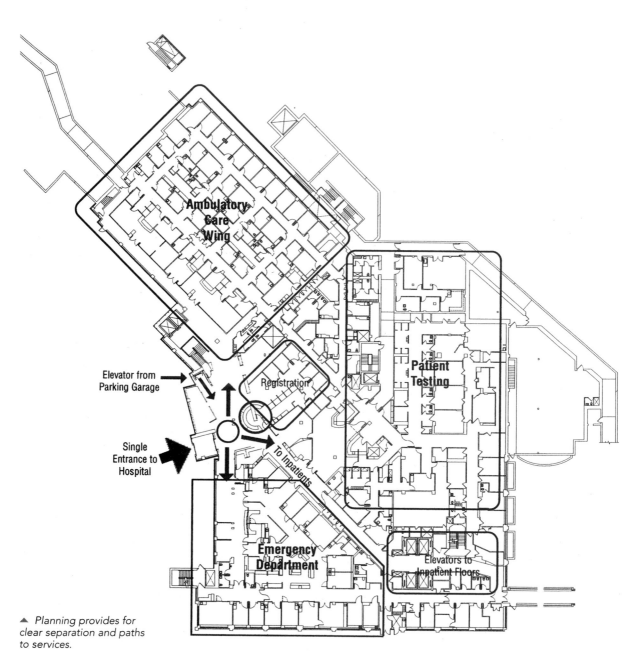

Ambulatory Care Wing

Patient Testing

Elevator from
Parking Garage

Registration

Single
Entrance to
Hospital

To Inpatients

Emergency Department

Elevators to
Inpatient Floors

▲ Planning provides for
clear separation and paths
to services.

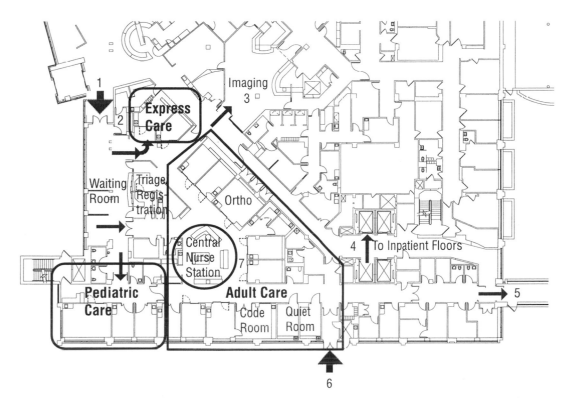

The following labels appear on the plan:

1

Imaging
3

Express
Care

2

Waiting
Room

Triage
Regis-
tration

Ortho

Central
Nurse
Station

7

4 To Inpatient Floors

5

Pediatric
Care

Adult Care

Code
Room

Quiet
Room

6

The lab is centrally located to serve all three areas and to provide rapid results.

Zoning of service areas

Several separate service "tracks" have become common in emergency departments. These designated areas help to provide improved care and control during hectic peak periods of operation:

- Adult care (traditional main treatment areas)
- Pediatric care
- Express care (primary nonemergency service within the ED)
- Isolated "quiet" room
- Observation (not a provided ED service at the Cambridge Hospital)

Flexibility of rooms

Of the 18 generic treatment beds at the Cambridge Hospital ED, all beds other than those in code rooms, which are used for extremely urgent care, were designed for flexible use on a case-by-case basis. As needs vary over the course of the day, the generic room design provides greater flexibility in scheduling the use of rooms. Rolling case carts, stocked for specific types of care, are brought from the nurses' station into the room. Rolling carts reduce the problem of patients having to wait an extended time in the waiting room until a case-equipped room frees up, while other rooms remain empty.

▲ Distinct zones of service have separate access.

Flexibility of staffing

The triangular plan allows the ED staff to serve the three populations efficiently, without crossing paths during their visits. It permits staff to move freely among these populations, while simultaneously minimizing patient-to-patient contact. In addition, it allows for beds to be used for adult care during peak times when separate tracks for express care or pediatrics may not be needed. The three main functional areas ring a central nurses' station. Two satellite stations (express and pediatrics) supplement the central location during peak hours. When patient flow decreases, staffing can be reduced by closing the satellite nurses' stations, obviating the need for additional staffing. Only the rooms surrounding the central nurses' station need be used. Benefits include high visibility of all patients and cost-effectiveness, through maximizing both patient flow and staff utilization.

Security for staff and patients

Security is a major concern in an urban ED. The diverse clientele includes prisoners and psychiatric patients. A number of security measures must he considered in designing an ED:

- Provide good visibility for both patients and staff.

- Avoid designing spaces where people can get cornered or trapped at nurses' stations and doctors' charting areas. Give particular focus to triage and registration areas.

- Install panic buttons (silent security calls) at each department control desk.

- If possible, situate the hospital's main security office near the ED, with direct oversight of the waiting area.

- Provide for a "quiet" track within the ED to isolate out-of-control patients.

- Provide a controlled access area where medications can be safely dispensed and where access can be monitored by the central nursing staff.

Patient privacy and safety

Patients facing life-threatening injury or illness in an emergency department are vulnerable and under extreme stress. Therefore, patient privacy is very important. Privacy features in the Cambridge ED include the following:

- Single-bed treatment rooms

- Curtains for visual privacy

- Glass doors for acoustical privacy

- Private interview space separate from the waiting area in triage

- Acoustical privacy for patient registration

- Grief rooms for doctors and family to discuss patient treatments and outcomes

Circulation

The ED is carefully placed to bridge associated hospital functions:

- Walk-in access is provided directly from the main entrance.

- The security office is placed for oversight of the waiting room and fast response to ED needs.

- The imaging suite is located directly across the main corridor from the ED and in line with the triage desk for easy and controlled patient access and quick procurement of X-rays and advanced imaging techniques.

- ED patients requiring extended admission into the hospital are provided direct access to the inpatient elevator core.

- Psychiatric referral patients are escorted separately to the hospital's psychiatric wing.

- Ambulance and police arrivals enter through a separate and discreet entrance drive.

- A dedicated dumbwaiter provides direct access from ED registration to the medical records department above.

Unique design concerns

Treatment rooms for express, adult, or pediatric care have common basic needs that follow code guidelines. The following summary list gives an indication of the elements to be located within the space. It is essential to develop exact positions for these elements within the treatment room with the ED medical staff, to match their work methods. Whether it is developed for major or minor treatment procedures, the identical layout of these common elements must be provided in all treatment rooms, allowing staff to work efficiently without reorientation:

- Treatment stretchers adaptable to gynecology (GYN) and positions for opthalmology patients

- Hand washing sink

- Counter for chart notation

- Overhead supply cabinets

- Examination privacy curtain

- Sliding glass privacy door

- Head wall supplying medical gases, vacuum, and power for equipment

- Patient monitor interfaced with central nurses' station

- Ultraviolet (UV) light for infection control

- Nurse call button

- Code Blue button

- Phone and intercom

- Code timing clock

- General time clock

- Examination light

- Ceiling-mounted intravenous (IV) track

- Sharp/hazardous disposal containers

- Typical diagnostic equipment

Treatment rooms identified for major procedures are primarily geared for cardiac and minor invasive work. To meet these demands, the rooms are larger to accommodate additional mobile equipment and staff. Additional provisions include the following:

- Medical gases and vacuum

- X-ray boxes

- Dedicated EKG cart

- Dedicated crash cart for use in treating heart attacks

With rooms developed in this typical generic fashion, specialization can be achieved within any room for common ED procedures. Carts stored around the central nurses' station carry specialized equipment, instruments, and supplies:

- Suture cart

- Cast cart

- GYN cart

- Eye cart

- EKG cart

- Crash cart

- Anesthetic cart

- Carts with specialized diagnostic equipment

All rooms in the Cambridge Hospital ED contain a single bed, except for the orthopedic rooms and one pediatric treatment room. Many rooms have natural light coming from a frosted glass window located above the head wall, which enlivens the rooms while maintaining privacy.

Specialized treatment rooms

Orthopedic treatment rooms

Orthopedic rooms are used for setting broken bones. They should be large enough to allow efficient maneuvering. They should be developed with the full array of minor treatment provisions and should include the following specialized items:

- Cast sink with plaster trap
- Cast saws—hand and electric
- X-ray view boxes
- Storage for supplies and crutches

Code room

This is the largest room, allowing maximum access to the bed by multiple caregivers. It is used for emergency heart attack treatment, other urgent resuscitation, or treatment requiring utmost speed and efficiency. The code room is located close to the ambulance bay to allow rapid patient transfer. Special provisions include the following:

- A highly advanced head wall
- Permanent EKG cart and crash cart
- OR scrub sink
- X-ray viewing box
- A rolling OR light
- Extensive cabinetry on one wall for fast, clear access to supplies

Quiet rooms

Quiet rooms are used for psychiatric, disorderly, or incarcerated patients. These rooms are located directly adjacent to the ambulance bay for quick transfer of patients. They include the following features:

- A standard head wall and sink that can be protected by lowering an automatic rolling door, controlled from the outside of the room
- A bed that can be locked to the floor to prevent overturning
- A tamperproof ceiling to prevent escape
- Soundproof walls and door to prevent disruption to other areas of the ED

Additional design concerns

- Provide as much natural light as possible for staff and patients.
- Maintain a calm, quiet atmosphere by having single-bed rooms, providing acoustic privacy between rooms, isolating noisy patients from the rest of the ED, and separating adults from children.
- Provide clear, easy wayfinding for patients to reduce the stress of the overall visit. The door to the hospital and the ED should be easy to find. Locate the triage station in the direct line of sight for the entering visitor.

Mechanical/electrical systems

The ED is an isolated suite within the hospital and is pressure balanced to maintain air isolation, with 100 percent fresh air supply and no recirculating air. Plan for all treatment rooms to have a high rate of exhaust air change. At the Cambridge Hospital ED, most treatment rooms are designed at isolation room exhaust rates, which helps protect staff and other patients from communicable disease. In compliance with code, two rooms have been dedicated to isolation, with the required pressure monitoring and alarms.

Electrical systems should be planned to provide emergency power, accessible at the treatment room head walls, for critical care equipment and monitoring. Plan to include provisions for increased use of computers at the bedside, allowing for future integrated patient record systems to be incorporated as they come on-line.

Operations/maintenance

- Plan the nurses' station to meet staffing needs, such as good sight lines for oversight of patients. Careful placement of the nurses' station can help minimize overstaffing and accommodate fluctuating daily staff requirements, thus reducing the hospital's operational costs.

- Provide a fixed location for staff medical reference manuals, to prevent their removal.

- Arrange an efficient interface between the triage nurse and the control nurse, to effectively monitor incoming patients and direct their flow into appropriate treatment spaces.

- Use seamless flooring in treatment rooms to eliminate buildup of contaminants in cracks.

- Protect lower walls with impact-resistant wainscoting.

- Use the more visually pleasing painted plaster above the wainscot, where damage is less likely.

WOMEN'S HEALTHCARE CENTERS

The highly personal nature of most procedures in the women's health arena requires design and layout uniquely sensitive to guarding patient confidentiality and allaying anxiety. Patients coming to a facility for gynecological examinations, particularly for nonroutine visits, are frequently concerned about both privacy and comfort. Facilities whose design addresses these concerns can alleviate unnecessary worry and enable patients to relax, despite the uneasiness inherent in their situation. Because these facilities cater to an all-female clientele and often a mostly female staff, the design of both medical and service areas should ideally be suited to female tastes and interests.

With this ideal as a guide, numerous centers have made it a shaping force in their design schemes. Whether facilities are designed for general women's healthcare or for special needs, the female healthcare industry has produced hybrid ambulatory care facilities that incorporate client needs and medicine in a way not previously envisioned. Made up of a range of services, from acupuncture and massage to high-tech imaging, and from on-site day care and play areas for patients' children to fully equipped laboratories and examination rooms, these centers focus on comprehensive treatment (from diagnosis to after care) of their female clientele in buildings that weave ambiance with functionality to provide medical services in a comfortable, aesthetically pleasing atmosphere.

Spence Center for Women's Health

Wellesley, Massachusetts

Architect: RUR Architecture P.C., Dobbs Ferry, New York
Architect of Record: Andrew Cohen, Cambridge, Massachusetts

Completed: 1996

Central Maine Medical Center The Sam & Jennie Bennett Breast Care Center

Lewiston, Maine

Architect: Harriman Associates, Auburn, Maine

Completed: 1998

Housing a facility that caters to the complete range of women's health issues, the Spence Center for Women's Health is designed to cloak its utilitarian purposes with the style and service of a contemporary spa or resort. Warm-toned halogen and incandescent lights supplant institutional fluorescents. Fresh flowers and custom-designed furniture create a relaxing, intimate environment. Its 6,000 sq ft floor plan utilizes sculptural forms to allow flowing circulation and increased levels of privacy as visitors move from the reception area to the examination rooms.

The Sam & Jennie Bennett Breast Care Center, located in a suite in a medical office building attached to the Central Maine Medical Center, specializes in exclusive attention to all phases of breast care—from routine mammography to prosthetics and support groups for women diagnosed with breast cancer and related diseases. Coordination between on-site experts allows patients to receive all the necessary services in one location and enables doctors to more speedily and effectively deal with each individual case.

The 4,200 sq ft suite is structured to maintain confidentiality and designed to allay patient anxiety with natural colors and comfortable furnishings.

Programming issues
The following are the principal programming requirements, listed in order of proximity to outside public space:

Spence Center

- Public: Reception/waiting, children's area, health care book shop, business office
- Semipublic: Education/class space, exercise space, dressing rooms and showers
- Alternative medicine services: Massage and acupuncture spaces
- Private: General examination rooms and services, internal waiting area
- Laboratories, technical and utility spaces, private offices, records storage

Bennett Breast Care Center

- Public: Reception/waiting area
- Semipublic: Education/support group space
- Private: Examination rooms, procedure rooms, lockers, dressing rooms, internal waiting and library area
- Technical and utility spaces, private offices, and records storage

Circulation
Spence Center
Within the facility, patient privacy is achieved through the staged succession of spaces from public to private and through the provision of a secondary, completely private waiting area that serves the examination rooms and radiology area.

1 Entry
2 Reception
3 Waiting
4 Staff Locker Area
5 Consult
6 Office
7 Dressing
8 Gowned Waiting
9 Stereotatic/Biopsy
10 Ultrasound
11 Exam
12 Soiled Utility
13 Clean Utility
14 Mammography/Exam
15 Mammography
16 Dark Room
17 Tech Work Area
18 Reading/Work
19 Lockers
20 Coffee Station

▲ *The layout of the Breast Care Center provides patients with privacy and confidentiality.*

Bennett Breast Care Center

Patient privacy and confidentiality are established by clearly separating patient and staff flows both physically and acoustically. The private changing rooms and robed waiting area are directly adjacent to examination rooms and separated from the public areas of the center.

Unique design concerns

Keeping in mind the unique issues involved in the treatment of an exclusively female clientele, designers of both facilities sought to reduce patient anxiety by cultivating a spa-like ambiance throughout the patient areas.

Spence Center

Using sculptural forms, contemporary lines, warm tones and textures, and residential-style lighting, designers avoided the institutional and impersonal aspects traditionally associated with healthcare facilities. Areas for additional on-site services, including health education and exercise courses, massage, and acupuncture, in addition to a children's play area, were incorporated in the design to encourage more frequent visits.

Bennett Breast Care Center

Facilitating collaboration between experts involved in all phases of breast care treatment and alleviation of patient

▶ *Modern lines and sculptural forms shape the atmosphere of the Spence Center.*

anxiety, the design team grouped and separated patient and staff areas. High ceilings, natural light, and a color scheme incorporating light woods and natural hues with seashore accents throughout, enhance the coordinated spa-like feeling of the center.

Site planning
As in any ambulatory healthcare facility, easy access and adequate parking were requirements for site selection, as was availability of adjacent space to allow future expansion, if needed.

Mechanical systems

Bennett Breast Care Center
The center is a suite in an existing building, so customized mechanical components are tied into the main systems. A minimum vertical clearance of 12 ft from the floor to the underside of the deck is required for installation of mechanical systems. A variable-air-volume system is required to provide individual control for rooms containing equipment that gives off heat, to allow adjustments for patient comfort. In addition, direct exhaust must be provided for plumbing in toilets and the darkroom.

Electrical/communication systems
Both centers feature an integrated system of telephone, intercom, and computer networks tied into the layout to allow for increased usage as healthcare technology develops. In addition, the systems (including a high-speed computer network, generator, fire alarms, and security and panic-duress systems) at the Bennett Breast Care Center are interfaced with the central network at the Central Maine Medical Center.

Acoustic control
Central to the acoustical plan for these facilities is the segmentation of areas by level of privacy. Carpeting, solid-core

doors, and acoustically insulated walls and ceilings throughout reduce noise transmission and contribute to a peaceful and private environment.

Lighting design

Spence Center

In public and circulation spaces, a mixture of low-voltage halogen incandescent ceiling fixtures, wall sconces, and compact, warm-tone fluorescents produces well-lit and comfortable spaces. In examination rooms, overheard fluorescents are combined with incandescent wall sconces to achieve the greatest visibility without harshness.

Bennett Breast Care Center

Large windows allow natural light to brighten both waiting areas. Table lamps in public areas provide a home-like atmosphere, as do accent lights that highlight artwork. Lighting in examination and procedure rooms is adjustable to suit a variety of situations and allow staff to read films and computer screens with ease.

Interior issues

Spence Center

The curved walls (ruled surfaces constructed of sheetrock on metal studs) of the center are neither difficult nor expensive to build, and they provide the basis for flowing circulation in a relatively small envelope. Colors and materials were chosen to create a spacious and comfortable atmosphere and to unify the graduated movement from public to private space.

Bennett Breast Care Center

A relaxed, spa-like environment is achieved through a unified color scheme and seashore motif in finishing details, furniture style, fabric patterns, artwork, and lighting design, which also lend cohesiveness to the center. The rich, yet neutral, colors coupled with the use of natural light enhance patient comfort.

Wayfinding

Custom signage, graphics, and logos for both facilities provide unity within the centers. Circulation patterns move patients along a single path compatible with the order of procedures in each center.

Finances, fees, feasibility

If a facility is privately owned (such as the Spence Women's Health Center), design and construction are financed through private investor cash. If it is hospital owned (such as the Bennett Breast Care Center), it is financed through institutional loans from the parent medical corporation and private donors. Donors can be recognized by plaques on the walls of entry and waiting room areas.

▲ The robed-waiting room emphasizes the spa-like environment at the Bennett Breast Care Center while protecting patient privacy.

HEART CENTERS

Heart centers offer comprehensive diagnostic, treatment, and rehabilitative programs for patients with disorders of the heart and vascular system. A successful design approach bases cardiology programs on wellness concepts—that is, programs providing early detection, prevention, psychosocial services, and education at one access point.

Morton Plant Hospital Heart and Vascular Pavilion

Clearwater, Florida

Architect: TRO/The Ritchie Organization; Sarasota, Florida

Completed: 1996

The Powell Cheek Heart and Vascular Pavilion at Morton Plant Hospital is a four-story, 102,000 sq ft freestanding building that focuses on offering disease management along with health management programs. Within a single building, the Heart and Vascular Pavilion provides an array of integrated services:

- Invasive and noninvasive diagnostics and surgery
- Cardiac rehabilitation
- Supervised exercise
- Nutritional and educational programs
- Diabetes management
- Wound care and hyperbaric therapies

The facility has a hotel-like atmosphere throughout its medical, physical therapy, and restaurant areas. A receptionist greets new visitors and guides them to their destination. The first floor components, which include a wellness center, restaurant, education kiosk, and lobby, are highly visible from both inside and outside the building. The second floor houses clinical programs, including invasive and noninvasive surgery, as well as conference space. Doctors' offices are located on the two upper floors.

Programming issues

Key programming issues to consider in designing a user-friendly heart and vascular center include the following:

- Site planning/ease of access
- Community outreach
- Comprehensive treatment services
- Flexibility for growth

Site planning/ease of access

In an effort to promote the heart-healthy concept and to allay any apprehension about cardiac treatment and rehabilitation, the Heart and Vascular Pavilion was sited to allow the public a clear view of the fitness area.

Patients and visitors expect convenient, "storefront" parking for doctors' office visits, as well as for clinical treatment. A five-story parking garage serves the Morton Plant's Heart and Vascular

▼ *Derived from the consumer-driven hospitality industry, this setting evokes a hotel-like atmosphere.*

Pavilion. To address the needs of the mobility impaired, yet eliminate the space considerations of excessive ramping, parking attendants shuttle patients/visitors to and from the parking garage in golf carts.

Basic site/access considerations

- Site the facility on a prominent hospital campus/community location to maximize public exposure and promote the concept of wellness.

- Provide a covered drop-off area for patients/visitors with special needs. Make sure the protected entry can accommodate two vehicles side by side.

- Provide accessible handicapped facilities.

Community outreach

The building is at the main entrance to the hospital campus, and was designed as a centerpiece to the entry, marking the presence of the hospital in the community.

The hospital provides open access to its community. The conference room is available to area community groups as a means to reach out into the hospital's constituency. The second floor conference room was strategically placed to cause community visitors to travel through the upbeat, user-friendly first floor, thereby promoting the services and facilities available.

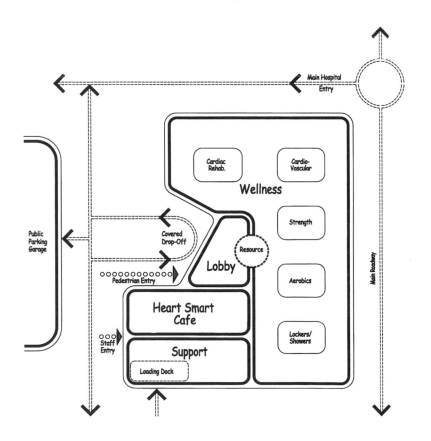

◀ Ease of access and visibility are basic considerations.

Comprehensive treatment service

Full-range cardiovascular programs, such as that of the Morton Plant Hospital, should include the following services:

- *Wellness center.* Exercise equipment, walking/jogging track, aerobics area, and specialized exercise/rehab classes. Place exercise areas in public view without compromising the users' privacy.

- *Cardiac rehabilitation.* Monitored exercise for patients recovering from heart attack or heart surgery. Place the cardiac rehabilitation program and the wellness center in the same area with minimal separation. Rehabilitation consumers are inspired by healthy, active wellness center consumers.

- *Evaluation.* Heart and vascular screening for proactive intervention and reduction of risk factors.

- *Invasive diagnostics/treatment.* Vascular catheterization laboratory with support and recovery areas.

- *Noninvasive diagnostics/treatment.* Cardiac stress testing, heart and vascular ultrasound, evaluation of the peripheral vascular system.

- *Physicians' offices.* Cardiology, vascular, thoracic, and radiology.

- *Community conference center.* Audiovisual resources, conference and meeting rooms, and storage.

- *Snack bar/restaurant.* Offers healthful meals, snacks, and beverages. The heart-healthy restaurant or cafe should be visible and easily accessible from the main entrance.

- *Resource library/education center.* Health-related books, brochures, and videos available for borrowing. Place the education center close to the main entrance; make print and electronic materials readily available to patients and visitors.

Flexibility for growth

Make sure future needs are taken into consideration. Although a provider may not have carefully thought out what its needs may be five to ten years in the future, steps can be taken early in the current project's planning to accommodate expansion.

- If possible, provide shell space adjacent to areas with potential for expansion, such as diagnostics and cardiac catheterization.

- Utilize a common plumbing wall between examination and treatment rooms to allow future reconfiguration.

- Incorporate duct systems into floors in wellness areas to allow for future recabling as equipment is moved or updated.

- Minimize elaborate detailing that may have to be changed in the future.

- Plan oversized cardiac catheterization laboratories to accommodate changing technology and equipment.

- The rehabilitation/wellness area should be open and flexible to accommodate rapidly changing equipment, which must be kept up-to-date in a competitive fitness/rehab facility.

- No equipment in the rehabilitation/wellness area should be permanently fastened.

- Procedure rooms of like use should be identical from the physician's point of view. The physician's position within the room relative to the patient and equipment should always be the same.

Additional programming considerations

- Use of focus groups (community, staff, administration, and physician) to determine the product/service mix for the facility (i.e., cardiac rehabilitation, restaurant, education, wellness, etc.)

- The number of visits, by age group and gender, for various services (fitness center, community, education, cardiac catheterization, dining, doctor's appointments, etc.) and anticipated length of visits

- Hours of operation for various services

- Number of clinical procedures, current and anticipated

Circulation/space planning

Circulation planning requires that a design

- Minimize travel distance within the building. A shallow U-shaped plan allows for central corridor circulation. This makes it easy to get to any portion of the building from the central core, and wayfinding is simplified. The rehabilitation/wellness area of the Pavilion was planned to house all of its respective components, including child care, lockers, fitness and rehabilitation area, and exercise rooms.

- Create reference points for the patient. At the center of the U a covered entry leads to the atrium lobby. The atrium is open to the second floor and provides a common space from which all circulation

emanates on the first two floors.

- Place consumer-oriented amenities in visible locations. The wellness center, resource library, and cafe are all in full view from the atrium, promoting the heart-healthy mission while acting as strong reference points.

- Separate invasive and noninvasive cardiology. Locate diagnostic/treatment areas apart from the more consumer-driven programs, such as wellness. These are clinical services, and the provider-patient relationship differs from that of the provider-consumer. However, invasive and noninvasive cardiology should share administrative space to operate more efficiently.

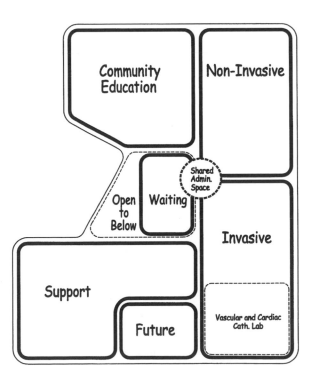

▼ Second-floor U-shaped plan showing invasive and noninvasive cardiology and community education areas.

- Create clear building zones to separate diverse programs and their respective customer types.

- Education and information areas should be clearly identifiable and centrally located.

- Clearly separate customer traffic to retail/wellness areas from traffic to clinical procedure and examination areas.

- Create a discreet, separate service entry.

Mechanical/electrical systems

To provide comfortable environments, air temperature zone controls should be built in to accommodate varying cooling needs. For example, wellness area customers have different climate control needs from customers waiting in doctors' offices on the above floors.

In the pavilion's wellness center, a recessed floor duct system allows for recabling to accommodate new or relocated equipment, such as treadmills and stationary bicycles. A floor duct system can also house a telemetry system that is hard wired to various pieces of exercise equipment. Telemetry is a means to monitor the basic vital signs of equipment users, then collect the data and store it at a central data collection point. Consumers are also made aware of their vital signs through individual screens mounted on the equipment.

Security

Consider hours of operation and the security required. The wellness center in the Heart and Vascular Pavilion is open 24 hours a day, thus requiring special security and surveillance measures.

Interiors

The choice and placement of interior materials, colors, textures, and lighting have a powerful influence on healing.

- Through the use of materials and finishes, try to achieve a hotel-like atmosphere, rather than that of a traditional hospital.

- Interiors should be stylish and contemporary but should not appear lavish or costly. Healthcare users assume that their medical bills pay for amenities. Use good quality materials, but avoid using marble, brass, and excessive amounts of wood.

- Lobby furnishing should be arranged in small, intimate groups to provide home-like settings and to ensure maximum flexibility for alternative uses such as community and support group meetings.

- Use glass in the wellness center to let in natural light, thus promoting the concept of a healthful environment. Use translucent interior shades to provide privacy.

- Equip conference and meeting rooms for multimedia presentations and provide movable partitions to accommodate two small groups or one large group.

- Place windows to maximize natural light and to allow for easy movement of interior wall partitions for changing needs.

- Vary color on doors and frames to differentiate between treatment areas. Colors are easily changed to reflect future case load mixes.

- All furnishings, finishes, and fittings should be easily maintained and updated.

Compliance with codes/ADA

Because of the variety of services and customers, the designer must show special sensitivity in meeting code requirements and the needs of the infirm patient/visitor.

Acoustic control

Because the preferences of patients and visitors vary, avoid piping music throughout the facility. Instead, provide wellness center customers with headphones.

Wayfinding

An organizing element is necessary in the building's design to provide landmarks and to help minimize customer disorientation. At Morton Plant, the center atrium serves as a wayfinding guide.

Other unique design concerns

- Create positive images for good health through openness and visibility.

- Allow for ease of remodeling, without service interruption, to keep abreast of changing style.

- The wellness and retail areas should have a spa/resort ambience. Avoid creating hospital and/or institutional environments.

- To meet reimbursement requirements, cardiac rehabilitation must be visually separated from the general rehabilitation/wellness areas, and its equipment can be used only for cardiac rehabilitation.

CANCER CENTERS

Freestanding cancer centers offer computer tomography (CT), radiology, radiation oncology, and magnetic resonance imaging (MRI) services to aid in the diagnosis and treatment of cancer. Housed within cancer centers are several clinical specialists, including medical oncologists, radiation oncologists, hematologists, surgeons, and chemotherapists. One of the challenges architects face when designing cancer centers is to physically place together as many of these specialists and disciplines to enable intercommunication, yet maintain privacy for diverse patient needs.

Greenwich Hospital Cancer Center

Greenwich, Connecticut

Architect: Payette Associates Inc., Boston Massachusetts

Completed: 1993

The Greenwich Hospital Cancer Center is a 72,000 sq ft, freestanding structure located adjacent to the hospital. The entire first floor is dedicated to the Cancer Center, with one floor of medical office suites above. Structured parking for 90 cars on five levels is located beneath the building. Planning the site of the Cancer Center required sensitivity to its residential surroundings through attention to scale, building design, and landscaping.

Programming issues

Programming determines design and merits acute attention:

- Diagnostic patients and treatment patients must be separate because of their varying needs.

- Space should be provided for family members in the treatment process.

- In chemotherapy areas, several levels of patient privacy should be provided, ranging from open cubicles to private

▶ Situating the parking area below the facility enables easy access for patients and use of green space to enhance the facility.

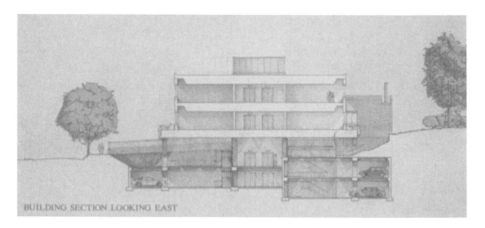

BUILDING SECTION LOOKING EAST

rooms. Such flexibility helps to accommodate the varying degrees of illness and offers separation between children and adults.

- At least one private room should be a positive/negative pressure room for immunosuppressed patients.

- At the Greenwich Center, physicians' office suites are situated on either side of the chemotherapy treatment area, enabling them to share one chemotherapy clinic. Distance between office and clinic is minimized, saving physicians time.

- The nurses' station is placed directly in front of the chemotherapy treatment stations, affording optimum sight lines to patients.

- Registration and central support areas (including a conference room, library, and group lounge) are centrally located.

- Chemotherapy and radiation therapy units have their own waiting areas.

- Involve patients in the design process to gain their perspective as users.

- Choose a structural module that allows for a range of configurations. A width of 28 to 30 ft is the most flexible; 26 ft is the minimum acceptable.

Plan for future needs

- Consider planning space for future linear accelerator (LinAc) equipment.

- Think about sizing for additional floors.

- Consider outfitting office spaces with plumbing roughed-in to allow for easy conversion to examination rooms in the future.

- Do not underestimate the needed size and activity of the blood draw/laboratory areas. The highest level of activity in cancer centers occurs in these areas, resulting in likely future expansion.

Site planning

At the Greenwich Center, an integrated, split-tray parking area conceals parking and driveways within the building footprint, allowing for optimum siting of a large building. In addition to shielding parking from its neighbors, this system also simplifies the arrival process for chronically ill patients. The patient remains under cover, has a minimal walk, and quickly arrives in the building. Arrival often can be one of the most stressful points in the process of care for a cancer patient.

Unique design concerns

Through careful expression of building mass, the institutional scale of the Greenwich Center project is broken down. Physicians' offices and examination rooms occupy the projecting portions of the building, and the recessed segments of the façade contain waiting rooms for each suite.

Techniques for fitting an outpatient center into a residential neighborhood include the following:

- Integrating the building with the community landscape, rather than creating a self-contained island. At Greenwich, a system of layers in the landscape gradually introduces the building to the streetscape through the use of indigenous stone walls and benches.

- Scaling down the massing to reflect more residential proportions and textures.

- Providing community conference rooms for after-hours support groups and counseling.

- Making sure exterior service areas are always visually inconspicuous.

- Allowing for both pedestrian and vehicular arrival. For Greenwich Cancer Center, the architects created a new bus stop for the convenience of patient access.

Natural light is a key design component in cancer centers. It helps orient patients and visitors and provides spiritual uplift

for chemotherapy patients, who often must endure hours of treatment at a visit, and for waiting family members. At Greenwich, each physician office and examination room has windows, and large windows sheathe the chemotherapy infusion and waiting areas, facing landscaped garden areas. Natural light and views

- help patients navigate through the building,

- reduce the amount of signage needed, as light acts as a means of wayfinding, and

- offer patients a change of scenery while they are undergoing lengthy treatment.

An integrated landscape connects exterior spaces to interior spaces, greatly enhancing the ambiance of the building's interior. The two main pedestrian entries are designed to create a sense of arrival and transition as one leaves the activity of the street edge, providing soothing spaces for patients and visitors within the garden walls. Along the southern entry walk, pedestrians encounter a series of garden

▲ *Garden spaces offer respite for ambulatory patients and people waiting in areas above.*

▶ *Windows to a small, private garden allow light to filter into the linear accelerator treatment area.*

spaces that correspond to patient waiting areas within the building above.

The linear accelerator (LinAc), a major piece of equipment used in radiation therapy, requires a dedicated room and entry maze surrounded by shielding, often yielding a cold and intimidating environment. Although the base building uses a steel system, the LinAc is housed in a concrete structure. At Greenwich, the LinAc is above grade, and a natural light well and small garden can be viewed from the entry maze, as well as from the LinAc table, helping to allay patients' fear and anxiety.

DIALYSIS CENTERS

The unique challenges of centers designed for patients and staff involved in the process of dialysis treatment differentiate these facilities from other ambulatory care facilities. Patients with

kidney disease require frequent treatment (usually on a weekly basis but, depending on individual needs, as often as daily) that lasts between two and six hours. During this time they must essentially remain immobile. This necessitates special attention by designers to aesthetic details and entertainment possibilities. The intensity of the treatment process requires the facilities to be fully functional medically while preserving a comfortable, residential atmosphere. Patients need to be in a space that is open enough to allow close observation without sacrificing staff efficiency, yet private and protected enough to keep patients comfortable. Reconciling these seemingly opposing goals can offer designers some interesting challenges— often including even the smallest details (location of scales and filing cabinets) in their plans.

Saints Memorial Medical Center Outpatient Dialysis Unit

Lowell, Massachusetts

Architect: Payette Associates Inc., Boston, Massachusetts

Completed: 1999

One of the major issues in planning the dialysis unit at Saints Memorial was siting. Patient input was central to the decision to keep it at the satellite campus of the center, although economic factors suggested a consolidation of facilities. Because dialysis patients spend several hours on a machine weekly, the opinions of patients and staff played a vital role in the design of the center where they would be spending so much time. The central dialysis area was designed to provide a warm and spacious light-filled environment to promote communication

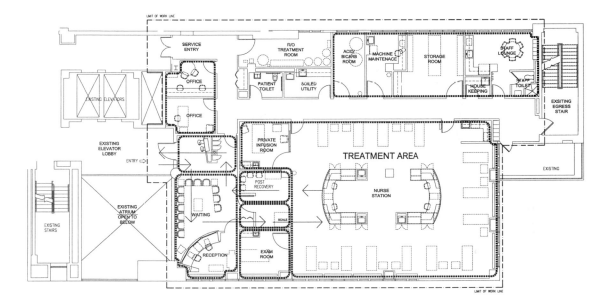

The floor plan shows labeled areas including:
SERVICE ENTRY, OFFICE, OFFICE, EXISTING ELEVATORS, EXISTING ELEVATOR LOBBY, ENTRY, EXISTING ATRIUM OPEN TO BELOW, EXISTING STAIRS, WAITING, RECEPTION, R/O TREATMENT ROOM, PATIENT TOILET, SOILED UTILITY, ACID BICARB ROOM, MACHINE MAINTENACE, STORAGE ROOM, STAFF LOUNGE, HOUSE KEEPING, STAFF TOILET, EXSITING EGRESS STAIR, EXISTING, PRIVATE INFUSION ROOM, POST RECOVERY, SCALE, EXAM ROOM, TREATMENT AREA, NURSE STATION, LIMIT OF WORK LINE

between patients and staff. The central nurses' station allows the staff to monitor the patients and also provides a semiprivate work zone. The dialysis unit was designed with a continuous central fluid delivery system that pipes R/O (reverse osmosis) water, acid, and bicarbonate to each station, keeping the tangle of cords and cables typical in such treatment areas out of sight and out of danger of accidental disconnection or tripping. This system alleviates the need for changing liquids at the stations and minimizes patient discomfort. Radiant heating panels built into the ceiling tile above each station warm each patient according to individual comfort preferences while preventing the drafts that accompany air-propelled heat systems. A wraparound soffit in the ceiling neatly hides individual patient television consoles, which can be used to watch videotapes and television programs.

Programming

Before a specific space program can be developed, the following issues must be clearly defined:

- The local regulatory requirements for licensure
- The projected growth of the number of dialysis patients
- The provision of acute care, chronic care, or both
- Hours of operation
- Staffing needs for functional operation of the unit

Once this data has been gathered, more detailed program information can be developed. Typical space requirements may include the following:

- Primary Activities:
  Treatment cubicles
  Isolation cubicles
  Acute care area
  Nurses' workstation
  Medication

▲ *The separation of areas by function allows for smoother patient circulation.*

233

AMBULATORY CARE FACILITIES

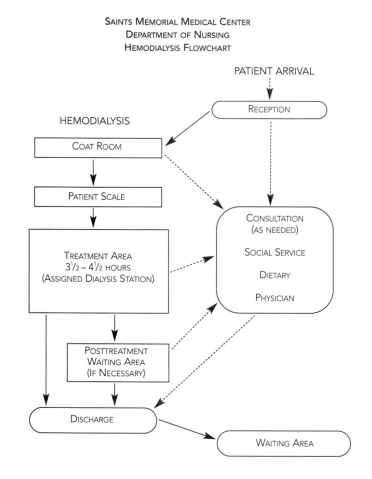

SAINTS MEMORIAL MEDICAL CENTER
DEPARTMENT OF NURSING
HEMODIALYSIS FLOWCHART

PATIENT ARRIVAL

RECEPTION

HEMODIALYSIS

COAT ROOM

PATIENT SCALE

TREATMENT AREA
3½–4½ HOURS
(ASSIGNED DIALYSIS STATION)

CONSULTATION
(AS NEEDED)

SOCIAL SERVICE

DIETARY

PHYSICIAN

POSTTREATMENT
WAITING AREA
(IF NECESSARY)

DISCHARGE

WAITING AREA

———▶ Patients with no scheduled consultations

--------▶ Patients *may* be scheduled for consultation using this patient flow

▲ *The arrangement of the center enables a flexible flow pattern to suit individual patient needs.*

Conference
Patient toilets
Waiting—posttreatment
Weighing alcove

• Support Areas:
Equipment storage
Reuse prep room
Rinse out prep room
R/O (reverse osmosis) water
    treatment room

Biomedical room
Wheelchair storage
Clean supply
Soiled utility
Janitor closet
Storage area
Special procedure room

• Administration/Staff:
Female change/locker room
Male change/locker room
Staff lounge
Staff toilet
Office—nurse manager
Office—social worker/dietician
Conference room
Billing alcove

• Family/Visitor Support Areas:
Waiting
Public toilets

Circulation

Circulation should be organized progressively to facilitate the different steps or stages associated with dialysis treatment. Patient circulation and service circulation should be separated. Circulation should be organized so that staff has a constant view of the patients.

At Saints Memorial Medical Center, patients circulate through the dialysis unit as follows:

• Patient arrives at reception/waiting.

• Proceeds to coat room.

• Patient is weighed.

• Proceeds to treatment area and assigned dialysis station for 3½ to 4½ hours.

• Proceeds to posttreatment/waiting.

• Patient is discharged.

Patients may be scheduled for social service, dietary, or physician consultation either before or after treatment.

Unique design concerns

Every project comes with its own set of unique design concerns. In this instance they included the following:

- Renovation of existing space. In assessing whether to renovate or restore a building for use as a dialysis center, the following factors should be considered:

  Whether the facility has adequate water pressure and flow

  Whether plumbing and special equipment installation is feasible

- Identify equipment manufacturers and vendors for R/O water, acid, and bicarbonate delivery systems.

- Determine mechanical, electrical, plumbing, structural, and architectural requirements for these and all specialized pieces of equipment.

- A centralized nurses' station is essential to allow the nursing or facilities staff to monitor and maintain the equipment.

- Some patients may arrive in wheelchairs alone or with family members, which increases space requirements to accommodate halls wide enough for maneuvering and generous closets or lockers for coat and wheelchair storage.

- Patients will spend four to six hours in the treatment facility on a regular basis, many for the rest of their lives. Special consideration should be given to creating a comfortable environment.

Site planning/parking/access

Access issues require that a design:

- Provide a convenient, preferably covered, patient drop-off area.

- Provide adequate and accessible designated dialysis-handicapped and visitor parking.

- Accommodate those patients who may require assistance with shuttle buses or taxicabs.

- Provide direct access for stretchers and emergency vehicles.

- Locate a delivery dock that is convenient but separate from patient and staff accesses.

Compliance with codes/ADA

- Universal design/ADA compliance is extremely important because of the age and physical condition of the majority of dialysis patients.

- Life safety issues, including adequate emergency power to sustain patients in critical situations and a review of the fire safety code in light of the prolonged periods of extreme incapacitation of patients undergoing treatment, are also very important because of the nature of patient care, especially in a hospital environment.

- Local plumbing codes must be carefully reviewed because of the special plumbing required for R/O water, acid, and bicarbonate fluid delivery.

Energy/environmental challenges

- Local and regional wastewater treatment procedures should be reviewed and considered in the facility's design because of the high quantity of water required for the dialysis process.

Structure system

Structural factors included the following:

- Large bays provide flexibility and minimize obstructions in the fluid delivery loop.

- Verify the pounds-per-square-foot loads required for different fluid containers and related equipment, which may include the following:

  Acid delivery tanks

  Reverse osmosis tanks

  Bicarbonate tanks and machinery

Mechanical/plumbing systems

- Oxygen should be provided to each of the dialysis stations, which requires gas hookups.

- HVAC (heating, ventilation, and air-conditioning) supply diffusers should be located to minimize air blowing over patients. This is important, as patients tend to become cold during dialysis treatment.

- Radiant-heated flooring below each patient chair or radiant-heated ceiling panels above provide a localized means to modulate the temperature.

- Plumbing for the continuous fluid delivery loop must not have any dead legs where bacteria may grow.

- Access to plumbing is important for regularly scheduled monitoring, cleaning, and testing, which will minimize downtime and intrusion for repairs.

Electrical/communications systems

Typical electrical systems required include the following:

- Closed-circuit television and remote door buzzer

- Nurse call and patient alarms

- Ground fault circuit interruption outlets on separate panels, because of the high amount of liquids used

- Voice/data outlets
- TV, VCR, cable, and radio connections

Special equipment

Because of the nature of dialysis centers, specialized equipment is needed, and the facility's design should be able to accommodate its spatial, plumbing, and maintenance needs. Consider the following points:

- Reverse osmosis (R/O) water treatment requires a dedicated room and is typically provided and maintained by a vendor who is either a consultant to the facility or a partner with the design team. The system should be designed and built in a continuous loop to deliver water to the dialysis stations in a way that minimizes dead spots.

- The acid delivery system fluid should be gravity fed to each station. This means raising the acid storage tanks above floor level. Special consideration should be given to the length of plumbing runs and the weight of the large acid containers.

- Bicarbonate can be mixed in small quantities on an as-needed basis and delivered to the individual stations in small jugs, or prepared in a large mixer and then delivered to the dialysis stations from a central location.

- A large, wheelchair-accommodating scale should be located near the entry of the patient treatment area.

- Dialysis machines are typically specified and purchased by the hospital or facility, but their selection must be coordinated with the design team.

- The "fluid delivery boxes," the connection points between the dialysis machines and the fluid delivery system, must be carefully designed and coordinated for ease of use, maintenance, and aesthetic qualities.
- Polypropylene tubing without 90-degree elbows and with minimal bends reduces bacterial growth but is extremely costly.

Materials

Generally, materials should not look or feel clinical. Dialysis patients spend a considerable amount of time in treatment. Materials should make them feel at home, regardless of their sedentary state.

- Flooring in the treatment area should be made of a water-resistant, continuous sheet with a 4 in. to 6 in. integral flashed base. In essence, this is a shallow "bathtub" to contain any potential spills. Durable sheet vinyl, linoleum, or rubber should provide some slip resistance and be easy to maintain.
- Consider epoxy paint on the walls, especially in the repair, water treatment, and acid and bicarbonate rooms.
- The water treatment, acid, and bicarbonate rooms should have a waterproof poured membrane or epoxy floor with at least a 6 in. integral flashed base. A ramp into these rooms aids the delivery of goods and satisfies ADA requirements. In addition, the floor should be slightly sloped to large, centrally located floor drains so that the rooms can be hosed down.

- A wainscot of easily maintained plastic laminate or similar water-resistant material throughout the treatment area helps with cleaning spills and protects the walls from damage caused by equipment or patient chairs.
- Wood should be used to provide a sense of warmth; however, it should be marine grade or sealed.

Acoustic controls

Unwanted sound can be a serious nuisance. Consider the following control measures:

- Because fluids are continuously moving through the plumbing loops within the walls, above the ceiling, and in the floor, batt and/or rigid insulation should be installed wherever possible to minimize noise.
- Extend gypsum wallboard partitions to the underside of the structure to help reduce sound transmission.
- Create variable ceiling heights within large, open dialysis areas to minimize noise reverberation.
- Movable fabric dividers, also used for acoustic control, help with patient privacy without interrupting sight lines required by the staff to monitor patients.

Lighting design

Lighting can be a powerful healing tool, as these measures show.

- Daylight should be used as much as possible. Daylight helps patients establish a sense of time while they are in treatment.
- A strategically placed mix of indirect and direct recessed lighting fixtures

helps to make the unit seem less institutional and clinical. Because most patients will be in a reclined position for long periods of time, place lighting to minimize glare, hot spots, and eyestrain.

Interiors

- Colors should be calming, yet not sedate or institutional.
- Water-resistant, durable materials should be specified for easy maintenance.
- Stimulation should be provided, such as personal television sets with VCRs or cable TV, radios, and windows with views.

Wayfinding

Careful selection of colors, lighting, and materials can help patients navigate and establish their bearings intuitively. Wayfinding elements should be incorporated to follow the logical progression of patient flow.

Operation and maintenance

- Establish a partnership with a reliable vendor of R/O water, acid, and bicarbonate.
- Prepare a functional operation plan for patient and facility staff.
- Schedule regular maintenance and cleaning to prevent bacterial growth.

Key cost factors

Construction costs for the dialysis unit at the center were $180 per square foot of fit-out space. Additional high costs will be incurred through plumbing design and installation, as well as for service fees associated with water treatment vendors.

ADAPTIVE REUSE OF SPACE

Innovative adaptation of existing structures to meet the needs of an entirely different purpose has opened possibilities for designers of ambulatory care facilities. For example, the huge, windowless structures used by large retail chains throughout the country seem suited only to the purpose for which they were built. They are essentially an open space—more than one story, but not quite two. When economic conditions in an area force retail establishments to close, it is difficult to find alternate uses for this space. Important issues include the responsible use or recycling of old materials, the adaptation of such an open space to fit the needs of a more compartmentalized facility, and the reshaping of existing structures to reflect their new purpose.

Maine Medical Center
Maine Center for Cancer Care

Scarborough, Maine

Architect: Harriman Associates, Auburn, Maine

Completed: 1998

This 104,000 sq ft facility not only represents the trend to deliver many services at one location, it is also an example of how a defunct retail plaza can be transformed into a modern ambulatory care center. The Maine Center for Cancer Care is a state-of-the-art outpatient oncology facility and diagnostic laboratory, created by recycling and reshaping an abandoned Kmart plaza. Housed in the facility are centers focused on radiation therapy, children's cancer, cancer medicine and blood disorders, IV therapy, endocrinology and diabetes, and breast care, in addition to a diagnostic

◀ Innovative design transformed this defunct retail plaza into a contemporary and patient-friendly medical center. ▼

laboratory, advanced imaging center, and a learning resource center. The location, just off a major highway, was a primary asset, offering easy access and ample parking space.

All but the steel framing of the Kmart store was torn down. The skin, walls, and flooring of the buildings, as well as the parking lot asphalt, were crushed on-site to become fill for a new parking lot. This not only reduced costs but also minimized truck traffic on the highway, thereby lessening congestion and pollution. A self-propelled crusher unit ground the old materials into a gravel-like mixture, which was then used as fill for the new parking lot.

The plain, boxy shape of the plaza was reshaped with pavilions connected by covered walkways at three main entrances. These provide shelter and convenience to patients and lead to glassed-in lobbies that overlook gardens and further the image of a patient-friendly center. A red brick façade, replacing the gray cinder block and precast concrete of the old store, adds to the effect.

▲ *Ample space allowed designers to include this playroom for young patients and waiting children.*

Inside, the huge, open area of the old Kmart was subdivided into hundreds of smaller spaces to accommodate the diverse healthcare services provided there. The corridor system was designed as a streetscape, with a series of connected spaces to avoid the look and feel of a long tunnel. Skylights flood the corridors with natural light, and artwork and plants lend a personal rather than institutional feel to the passageways. Soft colors and the warm tones of birch add up to a comforting atmosphere.

Transforming the windowless warehouse construction into a comfortable and inviting healthcare facility presented some unique design challenges. The depth of the building and its unusually high ceilings made it difficult to brighten the public and patient spaces. Using available natural light from windows and skylights and decorating in warm, outdoor colors, designers took advantage of the open space to create a comfortable, natural environment. The key cost factor for this project was $112 per square foot.

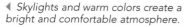

◀ *Skylights and warm colors create a bright and comfortable atmosphere.*

BIBLIOGRAPHY

Allen, Rex Whitaker and Ilona Von Karolyi. *Hospital Planning Handbook.* New York: John Wiley & Sons, 1976.

Ambasz, Emilio. *The Architecture of Luis Barragan.* New York: Museum of Modern Art, 1976. For the creation of light filled, modulated rooms and courts and the creation of a sense of place and calm.

The American Institute of Architects Academy of Architecture for Health. *Guidelines for Design and Construction of Hospital and Healthcare Facilities.* Washington, D.C.: The American Institute of Architects Press, 1996.

Burchell, Robert W. and David Listokin. *The Adaptive Reuse Handbook.* Piscataway, N.J.: The Center for Urban Policy Research, 1981.

Burns, Linda A. *Ambulatory Surgery: Developing and Managing Successful Programs.* Rockville, Md.: Aspen Systems Corp., 1984.

Byard, Paul Spencer. *The Architecture of Additions: Design and Regulation.* New York: W. W. Norton, 1998.

Capman, Janet R. and Myron A. Grant. *Design That Cares: Planning Health Facilities for Patients and Visitors.* American Hospital Publishing, Inc., 1993.

Fischer, Harry W. *Radiology Departments: Planning Operation and Management.* Edwards Brothers, Inc.

Hardy, Owen B. and Lawrence P. Lammers. Hospitals: *The Planning and Design Process.* Rockville, Md.: Aspen Publishers, 1986.

Leibrock, Cynthia. *Design Details for Health: Making the Most of Interior Design's Healing Potential.* New York: John Wiley & Sons, 2000.

Malkin, Jain. *Hospital Interior Architecture: Creating Healing Environments for Special Patient Populations.* New York: Van Nostrand Reinhold, 1992.

Matson, Theodore, ed. *Restructuring for Ambulatory Care: A Guide to Reorganization.* Chicago: American Hospital Association, 1990.

McCoy, Esther. *Five California Architects.* New York: Reinhold, 1960. For inside/outdoor integration: Irving Gill (pp. 59-101), Rudolph Schindler (pp. 153-160), Pueblo Ribera courtyard housing (p. 160), Lovell beach house (pp. 163-65).

Miller, Richard L. and Earl S. Swensson. *New Directions in Hospital and Healthcare Facility Design.* New York: McGraw-Hill, 1995.

Nesmith, Eleanor Lynn. *Health Care Architecture: Designs for the Future.* Washington, D.C.: Rockport Publishers, 1995.

Palmer, Mickey A. *The Architect's Guide to Facility Programming.* Washington, D.C.: American Institute of Architects, 1981.

Pearson, Paul David. *Alvar Aalto.* New York: Whitney Library of Design, 1978. See pp. 84-93 on Paimio Hospital.

Porter, David R. *Hospital Architecture.* AUPHA Press, 1982.

Putsep, Ervin. *Modern Hospital International Planning Practices.* London: Lloyd-Luke, 1981.

Riggs, Leonard M., Jr., ed. *Emergency Department Design.* American College of Emergency Physicians, 1993.

Rostenberg, Bill. *The Architecture of Imaging.* American Hospital Publishing, 1995.

Rostenberg, Bill. *Design Planning for Freestanding Ambulatory Care Facilities.* Chicago: American Hospital Association, 1986.

Symposium on Healthcare Design/Sara O. Marberry, ed. *Innovations in Healthcare Design: Selected Presentations from the First Five Symposia on Healthcare Design.* New York: Van Nostrand Reinhold, 1995.

Taylor, Brian Brace. *Pierre Chareau: Designer and Architect.* New York: Taschen, 1998. See pp. 103-149 on the Maison de Verre, Paris, for courtyard and manipulation of light for interior lighting

Wheeler, E. Todd. *Hospital Design and Function.* New York: McGraw-Hill, 1964.

Wheeler, E. Todd. *Hospital Modernization and Expansion.* New York: McGraw-Hill, 1971.

ILLUSTRATION CREDITS

CHAPTER 2

Page 10 (left): Photograph by T. S. Gordon. Page 10 (right): Photograph by Wes Thompson. Page 11 (St. John's Regional Medical Center): Photographs by Peter Malinowski. Page 11 (Mary Washington Hospital): Photograph by Rick Grunbaum. Page 21: Photograph by Greg Hursley, Tod Swiecichowski. Page 24: Photograph by Rick Grunbaum. Page 32: Photograph by T.S. Gordon. Page 33: Photograph by Wes Thompson. Page 34: Photograph by T. S. Gordon. Page 37: Photograph by Wes Thompson. Page 39: Photograph by Wes Thompson. Page 40: Photograph by Wes Thompson. Page 42: Photograph by Viscom Photography. Page 45: Photograph by Glen Arden/Rick Grunbaum. Page 50: Photograph by Michael Lowry. Page 59: Photograph by Kelly Peterson. Page 74: Photograph by Ed LaCasse. Page 78: Photograph by Rick Grunbaum. Page 81 (top): Photograph by Rick Grunbaum. Page 81 (middle): Photograph by Wes Thompson. Page 81 (bottom): Photograph courtesy HKS Inc. Page 88: Photograph by Wes Thompson. Page 89: Photograph by Rick Grunbaum. Page 91: Photograph by Rick Grunbaum. Page 97 (top): Photograph by Wes Thompson. Page 97 (bottom): Photograph by Rick Grunbaum. Page 108 (top and bottom): Photographs by Greg Hursley. Page 111: Photograph by Kelly Peterson. Page 112 (left): Photograph by King Graf. Page 112 (right): Photograph by Rick Grunbaum. Page 114: Photograph by Rick Grunbaum. Page 119: Photograph by Rick Grunbaum. Page 128: Photograph by Rick Grunbaum.

CHAPTER 3

Page 134 (top) and page 136 (bottom) are from John D. Thompson and Grace Goldin, *The Hospital: A Social and Architectural History* (New Haven: Yale University Press, 1975), pp. 32 and 152.
Page 136 (top) is from Nikolaus Pevsner, *A History of Building Types* (Princeton, N.J.: Princeton University Press, 1976), p. 150. Page 137 is from John Shaw Billings, et al., *Hospital Plans: Five Essays Relating to the Construction, Organization, and Management of Hospitals* (New York: William Wood and Co., 1875), appendix. All photographs in Chapter 3 by Michael Bobrow.

CHAPTER 4

All photographs courtesy of Payette Associates Inc.

COLOR PLATES:

University of Chicago Hospitals, Duchossois Center for Advanced Medicine: Photograph by Scott McDonald, Hedrich Blessing Photographers.
New England Medical Center, Patient Care Center: Photograph by Steve Rosenthal.
St. John's Regional Medical Center: Photograph by Peter Malinowski.
Yuma Regional Medical Center: Photograph by Wes Thompson.
Valley Children's Hospital: Photograph by Khaled AlKotob.
HealthPark Medical Center: Photograph by Michael Lowry.
Valley Children's Hospital: Photograph by Khaled AlKotob.
UCLA/Santa Monica Hospital Medical Center: Photograph courtesy BTA.
Arrowhead Regional Medical Center: Photograph courtesy BTA.
Daniel Freeman Memorial Hospital: Photograph courtesy BTA.
UCLA/Santa Monica Medical Center Women's Center: Photograph by Michael Arden.
Arrowhead Regional Medical Center, nursing tower: Photograph by John Edward Linden.
St. Luke's Medical Center: Photograph courtesy BTA.
Athens Regional Medical Center (both views): Photographs courtesy Payette Associates Inc.
Massachusetts General Hospital, Northeast Proton Therapy Center (both views): Photographs by Steve Rosenthal.
Greenwich Hospital Cancer Center: Photograph courtesy Payette Associates Inc.
Saints Memorial Medical Center: Photograph courtesy Payette Associates Inc.

INDEX